A GUIDE TO THE CONTENTS OF THE QUR'AN

A GUIDE TO THE CONTENTS OF THE QUR'AN

Faruq Sherif

Reading, 1995

Ithaca Press (Cased) ISBN 0 86372 190 7
Garnet Publishing (Paperback) ISBN 1 85964 045 1

British Library Cataloguing-in-Publication Data
A catalogue record for this book is available from the British Library

Cover design by David Rose
Typeset by Westkey Ltd, Falmouth, Cornwall
Printed in Lebanon

Typeset in 10/12 Baskerville

Ithaca Press is an imprint of Garnet Publishing

Published by Garnet Publishing Ltd,
8 Southern Court, South Street,
Reading, RG1 4QS, UK
Reprinted 1995

CONTENTS

THE QUR'AN: TABLE OF SURAS

Serial number of Sura	Title of Sura	Meccan (MC) or Medinese (MD)	Preceded by abbreviated letter	Containing an oath uttered by God	Serial number of Sura	Title of Sura	Meccan (MC) or Medinese (MD)	Preceded by abbreviated letter	Containing an oath uttered by God
1	The Exordium	MC			45	Kneeling	MC	H.M.	
2	The Cow	MD	A.L.M.		46	Sand Tracts (Ahqaf)	MC	H.M.	
3	The Family of Imran	MD	A.L.M.		47	Muhammad	MD		
4	The Woman	MD		*	48	Victory	MD		
5	The Table	MD			49	The Chambers	MD		
6	The Cattle	MC			50	Oaf	MC	Q.	*
7	The Heights	MC	A.L.M.S.		51	The Winds	MC		*
8	The Spoils	MD			52	The Mountain	MC		*
9	The Repentance	MD			53	The Star	MC		
10	Jonah	MC	A.L.R.		54	The Moon	MC		
11	Hud	MC	A.L.R.		55	Merciful	MC		
12	Joseph	MC	A.L.R.		56	The Inevitable Event	MC		
13	Thunder	MD	A.L.M.R.		57	The Iron	MD		
14	Abraham	MC	A.L.R.		58	She who pleaded	MD		
15	The Rocky Tract (Hijr)	MC	A.L.R.	*	59	The Banishment	MD		
16	The Bee	MC		*	60	She who is tested	MD		
17	The Night Journey	MC			61	The Battle Array	MD		
18	The Cave	MC			62	Friday	MD		
19	Mary	MC	KHYAS	*	63	The Hypocrites	MD		
20	Ta Ha	MC	T.H.		64	Cheating	MD		
21	The Prophets	MC			65	Divorce	MD		
22	The Pilgrimage	MD			66	The Prohibition	MD		
23	The Believers	MC			67	Dominion	MC		
24	Light	MD			68	The Pen	MD	N.	*
25	The Criterion	MC			69	The Sure Reality	MC		*
26	The Poets	MC	T.S.M.		70	The Ways of Ascent	MC		*
27	The Ants	MC	T.S.		71	Noah	MC		
28	Narration	MC	T.S.M.		72	The Jinns	MC		
29	The Spider	MC	A.L.M.		73	The Mantled One	MC		
30	The Romans	MC	A.L.M.		74	The Cloaked One	MC		*
31	Luqman	MC	A.L.M.		75	The Resurrection	MC		*
32	Adoration	MC	A.L.M.		76	Man	MC		
33	The Confederates	MD			77	Those sent forth	MC		*
34	Saba	MC			78	Tidings	MC		
35	The Creator	MC			79	The Soul-snatchers	MC		*
36	Ya Sin	MC	Y.S.	*	80	He frowned	MC		
37	The Ranks	MC		*	81	The Folding up	MC		*
38	Sad	MC	S.	*	82	The Cataclysm	MC		
39	The Crowds	MC			83	The Just	MC		
40	The Believer	MC	H.M.		84	The Rending Asunder	MC		*
41	Fussilat	MC	H.M.		85	The Constellation	MC		*
42	Consultation	MC	H.M./A.S.Q.		86	The Night Visitor	MC		*
43	Gold Ornaments	MC	H.M.	*	87	The Most High	MC		
44	Smoke	MC	H.M.	*	88	The overwhelming Event	MC		

Serial number of Sura	Title of Sura	Meccan (MC) or Medinese (MD)	Preceded by abbreviated letter	Containing an oath uttered by God	Serial number of Sura	Title of Sura	Meccan (MC) or Medinese (MD)	Preceded by abbreviated letter	Containing an oath uttered by God
89	The Break of Day	MC		*	102	Piling up	MC		
90	The City	MC		*	103	The Declining Day	MC		
91	The Sun	MC		*	104	The Scandal-Monger	MC		
92	The Night	MC		*	105	The Elephant	MC		
93	Daylight	MC		*	106	The Quraish	MC		
94	The Expansion	MC			107	Alms	MC		
95	The Fig	MC		*	108	Abundance	MC		
96	The Blood Clot	MC			109	The Unbelievers	MC		
97	The Night of Power	MC			110	Help	MD		
98	The Clear Evidence	MC			111	Lahab	MC		
99	The Convulsion	MC			112	Purity of Faith	MC		
100	The War Steeds	MC		*	113	The Dawn	MC		
101	The Day of Noise and Clamour	MC			114	Mankind	MC		

Summary:

There are 88 Meccan and 26 Medinese Suras.

29 Suras are preceded by abbreviated letters. With four exceptions they are all Meccan Suras.

CHAPTER ONE

INTRODUCTION

As is shown by the title of the book, the subject of this study is 'the contents of the Qur'an'. In conducting my research and developing its results in the pages that follow, I have kept strictly within the limits indicated by the title. Because of this limitation, many subjects which form part of the dogma and laws of Islam but which do not appear in the text of the Qur'an have been excluded from the scope of this study. I wish to make this point clear at the outset in case some readers, being under the wrong impression that everything that exists in Islam exists in the Qur'an, should expect to find in this book the discussion of more subjects than it actually covers.

It goes without saying that the Qur'an is the very essence of Islam. But the principles, doctrines and prescriptions of Islam have in the course of centuries been greatly developed by drawing on sources which are auxiliary to the Qur'an. Most important among these are the traditions (reported sayings, acts and oral teachings) of the Prophet also known as 'Hadith', to which the Shii community adds the traditions of the Twelve Imams who are deemed to be infallible like the Prophet himself.[1] The voluminous contents of the traditions together with additions from other sources (mainly the conclusions arrived at by doctors of Islamic jurisprudence) on all varieties of subjects have become necessary adjuncts to the Qur'an. It is significant that some of these additions relate even to essential ritual practices such as prayer, the fast and zakat, concerning which the text of the Qur'an, unless complemented by the reported practices of the Prophet, would not be sufficiently precise.

It is thus clear that the Qur'an together with the aggregate of contributions from other sources constitute the corpus of Islamic dogma, norms and prescriptions. To this corpus might be applied the term 'the contents of Islam' as distinct from the far more fundamental, but less extensive term 'the contents of the Qur'an', which is the exclusive subject of the present study.

There is obviously this important difference between the text of the Qur'an and the auxiliary sources that for the Moslem the Qur'an is

1

the very word of God, which does not admit of any doubt or questioning, while the traditions and other sources have often been the subject of dispute and controversy in regard both to their reliability and their content. It is not surprising that only a few of them have attained the degree of authority which is the special characteristic of the Holy Book.

In this book I have tried my utmost to reproduce, in miniature as it were, but faithfully, all the contents of the Qur'an. In so doing, it has in particular been my intention to avoid any treatment of the various subjects which would have the character of interpretation or interjection of a personal opinion or point of view. Maximum objectivity has been my unfailing guide in the preparation of this study.

Moslems believe in the Qur'an as the Word of God. Their attitude towards it is the attitude of faith. They read it with the sense of reverence and adoration which befits the meditation of divine utterances, but do not always understand the real meaning of its contents. The reader of the Arabic text is usually carried away by the rhythm and cadence of the verses in the same way that one who listens to music feels the charm of the melody without attributing an intellectual meaning to it. On reading or hearing the Qur'an the believer finds his faith strengthened. The Qur'an itself says that its revelations increase the believer's faith and bring joy to his heart. This in itself is a valuable consideration for those who find in their belief in God and the Hereafter a source of solace, comfort and support in their daily life. But where the context transcends the individual and affects the conduct of affairs of a society, it then becomes necessary to reflect on the objective meaning of the revelation. Besides, there are many who, were it only out of curiosity or desire for knowledge, are anxious to know what exactly the Qur'an has to say about the numerous subjects which its Suras cover.

Such seekers face a serious difficulty apart from that of language. The subjects discussed in the Qur'an do not appear consecutively or follow a chronological or other particular order. For any subject the student must search throughout the book with the help of an index to subject-matters, verses and words, and must then coordinate and harmonise the material collected.

This book has been written with the object of helping such students to acquire an objective understanding, albeit brief, of what the Qur'an has to say about each subject. This book contains, in addition to the introductory chapter, seven chapters subdivided into 68 sections, each covering one subject. An index corresponding to each section quotes the references to all verses relating to its subject, and a summarised description of the contents of the Qur'an is given for each subject without any attempt at interpretation or critical evaluation. Each subject has been recapitulated following the logical or chronological order, not the order of succession of the Suras in which the subject is discussed.

The contents of the chapters that follow are taken strictly from the Qur'an to the exclusion of all other sources customarily utilised for explaining, interpreting or complementing the commandments of the Qur'an, namely traditions, reports to the Prophet's sayings and actions, theology, jurisprudence, etc. There are two compelling reasons for such exclusive adherence of the contents of the Qur'an. One is that the other sources are often subject to controversy and do not always command universal recognition.[3] The other is the general tendency not to distinguish between the contents of the Qur'an and dictates which have their origin outside the Qur'an. Many examples can be quoted of the unfortunate consequences of an erroneous belief that a particular commandment or principle comes from the Qur'an when in fact it derives from some other source. One outstanding example, which has an important bearing on contemporary practices, is the subject of punishing adultery by stoning to death. It is often believed that the Qur'an provides for this punishment, whereas in fact the punishment prescribed for adultery in the Qur'an is flogging, not stoning. The latter is only supported by tradition, which evidently does not have the same value as the Qur'an. Another example concerns music. It is widely believed that the Qur'an prohibits music, but this belief is entirely unfounded, having its source only in a quite unjustified interpretation of the phrase 'idle tales' (Sura XXXI.5) or 'false words' (Sura XXII.31). It may be added that certain rules of conduct, believed to be prescribed by the Qur'an, really have their source only in reported sayings of either the Prophet or the Imams. Thus, while the Qur'an says that all religions are one and that no discrimination must be made by the Moslem in the matter of faith, it is reported that the sixth Imam enjoined upon believers not to make the first gesture of greeting when they meet non-Moslems. He is also reported to have said that if a Moslem happens to embrace a Jew, a Christian or a Zoroastrian he must purify himself with unpolluted earth.[4]

On the other hand, in order to enter into the spirit of the Qur'an and to understand the specific reasons for certain revelations and commandments, the student must familiarise himself with the habits and usages of the people of Arabia, with the general conditions – political, social and economic – which existed in Arabia and the neighbouring countries before and at the time of the appearance of Islam, and with certain outstanding events in the life of the Prophet. This insight into the characteristics of the time is the more necessary because all religions, philosophies, laws and ideas are the product of a particular time and place, and cannot be properly understood and judged except in the light of the circumstances in which they came into being.

One point that may strike the student is that certain parts of the Qur'an relate to a particular time and place and to circumstances which had only a temporary significance, and that these parts should be differentiated from those whose relevance is not affected by the passage of time. A few examples may be cited:

Sura CXI pronounces a curse on Abu Lahab, the Prophet's uncle. Sura CVI contains a counsel addressed to the tribe of Quraish. An important part of Sura XCVI reprimands and threatens Abu Jahl, an enemy of the Prophet. The whole of Sura LXVI concerns a passing crisis in the relations of the Prophet with his wives. The major part of Sura LXIII refers to certain episodes in the battle of Uhud and in the attack on the Mustaliq tribe. Several passages of the Qur'an relate to certain practices which were prevalent among the Arabs in the seventh century, but which have since disappeared. Examples are those of slavery and the arbitrary rejection of a wife without divorce in the forms known as zihar and ila'. Another example is the practice, tolerated in Arabia of the seventh century, of attacks by one tribe on the property and caravans of another, with the object of plunder, involving the then important question of distribution of the booty. It is obvious that such parts of the Qur'an lost their applicability in the course of history, and, if the rules embodied in them were to be considered enforceable forever, it would be necessary to revive the original conditions and circumstances. For instance if the rule contained in verse 4 of Sura LVIII (the obligation to free a slave in atonement of the breach of a previous oath taken when rejecting a wife) were to be applicable for all time, it would be necessary to revive two extinct customs, that of slavery and that of arbitrary rejection of wives. Another example is the permission given to a Moslem to marry an already married woman if her husband was an infidel (Sura LX.10).

A striking example may be given of how a commandment of the Qur'an can be misconstrued and misapplied if divorced from its proper context, and how such misapplication can, at the least, hinder the normal progress of a community, and, at the most, cause reversion to a primitive state. Verse 28 of Sura IX says: 'Truly polytheists [pagans] are unclean: let them not enter the Sacred Mosque *after this year of theirs is ended.*' A vast amount of post-Qur'anic literature has been devoted to the question of how believers should avoid physical contamination on meeting non-believers. But a careful examination of the context of the verse in question will show that the inference thus derived from it is unwarranted. The circumstances which gave rise to this commandment were the following: until the conquest of Mecca in AD 630 the pagans (polytheists) were in the habit of visiting the Ka'ba once a year in the sacred month in order to perform the ancient rites of pilgrimage (which were subsequently perpetuated by the Prophet) in honour of their divinities. In the year of conquest, when the season of pilgrimage (then as now the month of Dhu'l-Hijja) arrived both Moslems and pagans performed the pilgrimage together, but the Prophet did not take part in the ceremonies. In the following year the rites of pilgrimage were performed again in the same manner, but the Prophet sent a message to the effect that *after that year* the pagans should be treated as unfit (unclean) to enter the sacred precincts and that, once the sacred months were past, anyone who had not embraced Islam would be treated as an enemy.

Nearly all the penal provisions contained in the Qur'an reflect the social conditions which were characteristic of the Arabian tribes 14 centuries ago. An outstanding example is the law of talion. This law, which by present standards appears ruthless and inhuman, was a merciful innovation in 17th-century Arabia in that it restricted the then current practice of revenge to the sole person of the offender, not victimising his whole tribe as was the pre-Islamic custom.

It is to be noted that the spiritual orientation of the Qur'an, namely its emphasis on faith, its glorification of the ideals of the good and true, is bound up with a series of beliefs, concepts and commandments in which the Moslem is required to believe implicitly, but some of these require interpretation, figurative or otherwise, in order to be properly understood. More than one-fifth of the verses of the Qur'an, namely its emphasis on faith, its glorification of the ideals of the good and true, is bound up with a series of beliefs, concepts and commandments in which the Moslem is required to believe implicitly, but some of these require interpretation, figurative or otherwise, in order to be properly understood.

In the next few pages of this Introduction I give a brief exposition of a difference which exists between the Meccan and the Medinese Suras of the Qur'an. Believers in the Qur'an regard it as a homogeneous and indivisible whole, but are none the less conscious of some differences in the nature of its contents. According as to whether the place of revelation is Mecca or Medina, there is a noticeable difference between the Suras of the Qur'an in respect of style, tone and even spirit.

Eighty-eight Suras of the Qur'an were revealed during the Prophet's residence in Mecca after the declaration of his mission (twelve years) and 26 during his residence in Medina after the Hijra. The number of the Meccan verses (4,558) amounts to 73% of the total number of verses of the Qur'an, and if the length of the verses is taken into account (for the Medinese verses are in general longer than the Meccan) the Meccan part of revelation constitutes 63% of the whole. Although these two parts of the Qur'an cannot be considered as entirely distinct, there is an important difference between them in certain respects, as I will now try to explain.

Style

The Meccan verses are couched in a special style which is neither prose nor poetry, but lies between the two. It is a kind of rhymed prose with occasional refrains (such as the words 'then which of the favours of your Lord will you deny?' repeated in Sura LV as many as 31 times) that add to the poetic effect of the whole. The appeal of this style is evidently more emotional and spiritual than logical and intellectual. The difference between it and the style of the Medinese Suras is obvious. Though in the latter also some consecutive sentences end in rhymed words, on the whole the style is that of prose and lacks poetical appeal.

Revelation

A special feature of the Meccan Suras is that they dwell on the source and origin of the Prophet's mission and on the nature of its content. Fourteen passages emphasise that what the Prophet says is divinely revealed, and twice the Prophet is addressed in these words: 'Say I am but a man like yourselves,[5] only inspiration has come to me' (XVIII.110 and XLI.5). In verse XLVI.8 he is commanded to say: 'I am no apostle of new doctrines, nor do I know what will be done with me or with you; I follow only what is revealed to me, and my only duty is to give clear warning.' All these passages are contained in the Meccan Suras except one which is an exact repetition of a passage already contained in the Meccan Suras: 'This is part of the tidings of the things unseen which We reveal to thee.' Such insistence on the concept of revelation does not occur in Medinese Suras.

Preaching the Message

The subject of the Prophet's mission is proclamation of the Message, the Message of glad tidings as well as warning and admonition. Five passages emphasise that the Prophet's mission is only to proclaim the Message. He is to preach the essence of faith, which, as has repeatedly been stated in the Qur'an, is to believe in God as the one and only Lord who has neither associate, partner, nor offspring. Once the

Prophet has communicated this message, he has completed his mission, and if those who hear his message deny it, he must leave them to God. The Meccan verses reaffirm six times that the Prophet is not sent to manage people's affairs or to be their guardian. On the other hand, in the Medinese Suras the Prophet figures, not only as the bearer of a Message, but also as possessor of superlative authority to which all must submit. Indeed, he is joined to Allah as the source of absolute command (XLVII.35). Verse 36 of Sura XXXIII says: 'It is not fitting for a believer, man or woman, when a matter has been decided by God and His Apostle, to have any option about their decision. If anyone disobeys God and His Apostle he is indeed on a clearly wrong path.'

Glad tidings and warnings

In describing the nature of the Message, special emphasis is laid on the announcement of good tidings and warning. In no less than 17 verses the Meccan Suras affirm that the Prophet has been sent only as announcer of good news and giver of warning. Good news consists of promise of the joys of paradise to those who believe in Allah, the Apostle and the Resurrection, and warning consists of allusion to the tortures of hell for those who do not. Descriptions of paradise and hell are given in clear and realistic terms throughout the Meccan Suras. On the whole the threat of punishment prevails over the promise of reward, especially as the punishment of the unbeliever goes further than torments in the hereafter and includes penalties of all kinds in this life. One outstanding feature of Qur'anic narratives concerning ancient times and peoples is the reminder of the innumerable calamities that befell the cities and tribes which failed to listen to divine messages. The fact that threats of torments in the Hereafter specially abound in the Meccan Suras suggests that during the early phases the Message relied principally on the factor of fear inspired by the warning that the Day of Judgement was at hand. Naturally there existed also the counterpart to this threat, namely the promise of paradise as a reward of faith. These were the consequences of the Final Judgement to come. But after the Prophet's emigration to Medina, when the Message had become more established, the inducements to the Call of Islam became more worldly, such as the promise of participation in the booty of war or the threat of physical punishment.

Commandments

But the most important difference between the Meccan and Medinese Suras is the contrast between counsel and advice on the one hand,

and laws and commandments on the other. The Meccan Suras contain
no commandments in the legislative sense. The spirit throughout is
that of exhortation, guidance, announcement of glad tidings and
admonition. For example Sura XVII enumerates the qualities which
characterise the exemplary believer. He worships Allah, respects his
parents, assists the needy, fulfils his obligations, avoids wrongdoing,
etc. But these do not appear as rules supported by legal sanctions; they
are general counsels of moral perfection, not limited to any particular
time and place. The nature of these injunctions appears from verse 41
which says: 'These are among the precepts of wisdom which thy Lord
has revealed to thee.'

However, after the emigration to Medina, the Prophet's role for the
rest of his life was that of legislator, ruler, arbitrator and statesman. In
this capacity he was called upon to decide on all kinds of questions
as they arose from day to day. This new situation inevitably brought
about a change in the nature, content and tone of the Medinese Suras,
thus differentiating them from the Meccan revelation. There thus came
into being a body of commandments and rules necessitated by the
circumstances of the time.[6]

Reference to the circumstances of the Prophet's life

Except for a very few occasions, such as where the Prophet's enemies
are condemned, or where God reminds the Prophet of the favours
bestowed on him in early times when he was poor and helpless, the
Meccan Suras contain no reference to the circumstances of the outer
life of the Prophet. The Medinese Suras, on the other hand, often deal
with matters relating to the Prophet's personal circumstances. For
example, in one Sura (XXXIII, 'The Confederates') 20 out of its 73
verses are concerned with such matters as the legitimation of the
Prophet's marriage with the divorced wife of his adopted son, the
description of the categories of women that the Prophet could marry,
the manner in which the Prophet's wives were to wear the veil, to
address men, and generally to conduct themselves, the strict injunction against believers marrying the Prophet's widows after death, the
prohibition of entering the Prophet's house without his permission.
The Prophet's person is specially exalted over the persons of all
believers (XXXIII.6). It is singled out as the most fitting pattern for
the conduct of those who hope in God. It is stressed that God and the
Angels bless the Prophet (XXXIII.56) and that therefore the believers
must do likewise and not vex or ill-treat the Prophet. Sura LVIII
instructs believers as to how they should comport themselves in assem-
blies where the Prophet is present, and requires them to offer alms
when they wish to confer with the Prophet in private (verse 13). The

whole of Sura LXVI ('The Prohibition') is concerned with a crisis which occurred in the Prophet's relations with his wives. The episode of the charge against Ayesha and the resulting prescription concerning punishment for adultery form an important part of Sura XXIV. Other similar instances, which lay at the root of Islamic law, will be found in the relevant parts of this book. What has been said in this paragraph suffices to illustrate one important difference between the Meccan and Medinese Suras.

The Hypocrites unmasked

The Meccan Suras contain no reference to that category of the Prophet's opponents who came to be called 'the hypocrites'. Hypocrites, in the specific sense in which the term is used in the Qur'an, did not exist in Mecca. Shortly after the emigration to Medina, when the Prophet had organised the Moslem community and had established his power as a leader, certain envious and ambitious persons who desired to acquire a position of leadership and access to material benefits, but who had no chance of achieving their end by open activity, began to play a role of duplicity. While swearing allegiance to the Prophet, they secretly engaged in intrigues in order to frustrate his work and campaigns. Their disloyalty was first detected at the battle of Uhud (early 625), and in spite of the determination with which the Prophet countered their activities they continued to weave their plots and to cause disaffection and desertion in the ranks of the Moslems during the Prophet's life. Consequently, frequent reference is made to them in the Medinese Suras, one of which (LXIII) concerns them only. In these texts the believers are warned of the danger of the activities of these real enemies and are commanded to abstain from befriending them, and to seize those of them who desert the ranks of the believers and to put them to death whenever they find them. 'The hypocrites', says verse IV.144, 'shall be cast into the lowest depths of Hell: there shall be none to help them.' A fuller account of the hypocrites is given elsewhere in this book. In this paragraph I only intend to point out that the part of the Qur'anic revelation which relates to the hypocrites belongs only to the Medinese period.

The Prophet's treatment of his opponents

There is a striking change in the attitude of the Prophet towards his adversaries as reflected in the Meccan Suras and as shown in his comportment in Medina. Victim in Mecca, he becomes avenger in Medina.

During his Meccan years the Prophet met with bitter hostility from the pagans in various forms: rejection of his message, contempt, abuse and persecution. His revelations were treated as ancient fables dictated by strangers, hallucinations of a deranged mind, babblings of a soothsayer, and a pack of lies (XVII.50, XXV.5–6, LXIX.41 to 42). His arch-enemy Abu Jahl even succeeded in forming a confederacy of the different clans of Quraish to boycott the Hashimi (the Prophet's) branch. The members of this branch, whether or not converts to the new religion, held themselves bound to protect their kinsman, and they submitted to the boycott which meant that they were virtually blockaded in the isolated quarter of Abu Talib for over two years (619–20). This situation also brought about a disaffection within the Hashimite clan in that Abu Lahab, the Prophet's uncle, joined the boycott and, when he succeeded to his brother Abu Talib on the latter's death in 619 as chief of the tribe, became a violent enemy of the Prophet. The hostile league against the Hashimites was at last broken up by the intervention of certain well-wishing members of the tribe, but Muhammad continued to be visited by persecutions even severer than those he had suffered before. In addition to these trials and the death of his guardian and protector Abu Talib he lost his greatest companion and counsellor, his wife Khadija. This made his heart and his home desolate and his solitude complete. There was now no one to protect him from his foes. The new chief of the tribe, his uncle Abu Lahab hated his nephew's innovation which set at nought the faith of the tribe's forebears. Disheartened by the attitude of the members of his own tribe, Muhammad thought of carrying his message elsewhere and decided in favour of Ta'if, some 70 miles east of Mecca, the home of the tribe of Thaqif, idol-worshippers but jealous rivals of the Quraish. But far from attracting the sympathy of the Thaqif during his ten-day residence among them, he found them as hostile as the Meccans and was at last driven away from Ta'if by being hooted through the streets and pelted with stones. Dejected, he returned to Mecca to face again the enmity of his own tribe.

In the face of his Meccan persecutors, the Prophet, having no power to react otherwise than by words, gave vent to his rancour by reciting verses in which Allah uttered curses and threats against them. The Qur'an refers to the Prophet's opponents once by name and several times by implication. The one opponent mentioned by name and subjected to a strong invective in a Sura of 5 verses (CXI) is the Prophet's uncle Abu Lahab. Once, when the Prophet had called his kinsmen together to announce his mission, Abu Lahab had cried out: 'May you perish! Was it for this that you called us together?' The curse came home to roost in Sura CXI: 'May the hands of Abu Lahab perish! May no profit come to him from all his wealth . . . He shall go down to burn in a flaming fire; his wife also . . .'

Apart from Abu Lahab none of the Prophet's enemies has been mentioned by name, but certain persons alluded to in different Suras have been identified by almost unanimous agreement. Prominent among them is Abu Jahl who in his opposition to the Prophet attempted to prevent him and his followers from going to the Ka'ba to pray. Verses XCVI.9–16 refer to this act of repression. 'Do you see the one who forbids God's servant from going to pray? . . . Let him beware, for if he does not desist, We will drag him by the forelock, the lying sinful forelock' Abu Jahl perished in the battle of Badr.

Ibn Wa'il is believed to be one of the two ill-wishers of the Prophet (the other being Walid ibn Mughaira) who were known to refer to the Prophet as 'abtar', meaning childless, thus venting their spite against him by taunting him with the loss of his infant son Qasim as a mark of divine displeasure. This appellation also boomeranged: 'Abtar shall be he who hates you!' (Sura CVIII). Here the term also covers the figurative meaning of one who is cut off from all hope.

The other originator of the title 'abtar', Walid ibn Mughaira, was an inveterate enemy of the Prophet. A plotter and a ringleader in slandering the Prophet, he supported his calumnies with oaths. In versed LXVIII.10–13 Allah so commands the Prophet: 'Do not obey the despicable man of many oaths, the defamer going about with calumnies, the opponent of good, the sinful transgressor, the bully who with all that is also base-born.' He is again referred to in LXXIV.19–26: 'He plotted . . . how he plotted! Then he said "this is nothing but magic derived from of old, nothing but the word of a mortal." Soon will I cast him into hell-fire.'

The Meccan opponents (Abu Jahl, Walid, Ibn Wa'il and others) are collectively condemned in Sura LXXXIII.29–35: 'Those in sin used to laugh at those who believed . . . but on the Day of Resurrection it is the believers who, reclining on raised couches, shall laugh at the unbelievers.'

Nothing angered the Prophet more than casting reflections on his recital of the Qur'an. To refer to the Word of God as 'ancient fables' and outpourings of a deranged mind was not only calumny, it was unpardonable blasphemy. Several passages in the Qur'an show that such accusations were currently made, and the commentaries identify the authors. The one who excited the Prophet's wrath in particular was a pagan named Nadhr ibn Harith who indulged in reciting Persian romances before gatherings of the Quraish, declaring them to be superior to the tales told in the Qur'an. No wonder that the Qur'an doomed him to a grievous fate: 'Some there are among men who would pay for idle tales in order in their ignorance to mislead others from the path of God and laugh it to scorn. For such there shall be a grievous punishment (XXXI.5).' In 624, after the battle of Badr,

Nadhr ibn Harith was executed. So was another prisoner named Uqba ibn Muit for a similar offence.

The theory of the three periods

The theme of the difference between the Meccan and the Medinese Suras finds an interesting illustration in the attempts which have been made at dividing the Qur'anic revelation into periods. One tripartite division assigns two periods to Mecca and one to Medina, the former being respectively lyrical and admonitory, the latter being journalistic and legislative. But another tripartite division applies only to the Meccan Suras. According to this division the Meccan revelations begin with the lyrical expression of an initial experience accompanied by an apocalyptic vision of the Last Judgement and an emphasis on the transcendence of the prophetic mission. Then they go on to voice the anguish of a 'prophet crying in the desert', warning, threatening, harping on the theme of the dire penalties inflicted on the people of ancient times who failed to heed the admonitions of divine messengers. The Prophet is overwhelmed by his enemies and cries out in despair. At this stage the style of poetry changes to that of diatribe. In the third period the tone becomes one of homily, sermon and prediction addressed not only to Meccans but to all Arabs, and the way is prepared for the organisation of the community of the faithful. Then the scene moves to Medina, where the community is formed, and the tone of the Suras changes accordingly. Whilst it was persuasive, promising or threatening in Mecca, it becomes mandatory and imperative in Medina. Muhammad is no longer a 'prophet crying in the desert'; he rules over an established community and demands obedience in Allah's name and in his own. 'He that obeys Allah and His Apostle shall dwell forever in gardens watered by running streams . . . But he that defies Allah and His Apostle . . . shall be cast into hell-fire and shall abide in it for ever' (Medinese Sura IV.13–14).

The 'Suras of Wrath'

Typical of the revelations of the second Meccan period (the period of anguish and travail) are the so-called 'terrible' or 'awesome' Suras. According to numerous traditions, this epithet was applied by the Prophet to Suras XI, LVI and CI and to 'their sisters'. The latter have been identified as Suras XXI, LXIX, LXXVII, LXXVIII, LXXXI. The occasion which gave rise to these Suras being qualified as 'Suras of Wrath' is reported to have been the following. In the latter days of the Prophet, Abu-Bakr once remarked sorrowfully to him that grey hairs were hastening on him. The Prophet raised his beard, looked at the grey hairs in it and said: 'It is the travail of inspiration which has done this.' Now quite plainly the common feature of these eight Suras is their terrifying apocalyptic tone. The Resurrection, Last Judgement and horrors of Hell are evoked in them in fearsome terms. Doomed to eternal perdition are the false gods and all those who have mocked and rejected the messengers of God. The horrors that lie in store for them are described in these as in other Suras. A brief exposition of them will be found in Chapter 7 in the section headed Hell and the Doomed.

The compilation of the Qur'an

During the lifetime of the Prophet the Qur'an did not exist in the form of a book containing the entire Revelation as it is known today. As the Revelation came to the Prophet, and as he uttered it, it was noted down by different scribes on such material as came to hand (palm fronds, bones, leather etc.). But this did not happen always; where the utterance was not immediately reduced to writing, it was preserved in the memories of men. Certain of the Prophet's companions formed, from these two sources, their own copies of the Revelation and arranged it in such order as seemed best to them, mostly following the Arab preference (in, for instance, recording poems) for placing the longer pieces before the shorter. Tradition has supplied posterity with the names of the Prophet's scribes, of those few who knew the Revelation by heart, and of those who possessed small collections of the Prophet's utterances for their own use. Although no complete transcription of the Qur'an was made during the life of the Prophet, the conception of the Revelation as a Book, like the Jewish and Christian scriptures, was clearly present in several passages in the Qur'an such as: 'This *book* is not to be doubted' (II.2); 'The glorious Qur'an is inscribed in a well-guarded *book* which none but the pure may *touch*' (LVI.77–79); '. . . an apostle from Allah reading pure and sanctified *scriptures*' (XCVIII.2). The opinion expressed by some commentators to the effect that the entire Revelation was put together, and the arrangement of its chapters was ordained, by the Prophet under divine guidance is evidently prompted by a passage in the Qur'an (LXXV.17) which says: 'We Ourselves will see to its [Qur'an's] collection.' Those commentators who recognise that the Prophet did not direct the compilation of the Qur'an under his supervision are so puzzled thereby that they resort to far-fetched conjectures, one of which is that the Prophet regarded it as sacrilegious to create an earthly transcript of the Celestial Archetype or the Guarded Tablet mentioned in LXXXV.22, where Allah has recorded His eternal laws and which is the original of all divine scriptures including the Qur'an.

Thus at the Prophet's death no authoritative compilation of the Qur'an was in existence. A number of scattered fragments and a few more or less complete copies of the Qur'an were in the hands of individuals, while a few of the Prophet's companions knew the Qur'an by heart and were able to reinforce and add to the written record by oral recitation. A year later the war with the false prophet Musailama broke out, and some of the Prophet's companions lost their lives in the fighting. This gave rise to anxiety lest, with the disappearance of those who had been close to the Prophet and who were the last remaining guardians of the Revelation, an important part of it should be lost forever. This fear was expressed by Umar to Abu Bakr who decided to ward off the danger. He summoned the Medinese Zaid ibn Thabit who had been one of the Prophet's scribes and who knew the entire Qur'an by heart, and commanded him to prepare a complete transcript of the Revelation. Zaid is reported to have demurred at first, saying that this task would require him to bear a burden heavier than that of lifting a mountain. But he obeyed Abu Bakr's command and devoted himself to the mission. He brought together the existing fragments of the Revelation and had recourse to his own memory and that of others for verifying and completing the written record. He then recopied the entire collection on leaves (suhuf) probably of parchment, and handed them to Abu Bakr from whom they passed to the possession of the second caliph Umar and were in due course inherited by the latter's daughter and the Prophet's widow Hafsa.

The copy thus made for Abu Bakr was not intended to become the authorised version for the use of the whole community; it was the personal property of the caliph. Side by side with it existed other collections which belonged to private individuals, notably those of Ali, Abdullah ibn Abbas, Ibn Mas'ud, Abu Musa Ash'ari and Obay ibn Ka'b, and which differed from each other in the ordering of the chapters and in certain details. Each possessor of a private copy naturally held his version to be authentic to the exclusion of all others, and this gave rise to differences in reading which endangered the emergence of a universally accepted text and consequently the unity of the creed. The realisation of this danger caused the third caliph Uthman (AD 644–656) to undertake the task of producing a unified, authoritative text which would eliminate all competing versions. This mission was again entrusted to Zaid ibn Thabit, aided by three companions of the Prophet. Uthman called upon Hafsa to entrust him with the 'leaves' prepared for Abu Bakr, and thereupon the commission of four (or more, the number having been set by some historians at twelve) embarked on a revision of the 'suhuf', taking into account, for additions and alterations, new fragments which had come to light as well as the memory of persons who had not been consulted on the first occasion. The result was a complete recension of the 'suhuf', the assemblage of which received the name of 'mus-haf', synonym of the

Qur'an. The 'suhuf' were then returned to Hafsa, on whose death some thirty years later they were destroyed. Thus came into being the official version of the Qur'an, fixing for all time, and without any possibility of variation, its contents as well as the ordering of its chapters and the sequence of the verses within each chapter. By order of Uthman copies were made for, and forwarded to, the four important Islamic centres of Mecca, Koufa, Basra and Damascus.

A word must be said about an alternative arrangement of the Suras. In the official version the Suras are not arranged in chronological order; indeed the order is partly the very reverse of chronological, the earliest Suras coming last. In the middle of the 19th century certain orientalists initiated a research with a view to discovering the order in which the different Suras were revealed. To this end they carefully studied the style of each Sura, the subjects treated in the different Suras and their probable connection with known historical events. They also examined an ancient chronological list which had existed but had not affected the Abu Bakr and Uthman recensions. The result of this investigation was the composition of chronological lists, principally by Weil and Nöldeke, and their adoption by historians and translators of the Qur'an, notably Rodwell and Sir William Muir. However, these new classifications have not supplanted, nor can they be expected to supplant, the order of sequence of the Suras established by the official recension.

I close this Introduction by giving some idea of the relative weight that the Qur'an attaches to the subjects it addresses. The following table shows the divisions of the subjects adopted in this book, the numbers of verses relating to each subject and the ratio (weight) of the number of verses in each chapter to the total number of verses in the Qur'an.[7]

For example, more that one-fifth of the verses of the Qur'an (1,390 verses) are devoted to the description of Resurrection, paradise and hell in clear and realistic terms which, however, are perhaps not to be taken in the literal sense. And if to these verses are added those concerning the consequences of faith, unbelief, polytheism and sin, the resulting number will amount to over one-third of all the verses of the Qur'an. Nearly one-fifth of all the verses describe the lives and experiences of prophets and certain historical or legendary figures of ancient times. These correspond more or less to the accounts existing in pre-Islamic sources; the reason for these descriptions, often involving repetition, is to lay emphasis on spiritual and ethical precepts which can be summarised in a few pages. Nearly 28% of the verses (1,787 in all) recite the glory, essence and attributes of God, and reiterate the divine origin of the Prophet's mission and of the Qur'anic revelation. Finally, over one-tenth contain religious, moral, judicial and social commandments.

Title of chapter and number of verses corresponding to each	Title of section	Number of verses corresponding to each section	Number of verses relevant to each chapter as percentage of all verses
Chapter Two: The Creator and His Creatures *1035 verses*	Allah	262	
	Creation	451	
	Angels	24	
	Jinn	22	
	Satan	91	
	Allah's Message to His Creatures	185	
			16.0%
Chapter Three: The Prophet and the Qur'an *752 verses*	The Prophet	355	
	The Qur'an	323	
	The abbreviated letters		
	Oaths uttered by Allah	74	
	The language of the Qur'an		
	The Prophet: neither a madman nor a soothsayer nor a poet		
	Some Qur'anic parables		
	The doctrine of abrogation		
	The Qur'an as seen by itself		
	The Qur'an and miracles		
	Explanation, interpretation and exegesis		
			11.6%
Chapter Four: The Previous Bearers of the Divine Message *1453 verses*	Adam	26	
	The sons of Adam: Abel and Cain	5	
	Noah	118	
	Hud and Salih	130	
	Abraham	209	
	Lot	73	
	Joseph	100	
	Elias	10	
	Jonah (Jonas)	16	
	Job	7	
	Shuaib	40	
	Moses and the Israelites	510	
	David and Solomon	63	
	Zacharias, John, Mary and Jesus	93	
	Some minor prophets		
	Some legendary figures	53	
			22.5%
Chapter Five: Some Historical Events *211 verses*	Description of past events	84	
	Destruction of past generations	117	
			3.3%
Chapter Six: Faith and Religion *830 verses*	The words Islam and Moslem	12	
	Faith (Belief)	220	
	Unbelief	367	
	Polytheism	89	
	Idols	33	
	The Hypocrites	47	
	The People of the Book	27	
	Attitude towards other religions	35	
			12.8%

Title of chapter and number of verses corresponding to each	*Title of section*	*Number of verses corresponding to each section*	*Number of verses relevant to each chapter as percentage of all verses*
Chapter Seven: The Other World *1390 verses*	The Hereafter	52	
	Resurrection	584	
	Responsibility	68	
	Hell and the doomed	367	
	Paradise and the blest	312	
	Purgatory	7	
			21.5%
Chapter Eight: Commandments *792 verses*	Religious commandments	95	
	Prayer, fasting, pilgrimage, Purity, prohibition of wine, fighting	141	
	Emigration	15	
	Booty of war	14	
	Morality and social behaviour	218	
	Usury	5	
	Civil law matters	19	
	Oaths and imprecation	90	
	Inheritance	19	
	Women mentioned in the Qur'an		
	The condition of women		
	Marriage	55	
	Divorce		
	The veil		
	The Prophet's wives		
	Slavery	14	
	Government	19	
	Criminal law	88	
			12.2%

Note: According to the Arabic edition of the Qur'an published in Cairo 1923, the total number of verses is 6252, whereas the total number represented in the table amounts to 6463 showing a difference of 211. This is due to the fact that a number of verses, dealing with two unconnected subjects, have been counted twice.

Notes to Chapter One

1. The doctrine of the infallibility of the Prophet requires interpretation in view of verses XL.57 and XLVII.21 in which Allah commands the Prophet to implore Him to forgive his sin (zanbika), and of verse XLVIII.2 where reference is made to Allah forgiving the Prophet's past and future sin (ma taqaddama min zanbika wa ma ta'akhkhara). That the Prophet had been in error before divine guidance came to him is stated in verse XCIII.7.
2. The chapters of the Qur'an are called Suras. The Roman figures appearing after Suras in this book indicate the traditional serial numbers of the Suras.
3. The vast corpus of Islamic faith, dogma, law and morality is made up of the Qur'an, the traditions of the Prophet, the first four Caliphs and the Shia Imams, the judicial doctrines of the four great schools of Sunni jurisprudence, and the principles arrived at through analogy and rational deduction. Among these sources absolute authority belongs of course only to the Qur'an; the others, though they play an important role in laying down the criteria of faith and conduct, are only valid to the extent that their conformity to the prescriptions of the Qur'an is established. The validity of a great number of traditions has in fact been called in question. To mention only the traditions of the Prophet, one of the principal collectors of these (Bukhari: 9th century) is reported to have examined 600,000 of them, of which he chose no more than 7,000. Doubt as to the authenticity of the traditions was expressed, at the time that the search for them was the most intense (9th century), in these words: 'In nothing do we see learned men more prone to untruth than in the fabrication of traditions'. (G. H. Jansen, *Militant Islam* New York, Harper & Row, 1979, p. 23.)
4. Dr J. E. Polak, who lived many years in Iran around the middle of the 19th century as Nasereddin Shah's doctor, writes in his memoirs that Mirza Saeed Khan, the then Minister of Foreign Affairs used to wash his eyes every time he saw a European in order to preserve his sight from impurity. (*Persien: Das Land und seine Bewohner*, Leipzig 1865.)
5. The human nature of Muhammad is emphasised in the Qur'an. Allah commands him again and again to say that he is only a messenger, that his knowledge does not extend to the unseen, that he is no angel, that he has no access to Allah's treasures, nor any unusual power over himself (VI.50, VII.188). At the ill-fated battle of Uhud Allah keeps up the spirit of the flinching combatants with these words: 'Muhammad is only a messenger; messengers have passed away before him. If he died or were slain, would you turn back on your heels?' (III.138). As a human being he is exposed to error. When he is close to falling into error, Allah sustains and saves him: 'Indeed the unbelievers were near to tempting you away from that which We revealed to you so that you might forge some other scripture in Our name, and then they would have taken you surely as their friend. If We had not given you strength you would almost have inclined somewhat to them and would then have incurred a double punishment in this life and in the next' (XVII.73–75).
6. A celebrated student of Islam, referring to the striking change which occurs in the Qur'anic revelations after the Prophet's emigration to Medina, comments as follows on the peculiarities of the Medinese revelations: 'In the Medinese predications . . . expression becomes less colourful, is brought to a less elevated level by the nature of the daily subjects which

are to be treated, and sometimes descends to the level of current prose . . . The Prophet now struggles against his adversaries, both within and outside the community, who frustrate his designs; he organises his followers and establishes a civil and religious law for the new-born community, and lays down rules for the practical circumstances of life.' (I. Goldziher, *Le dogme et la loi de l'Islam*, Paris, Geuthner, 1973, p. 10.)

7. The text of the Qur'an adopted as the basis of this work is the edition (Arabic) published in Cairo in 1923. The order of the Suras as well as the numbering of verses in each Sura as they appear in this work conform to the same edition. My justifications for using this text are the same as Régis Blachère's from which I quote as follows: 'The text adopted as the basis of this translation is that of the edition published in Cairo in 1342 of the Hegira (AD 1923) under the aegis of King Fouad the First of Egypt. It seemed indeed preferable to start from a text which is *recognised by Islamic orthodoxy* rather than from the Flugel recension which is generally used in Europe. It is also known that the Cairo Vulgate and the Flugel edition differ as to the division into (i.e. the numbering of) verses and that the division used in the first is in general more satisfactory than that used in the second.' (Italics are mine.) (Régis Blachère, *Le Coran*, Paris, G.P. Maisonneuve, 1947.)

CHAPTER TWO

THE CREATOR AND HIS CREATURES

Allah

The verses of the Qur'an make it clear that both the concept of Allah as the Supreme Being and the very name Allah existed in the Jahiliyya or pre-Islamic Arabia, not only among the Jews and the Christians, but also among certain Arab Bedouin tribes. Besides, the word occurs often in the poetry of the Jahili period and also in composite pre-Islamic names such as Abdullah (servant of Allah). Certain pagan tribes believed in a god whom they called 'Allah' and whom they believed to be the creator of heaven and earth and holder of the highest rank in the hierarchy of the gods. It is well known that the Quraish as well as other tribes believed in Allah, whom they designated as the 'Lord of the House' (i.e. of the Ka'ba). The polytheists conceived of a number of divinities, goddesses, angels and even jinns as mediators between the creator and his creatures. All Arabs attached special importance to the notion of an other-worldly being interceding on their behalf on the day of Judgement. Indeed their religion consisted of belief in the existence of such heavenly intercessors. Certain verses of the Qur'an state clearly that the polytheists worshipped their gods only as mediators between themselves and Allah. Verse 4 of Sura XXXIX quotes them as saying: 'We only serve them [i.e. their gods] in order that they may bring us nearer to Allah.' Verse 27 of Sura XLVI also mentions the pagans' trust in their gods as mediators, and asks: 'Why then was no help forthcoming to them from those whom they worshipped as gods?'

The Qur'an refers in several places to the fact that the Jahili Arabs believed in Allah as the possessor of greatness and supreme power, and expresses astonishment therefore at their obstinate refusal to submit to Him. Verses 61–65 of Sura XXIX say: 'If you ask them who it is that has created the heavens and the earth and subjected the sun and the moon they will say "Allah" . . . If you ask them who it is that sends down water from the sky and thereby quickens the dead earth, they will reply "Allah" . . . When they embark they pray to Allah with

21

all fervour, but when He brings them safe to land they serve other gods besides Him.' The same remark is made in verse 32 of Sura XXXI as follows: 'When the waves, like giant shadows, envelop them, they pray to Allah with all devotion, but no sooner does He bring them safe to land than some of them falter between faith and unbelief.' Verses 86 to 92 of Sura XXIII repeat the above-quoted question and answer, and go on to ask further: 'In whose hands is the sovereignty of all things; who is it that protects all, while against him there is no protection' and then echo the answer "Allah".' Verse 37 of Sura XVI and verse 42 of Sura XXXV point to the fact that when the pagans take a solemn oath they invariably invoke the name of Allah. Thus, reiterating the absolute belief of the pagans in the greatness of Allah, the question is asked: 'Then why do they not reflect; why do they persevere in their bewitched worship of other gods?'

It is therefore clear that the Qur'anic conception of Allah is not entirely new, but it transformed the Jahili conception so radically that is can be said that the two divinities have nothing in common. The Jahili Allah has associates, even though inferior to him in rank; the Qur'anic stands strictly alone. The Jahili Allah is a far-away object of ritual practices; the Qur'anic dominates every phase of man's life from birth to death. In the full sense of the word, Allah is a presence, a person and a living force.

The personality of Allah stands out in almost every verse of the Qur'an, but the substance of the description can be condensed into a few sentences, because the treatment of this theme in the Qur'an is characterised, more than that of any other theme, by repetition.

All the Suras of the Qur'an except one (IX: Repentance) begin with the phrase 'In the name of Allah the Most Gracious, the Merciful'. But from this it should not be inferred that Allah is all compassion and mercy. Over and over again we find Allah described in the Qur'an as revengeful, unforgiving, stern in retribution, and terrible in His wrath. His outstanding attribute is His oneness. The Prophet is quoted as having said that the Qur'anic injunction, 'Say, He is God, the One and Only', contained in Sura CXII is equal to one-third of the whole Book. In this Sura Allah commands the Prophet to describe Him to the believers in these words: 'He is eternal, absolute, He does not beget, nor is He begotten, and there is none like Him.' But in the last analysis Allah cannot be defined; His qualities include all contraries and are innumerable. The mind of man cannot encompass knowledge of the divine. Nevertheless the Qur'an effectively helps believers to form a mental image of the deity by describing His action in the universe in language which is comprehensible to man, and by calling Him by numerous names each of which represents a perceptible attribute. Verse 179 of Sura VII says: 'The most Beautiful Names belong to Allah, so call on Him by them.' The attribution of the Most Beautiful Names to Allah also appears in verses XVII.110 and XX.7. Tradition has elaborated a list of 99 Names taken mostly from the contents of the Qur'an for purposes of celebrating the praise of Allah. But what are the names by which believers should invoke Allah in their prayers and in moments of communion? Quoted below are the names and attributes which accompany the mention of Allah throughout the Qur'an:

Master of the worlds; forgiving, compassionate; Lord of the day of Judgement; creator, preserver and destroyer; Lord of the East and the West; He who has no need; living, wakeful and everlasting; owner of the earth, the heavens and all that exists in between; holder of the keys to the worlds both visible and invisible; He who has no equal, no associate and no offspring; the first and the last; the manifest and the hidden; all glorious; omnipotent, omniscient and richest of the rich; He on whose will there is no constraint; watchful over His creatures; ever ready to receive man's gratitude and man's repentance; forgiver of all sins save that of idolatry; dispenser of rewards to the virtuous and punishment to evildoers; just, swift in reckoning; stern in retribution; grievous tormentor of the wicked; exacting and revengeful; best judge; nourisher; He who guides and leads astray; friend to believers and foe to unbelievers; superlatively wise; the best of all plotters; He who hears and sees; He who causes the living to die and the dead to rise again.

Many of the attributes associated in the Qur'an with the name of Allah are equally applicable to man. The Qur'anic conception of the nature of the divinity is essentially transcendental. Allah is above and beyond all description. He resembles nothing, and nothing resembles Him. 'There is nothing whatever like Him' (XLII.9). But at the same time the Qur'an presents throughout its verses a substantial image of Allah, often in corporeal terms. The verse just quoted is completed by the words 'and He hears and sees'. Another verse (XX.46) cites Allah as saying to Moses and Aaron: 'Fear not, for I am with you: I hear and see.' Indeed the scriptures of the monotheistic religions speak so frequently of God in physical, corporeal and moral terms that the notion of transcendence is sometimes obscured.[1]

There exists an apparent difficulty in the Qur'an in regard to references to God's knowledge. In almost every page of the Qur'an there is mention of God's omniscience. To quote a few examples from among a multitude: God's knowledge encompasses everything; He knows what is in the heavens and on earth; the visible and the invisible; the past, the present and the future; the promptings of men's souls; every word that is spoken in the heavens or on earth. Man does not embark on any action but God watches him; He knows who goes astray and who follows the straight path. Nothing can be hidden from Him.

One of the sentences most frequently repeated in the Qur'an is: 'He knows the secrets of all hearts.' Verse LVIII.8 puts emphasis on God's insight into the machinations of men: 'If three men talk in secret together He is their fourth, if four He is their fifth, if five He is their sixth; whether fewer or more, wherever they be He is with them.'

These descriptions show clearly that God's knowledge belongs to His essence, i.e. it is not accidental or adventitious. Being all-comprehensive, it needs nothing to be added to it. But a difficulty arises here: several passages in the Qur'an imply that God seeks knowledge which He did not possess before: a few examples follow: 'We alternate these vicissitudes among men so that *Allah may know* the true believers' (III.134). 'We decreed your former qibla only *in order that We might know* who followed the Apostle and those who would turn on their heels' (II.138). 'The defeat which you suffered when the two armies met was ordained *by Allah so that He might know* the true believers and the hypocrites' (III.161). 'We roused them *in order to know* which of the two parties could best tell the length of their stay' (XVIII.11). And, as if to answer the question why Satan was able to mislead men, verse XXXIV.20 says: 'He has no power over them except *that We might know* who believes in the Hereafter and who is in doubt concerning it.'

In order to overcome the difficulty some translators have rendered the phrase 'that He may *know*' (*la ya'lam*) by the words 'that He may *test*', but this does not remove the difficulty because testing also implies an attempt at ascertaining what was in doubt before. Indeed, in one instance God actually 'tests' in order to 'know': 'Allah will test you in a little matter of game ... *so that He may know* those who truly fear Him unseen' (V.95).

Adjectives describing Allah's attributes (numbering over 50) occur repeatedly throughout the Qur'an. Thus the sentence, 'Allah is oft-forgiving and merciful', occurs 84 times (apart from the use of the word 'merciful' 113 times in the sacred formula with which all the Suras except one begin). The description 'Allah is Exalted' is repeated 72 times, Omniscient 68, Wise 64, Hearing and Seeing 54, Omnipotent 32 and Stern in retribution 32 times. The epithet least repeated (only twice) is 'the Best of Plotters'.

It follows clearly from the Qur'anic revelation that Allah does not reveal Himself through incarnation in human form or human attributes. The absolutely transcendent Deity cannot be directly apprehended by man. 'The vision of man does not apprehend Him' (VI.103). 'Man can apprehend nothing of His knowledge except what He wills' (II.256). But when God so wills He vouchsafes knowledge of Himself to man by opening his bosom (VI.125) and his eyes (VI.104) to the perception of the 'signs' and proofs which He places before him and within him (XL.153). The Qur'an abounds in passages which emphasise the approach to knowledge of God through the contemplation of His signs. 'In the heavens and the earth are signs for those who believe' XLV.2. 'In the creation of the heavens and the earth, in the alternation of night and day . . . in the movement of the winds . . . are indeed signs for a people who understand' (II.159). It is no paradox to say at the same time that God cannot be apprehended directly and that He can be seen everywhere.

Among the Qur'anic expressions which have occasioned attempts at exegesis the most important is that of the 'Word of God'. The use of the term 'Word' with a divine connotation (Logos in Greek and kalima in Arabic) precedes the Qur'an. In monotheism it goes back to Judaism, and in philosophy to the Stoics. In both contexts 'Word' symbolises the creation, design, ordering and governance of the Cosmos. A clear expression of its meaning is contained in the Gospel according to St John which says that 'in the beginning was the Word, and the Word was with God, and the Word was God'. And it goes on to identify the Word with Jesus Christ in whom it says that the Word became flesh. This statement finds a parallel in the Qur'an where (III.40) it is said that the angels brought glad tidings to Mary from God: a Word from Him bearing the name Christ Jesus son of Mary. Thus in Christianity the Word of God is the person of Jesus enshrined in Mary, while in Islam the Word of God is the Holy Qur'an revealed to the Prophet through Archangel Gabriel. 'He brings down the Revelation to thy heart by God's will' (II.91). It should be added that in the language of the Qur'an 'Word' has a wide range of connotation including: the fiat of creation (III.52), divine utterance (IV.162), creation independently of father or seed (IV.169), revelation (IX.6), warning (XXXIX.71), God's bounties (XXXI.26).

A brief reference is necessary here to another Qur'anic term to which commentators have devoted especial attention: the term 'Rahman'. The Arabic words 'Rahman' (differently translated as 'Most Gracious', 'Compassionate' or 'Most Merciful') and 'Rahim' (translated as 'Merciful') which appear in the invocation of the name of Allah at the beginning of the Suras both represent aspects of the quality of mercy; Rahman in a universal, characteristically divine sense, Rahim in a more restricted sense especially applicable to Allah in His relation to man. That 'Rahman' has an exclusively divine connotation follows from the fact that the Qur'an frequently uses it as a synonym of Allah. Verse XVII.110 says 'Call upon Allah or call upon Rahman'. In only one Sura (XIX) the word 'Rahman' has been used no less than 13 times in lieu of Allah, e.g. 'It is not consonant with the majesty of the Rahman to beget a son' (verse 93): 'Satan was a rebel against Rahman' (verse 45). Verse XX.4 says 'Rahman sits in majesty on the

Throne'. These verses point to the conclusion that 'Rahman' is another word for 'Allah', which identification puts emphasis on 'mercy' as a characteristic of Allah.[2]

One aspect of Allah's Rahmaniyya (attribute of mercy) is that He is self-subsisting (hayy ul qayyum, II.256) and free from all want and yet He is solicitous for man, His creature who is all want, and shows him the way to redemption. 'O man, it is you that have need of God, but God is the One Free of all wants [Ghani], worthy of all praise' (XXXV.15). 'Thy Lord is self-sufficient, the Lord of Mercy' (VI.133). The quality of 'rahmaniyya' embraces other divine attributes such as that of being 'all-forgiving' (ghafur, ghafer) on which the Qur'an lays especial emphasis (as in VII.152 and XL.2 and indeed throughout the Qur'an).

Creation

Allah is the creator of all things, the producer of being from non-being; that is His greatest and most manifest attribute. There is no creator but He. He is the preserver of heaven and earth. All that exists will vanish save He. Whatever exists on earth, in the heavens and in the souls of men is a sign and symbol of His power and His greatness, and is a reminder of the innumerable favours that He has bestowed on mankind, for which mankind must be eternally thankful to Him. All creatures that exist, angels as well as animate and inanimate beings, prostrate themselves before Allah and praise Him. His creatures are not only things that can be seen with the eye; the Qur'an frequently refers to invisible things: the Spirit (Gabriel), angels, jinns and demons. A great many verses of the Qur'an enumerate the things created by Allah. In order to create, Allah need only say, 'be, and it is' (II.111). This is how everything has come into being.

The Qur'anic cosmogony can be briefly described: Allah has created seven heavens and has placed them one above the other over our earth, in perfect and flawless order, each orbiting in its appointed course. The sevenfold superimposition of the heavens repeated in five verses (II.27, XXIII.17, LXV.12, LXVII.3, LXXVIII.12) is complemented by mention of the zodiacal signs, of the sun and the moon, and of beautiful stars and flashing meteors, the latter serving as missiles to be hurled at the devils when they go eavesdropping outside the Celestial Concourse (LXVII.5, XV.16–18, XXXVII.6–10, LXXII.9).

The Qur'an emphasises that Allah is never unmindful of His creation (XXIII.17). He has created as many earths as He has created heavens: 'Allah is He Who created seven heavens, and of the earth a similar number' (LXV.12); and for those who inhabit the earth He has provided all that is needed to ensure their physical and spiritual well-being. In the entire range of visible objects of creation there is nothing which the Qur'an does not mention over and over again in the context of their usefulness to man: heavens, sun, moon, stars, night, day, clouds, wind, rain, earth, ways, seas, rivers, fountains, mountains, plants, certain fruits specially dates, grapes and pomegranates, minerals (iron), animals, etc. If it is asked what is the reason for such repetitious mention of objects which lie before our eyes, the answer is that no amount of emphasis on God's signs and symbols will be sufficient for testifying to God's greatness, His power and the favours that He has vouchsafed to humanity. Mankind is the noblest object of divine creation. At the very inception of creation, Allah set up Man as His vicegerent on earth, to him alone did He teach the names of all things; He commanded the angels to prostrate themselves before Adam; He placed Adam in the eternal garden of Eden. He created all things for the sake of Man. He made the earth to serve as Man's dwelling place, He made the stars in order to guide Man in his navigation, and the sun and moon in order to serve as the basis of Man's calendar. Verse 36 of the Sura IX says that on the day when God created the heavens and the earth He divided the months into twelve, four of which were destined to be sacred. He created animals so that their flesh would nourish Man and that they would bear Man's burdens. He sent down the rain to fertilise the land in order to bear food for Man and his animals. The process by which Man grows by stages from the embryo to maturity, then to old age and finally to death has been repeatedly described. But God, after having created Man in the best of moulds, abases him, except those who believe and do good deeds, to the lowest of low degrees (XCV.5 and 6).

As regards the length of time during which the Creation has taken place, the Qur'an says in numerous verses that God created the universe in six days,[3] and that God's day equals one thousand years. Therefore according to the Qur'an Creation has taken place in 6,000 years. Certain commentators have expressed the opinion that the word 'year' in this context has been used, not in the ordinary sense, but figuratively to mean an unlimited period of time. Others, however, maintain that this interpretation does not seem justified in the face of the precise wording of the relevant verses in which it is clearly stated that 'a day in the sight of thy Lord is like a thousand years *of your reckoning*' (XXII.47 and XXXII.4).

The Qur'an is at pains to demonstrate that Allah's act of creation is no idle sport, play or pastime (XXI.16), but, apart from the hint that everything was created to serve man's needs, does not reveal the nature of the divine plan or the rationale and teleology of creation. It does state that the creation of mankind and the jinn was motivated alone by Allah's desire to be worshipped (LI.56), but men and jinn are only a minor part of creation. The Qur'an says that the creation of heaven and earth is much greater than that of man (XL.59). In Allah's entire creation there are signs for those who understand: the man of faith should, with every posture that his body takes, reflect on the wonders of the universe and say: 'Lord, you have not created all this in vain' (III.188). Allah's motive in creating the entire universe (which causes Him no fatigue or weariness: II.256 and XLVI.32) does not appear in the Qur'an but is reported in Hadith literature. Thus, according to one tradition attributed to the Prophet, Allah says: 'I was a hidden treasure. Then did I feel the love of being known, and I created the Creation in order that I should be known.' According to another tradition Allah addresses the Prophet in these words: 'Were it not for thee, I would not have created the heavens.'

Creation is not an act done once and for all, but may be renewed whenever Allah so wills (XXIX.18, L.15). As a retort to unbelievers who denied the possibility of resurrection, the Qur'an says several times that a 'second or new' creation is as easy to Allah as the first (XXI.104, XIII.5, XVII.52,100,101).

Just as the Old Testament, representing God as being well-pleased with His creation (Genesis I.31), says that on completion of the work of each of the six creative days He saw all that He had created and 'it was very good', so does the Qur'an quote Allah as saying, in the context of the creation and evolution of Man, 'Blessed be Allah, the best of creators' (XXIII.12–14).

Nevertheless Allah does not appear, from the contents of the Qur'an, to be wholly satisfied with His creation. Man, most favoured of His creatures, has proved to be ungrateful and arrogant, and has provoked Allah's wrath and terrible vengeance as reflected throughout the Qur'an. But Allah's displeasure appears to extend to the whole of His creation as is implied in the contents of two Suras, CXIII and CXIV. In the former, God commands the Prophet to say: 'I seek refuge in the Lord of Daybreak from the *mischief* of His creation.' Then follows a reference to the mischiefs of darkness, witchcraft and envy. In the latter Sura God commands the Prophet to seek refuge in the Lord of Men from the *mischief* of temptation, personified as 'the slinking prompter who whispers in the hearts of men'. These mischiefs of creation constitute the core of the problem of evil.

Angels

According to the Qur'an the universe does not consist only of visible beings and objects; there are also things that cannot be seen with the eye. Ontologically there is no difference between visible and invisible things. In Allah's sight all things created are real, eminently real since He swears by them in declaring the glory of the Prophet (LXIX.38,39). The invisible beings mentioned in the Qur'an are angels, jinn and demons. Of these only angels manifest themselves occasionally to the elect of God; in respect of the other two species, the Qur'an makes no mention of their being visible to men, though reference is frequently made to their doings.

The Qur'an commands men to believe in angels as they believe in Allah, the Book and the Prophet. Angels are the purest and noblest beings created by God. Whilst man was fashioned from moulded clay into which God then breathed of His Spirit, angels were created from pure spirit unmixed with any earthly substance. Nevertheless the spiritual plus material nature of man gave him an advantage in the sight of God over the purely spiritual nature of angels. Thus He chose man as His vicegerent on earth (disregarding the angels' protest) and taught Man the names of all things (II.28,29).

The eternal dwelling of angels is the heavens where they form the celestial concourse and ceaselessly celebrate the glory of the Lord and sing His praise. Of the deliberations which take place in the celestial concourse none, not even the Prophet, can obtain any knowledge (XXXVIII.69). But angels are not forever confined to their heavenly home. They also descend to earth, flying on two, three or four pairs of wings to do God's errands (XXXV.1). Whole hosts of angels glide swiftly on all kinds of missions: tearing out the souls of the wicked, drawing out gently the souls of the blest (LXXIX.1–5).

At the time of the appearance of the Prophet the public believed firmly that any message purporting to be divine must be brought to earth visibly by angels. They therefore refused to believe in the divine origin of Muhammad's message because it had not been brought to them by angels.

In one important respect, angels are superior to men. They are the intermediaries for conveying God's message to those chosen by Him (XVI.2). The Qur'an recites how the Archangel Gabriel conveys Allah's message to the Prophet (LIII.5 *et seq.*, LXXXI.20,23). A description in realistic terms is given of the meeting that takes place between Gabriel and Muhammad. Moreover, the word of command 'Recite' with which Sura XCVI begins is uttered by Gabriel who thus begins the cycle of revelations. Verse XVI.104 calls Gabriel 'the Holy Spirit'. Verses II.91 and 92 also refer to Gabriel as the angel who brings inspiration; in this context it is said that whoever is an enemy of the angels Gabriel and Michael incurs the enmity of Allah. Sura XCVII says that on the Night of Power (Revelation) the angels and spirit (Holy Spirit or Gabriel) descend to earth, being bearers of divine commands on all matters.

The verses of the Qur'an establish a close relation between the words Spirit, Holy Spirit, Gabriel and inspiration. Spirit is synonymous on the one hand with Gabriel and on the other with inspiration as a threefold mystery: its origin is God's command, its bearer is Gabriel and its recipient is Allah's Apostle. No greater knowledge than this is vouchsafed to Man on this primordial question of inspiration (XVII.85).

Many verses of the Qur'an contain references to angels as spiritual agents and trusted servants of God. The Throne of God rests on the shoulders of eight angels (LXIX.17 and XL.7). Other angels stand around the Throne, continuously serving and praising God and imploring for mercy on behalf of sinners (II.28, XLII.3, XXXIX.75). The guardians of Paradise are angels. Hell is guarded by 19 stern angels (LXVI.6 and LXXIV.30); their leader, a most severe angel, refuses all mercy to the doomed (XLIII.77). The heavenly hosts consist of angels (XLVIII.4). At the battle of Badr Allah sends down a host of 1,000 angels to help Muhammad's army (VIII.9). In connection with the battle of Uhud the Prophet says to his troops that if they were steadfast Allah would send 3,000 or even 5,000 angels to help them (III.120,121). In verse XXXIII.9 Allah reminds the Moslems that He had sent down hosts of invisible angels to help them at the battle of the Trench.

There is mention by reference in the Qur'an of the fall of an angel. This is Iblis (Satan) of whom the Qur'an says (II.32, VII.10, XV.30) that when God commanded the angels to prostrate themselves before Man they all obeyed *except Iblis* who rebelled by saying in arrogance: 'You created me from fire and him from clay.' There is also an allusion to the fall of the two angels Harut and Marut (II.96) who came down to earth but became the victims of an accusation of sorcery and were punished. This charge is denied by the Qur'an, but is claimed by Jewish and Christian tradition according to which the two angels had entreated God to send them to earth to judge men for sinning. But when they came they fell prey to the charms of a beautiful woman and committed several sins in order to win her favours. For this God refused them re-entry into heaven and gave them a choice between being punished in this life or in the Hereafter. Having chosen the former they were suspended head downwards in a pit in Babylon where they will remain until doomsday. As for the woman she ascended to heaven by using the 'Most Great Name of God' which the angels had taught her. But she was refused entry into Paradise, and

God transformed her into the star Venus. The New Testament also refers to angels who having sinned were put by God into a gloomy dungeon to be held for judgement (2 Peter ii.4 and Jude 6).

A special mission which is entrusted to angels by Allah is that of watching over men as protectors and witnesses. Each person is flanked by two angels, sitting one on his left and one on his right. Verse XIII.12 says: 'Each person has a succession of angels before him and behind him who watch over him by God's command.' Verse VI.61 likewise states that God watches over His servants by sending angels to guard them. The *Kashf al-Asrar* commentary quotes a tradition which says that the angel sitting on the right of each person records his good deeds, while the angel on his left records his evil deeds. 'Kind, honourable . . . knowing and understanding', they observe, listen and record. Thus is prepared in respect of each person the conclusive record of his deeds, which is produced on the day of Judgement (LXXXII.12, L.16, XLIII.80). Angels descend on steadfast believers and say to them: 'Fear not and do not grieve . . . we are your protectors in this life and in the Hereafter' (XLI.30-31). Conversely they fulfil the task of torturers when they descend to take the souls of apostates while smiting them on their faces and their backs (XLVII.27). These torturer-angels should not be confused with the principal taker of souls: 'The angel of death who has been given charge of you will carry off your souls; then to your Lord you shall return' (XXXII.11).

Finally, two passages occur in the Qur'an concerning the descent of angels and Spirit to earth and their ascent heavenwards. Sura XCVII says that on the Night of Power[4] which is better than 1,000 months, the angels and Spirit come down with Allah's permission on every errand. Sura LXX says that angels and Spirit accomplish the ascent to heaven in the space of one day, whose measure is 50,000 years.

Jinn

Jinn have been mentioned in 40 Suras. Sura LXXII is entitled 'The Jinn'; 15 out of the 28 verses of this Sura speak consecutively of these creatures. A group of them have assembled together and discuss the Qur'an, their beliefs and the beliefs of mankind. The Prophet gains knowledge of this discourse through revelation. The Jinn have heard a recital of the Qur'an and have found it to be a wondrous Book which shows the straight path and teaches a faith which saves men and Jinn from eternal doom. The Jinn have now realised that what some of them or indeed all men used to say in their folly was vain: God has neither associates, spouse or offspring. Those people who had believed the Jinn to be God's associates were in grievous error. Those who have not ceased to seek shelter with the Jinn will be sorely disappionted, for their appeal to the Jinn will only increase their insubordination. The Jinn have now determined to mend their ways. In the past they used to climb to the sky in order to approach the Heavenly Concourse and, by stealing a hearing, to acquire knowledge of the mysteries of the world above, but now they have become aware that the heavens are watched over by stern guards who are armed with flaming fires to drive away intruders and eavesdroppers. They know now that they cannot frustrate God either on earth or in heaven. Now that guidance has come to them, some of them have surrendered to God's will and will therefore be saved, while others have remained recalcitrant and will become the fuel of Hell. Nevertheless they are in doubt as to whether God's intention is to inflict evil on His creatures or to bring guidance to them (LXXII.10).

A short reference is made in XLVI.28–30 to the vision in which Muhammad acquires knowledge of the deliberations of the Jinn. The commentators explain that the vision occurred at the end of a visit which the Prophet paid to Taif, the nearest important city to Mecca, in 620 when, having suffered persecution at the hands of the Meccans after the death of his uncle and protector, he decided to look for sympathy and help elsewhere. In this he was disappointed, for the people of Taif maltreated and finally expelled him after ten days. He then started, in a mood of utter despair, on the return trip to Mecca. Halfway lay the vale of Nakhla, where he halted for the night. In the middle of the night he rose to offer, in an excited frame of mind, a prayer of entreaty for divine help, which has been preserved in the commentaries. Then in his mind's eye he witnessed a scene which dissolved his despair. A company of the Jinn passed by as he was reciting the Qur'an, and being attracted by the chanting stopped to listen. Then they went back to their people and said: 'We have just been listening to a scripture revealed since the time of Moses, confirming the previous scriptures and directing to the truth and to a straight path. O our people, listen to this one who invites you to God and believe in Him. He will forgive you your sins and deliver you from a grievous penalty.'

The Jinn form part of God's creation like mankind, but they are distinct from men, having been created before Adam (XV.27). Adam was created from clay, but the Jinn from smokeless fire. Satan was also created from fire, and is therefore congeneric with Jinn. 'Iblis', says verse XVIII.48, 'was one of the Jinn.' The phrase 'Jinn and men' which occurs frequently in the Qur'an (VI.130 *inter alia*) shows that these are two distinct species of creatures, which have this in common that God addresses them alike. The Jinn has been created from fire but possesses a body since the Qur'an speaks of 'a company of Jinn' (LXXII.1) and of 'persons' among them with whom some seek shelter (LXXII.6). Also the Jinn formed part of Solomon's army and attendants. They cannot therefore be disembodied spirits as some commentators have suggested. Yet another argument can be advanced for the corporeality of the Jinn; verse 120 of Sura XI says: 'The Word of your Lord shall be fulfilled: "I will fill Hell with Jinn and men all together." ' The Jinn must therefore have physical substance to be consumable by fire.

Commentators suggest that the 'company of Jinn' mentioned in XLVI.28 and LXXII.1 who heard the Qur'an recited and, bowing in veneration before its grandeur, embraced Islam and proselytised their people, were not ethereal, semi-spiritual beings, but were men of a type unfamiliar in Arabia, perhaps leaders of a Jewish community of Nisibin. The word 'company' being the translation of 'nafar' which in Arabic is a unit of counting and denotes any number between three and nine, commentators set its exact number at nine and even go so far as to give names to the nine members of the 'company'.

The Qur'anic references to Jinn show clearly that these are real creatures separate from mankind but bound by the same obligation towards the deity as men in the matter of worship and obedience. On two occasions Jinn and men are addressed collectively in the Qur'an: once, on the Day of Judgement, they will be reminded that God sent messengers to warn them but they did not heed the divine admonition; and on another occasion it is brought home to them that they would in vain try, in the absence of authority from God, to pass beyond the limits of power that God has prescribed for them (LV.33).

When Allah addresses the assembly of the Jinn on Judgement Day, he calls them to account for having seduced mankind on earth and dooms them to hell-fire. On hearing Allah reprove the Jinn (verse VI.128), the votaries of Jinn among men speak up as if to defend their seducers. They say: 'Our Lord, we have indeed profited from one another's company, but we have now reached the end of the term that You had allowed us.' Allah then says: 'The fire shall be your dwelling-place forever unless Allah decrees otherwise.'

Satan

Satan (also called Iblis) is the personification of arrogance, insubordination and all that is evil. He is the inveterate enemy of mankind; he leads men into temptation and prompts them to disobey God's commandments and lead a sinful life. The Qur'an relates several times how

Satan refused to bow down to Adam when all the angels were ordered by God to do so. He claimed superiority over Adam who was created from clay whilst he had been created from fire. Satan belonged to the category of the Jinn, whose creation had preceded that of Man (XVIII.48). It is also implied that Satan was one of the angels. Verses VII.10 and XV.30 *et seq.* say that when Allah ordered the angels to prostrate themselves before Adam, *all the angels* did so *except Iblis* who refused.

For Satan's act of rebellion Allah uttered a curse on him until the day of Judgement, but Satan asked that, although thus condemned, he should be granted a 'respite' until Resurrection, and Allah granted him such respite (XV.37 and VII.14).

Satan, thus reprieved, discloses the motive of his request. Addressing Allah in response to His verdict, he says: 'Since You have led me astray, I will waylay Your servants as they walk on Your straight path and spring upon them from the front and from the rear, from their right and from their left; then You shall find the greater part of them ungrateful' (VII.15, XV.38 and XXXVIII.83). With a rebellious arrogance in the face of the curse laid upon him, Satan exposes further the plan of his future deeds: 'I will take my toll of a goodly number of Your servants. I will lead them astray, will arouse in them vain desires, will order them to slit the ears of cattle[5] and to deface Allah's creation' (IV.118 *et seq.*). Allah's rejoinder is that Satan shall have no power over His servants, except such as put themselves in the wrong and follow Satan, and these shall become the fuel of Hell (XXXVIII.85). Allah is of course conscious of the mischief that Satan introduced into His creation, a mischief so great that when Allah makes Muhammad a Prophet He warns him to protect himself from it by taking refuge in Him (Sura CXIV).

Satan lost no time in making use of his 'respite'. No sooner was Adam placed in Paradise and blessed with the company of Eve than Satan seduced them and made them disobey Allah's command, thus bringing about their fall. The part played by him bringing suffering and frustration into the lives of prophets and saints, notably in the case of Job, is well known. In short he has always tried, and continues to try, to seduce mankind; he stimulates conspiracies, provokes and encourages sedition and sinful acts, and attempts by all kinds of means to obstruct Allah's work. His chances of success are to be taken seriously, for Allah warns believers repeatedly and emphatically to beware of him, and calls him mankind's bitterest enemy. Verses VII.199 and XLI.36 contain the following injunction addressed to the Prophet: 'If Satan tempts you, seek refuge in Allah.' Verse VI.67 refers to the possibility of Satan causing the Prophet to forget God's revelations.

In verse XXII.51 Allah reminds believers that He has never sent a Prophet without Satan trying to interject an evil suggestion in his recital of Allah's message. This is a clear reference to the Satan-prompted words pronounced by the Prophet in regard to the three principal idols Lat, Manat and Uzza, as explained in the Section on Idols. In this connection the Qur'an says (XII.52) that Allah makes void Satan's prompting, but permits it as a trial of those whose hearts are diseased. Verse XVI.100 says to the Prophet: 'When you recite the Qur'an, seek refuge in Allah from accursed Satan,' but the next verse affirms that Satan has no power over those who put their trust in Allah. There are numerous verses which counsel believers to take refuge with God in order to preserve themselves from the temptation of Satan and his host of evil ones. Verse XXIII.99 contains this counsel: 'Say, "Lord, I seek refuge in You from the promptings of the devils; I take refuge in You from their presence." '

The inference to be drawn from the foregoing is evident: since Allah in His wisdom did not destroy Satan but allowed him to waylay mankind until the Last Judgement, the incidence of temptation on the destiny of man will last as long as life on earth, though Allah will protect the faithful.

Allah's Message to His Creatures

The necessity for a mediator between the human and the divine is the essence of the Qur'anic Revelation. God's message to mankind has always been conveyed through prophets and apostles.[6] To each people God has sent a messenger with miracles, clear proofs and a Book in its language. The mission entrusted to these messengers has been to teach men the way of justice, virtue and forbearance and to bring to them glad tidings as well as warnings by announcing the rewards and punishments of the Hereafter. The mission of all the prophets has been one and the same, i.e. to baptise or anoint men (literally 'give the colour of God': II.132) in God. In the fulfilment of the divine mission all prophets are alike, in the sense that men must make no distinction between them (II.130 and 285), though God has given them different degrees of rank. Verse II.253 says: 'Of these messengers We have exalted some above others. To some Allah spoke directly; others He raised to a lofty status. We gave Jesus son of Mary veritable signs and strengthened him with the Holy Spirit.' It is frequently repeated that Allah sends apostles to guide mankind, but it is as frequently affirmed that the only guide is Allah Himself. No one, not even the Prophet can guide whom he desires (XXVIII.56). Only God resolves whom to save and whom to condemn to perdition (XXX.13).

The experience of all prophets in this world has been essentially the same. They conveyed God's message to men; with but few exceptions, the people to whom they had been sent denied, mocked and opposed them; demons also put obstacles in their way; thus frustrated on all sides, they became despondent; thereupon God sent down calamities which destroyed the wicked and spared the believers. But whatever has happened to the prophets, and the enmity to which they have been subjected, has been part of God's plans. Verse XXV.33 says: 'Thus to every prophet We have appointed an enemy among the wrongdoers.' Moreover the verse which mentions the different ranks assigned to the prophets by God ends by saying that had it been God's will men would not have fought among themselves on account of the divine messages conveyed to them.

Underlying the accounts of the prophets' experiences is the persistent warning to future generations to desist from any resistance to God's will; in this context verse XII.111 says: 'There is, in their stories, instruction for men endowed with understanding.'

Notes to Chapter Two

1. The Bible quotes God as saying: 'Let us make man in our image, in our likeness' (Genesis: I.28).
2. Among the people of Southern Arabia the god of Jews and Christians was referred to as 'Rahmanan', a word of Aramaic or Hebrew origin. The word 'Rahman' was also adopted by Musailama (the false prophet of Yamama) as the name of the god of his creed.
3. After creating the universe in six days, Allah sits firmly on the Throne (X.3). This is not by way of taking a rest conforming to the statement in the Bible (Genesis II.2) where God 'rested from all His work on the seventh day'. Allah's establishment on the Throne is a symbol of divine Power.
4. Commentators generally agree that the 'Night of Power' is a mystic conception, but literalists have identified it with dates in the calendar, i.e. the 23rd, 25th or 27th of the month of Ramadan.
5. Allusion to pagan Arab practice, resulting from superstition, of dedicating camels and other beasts to a god by splitting their ear.
6. In the manner of delivery of God's message to mankind there is resemblance between the Qur'an and the scriptures of Judaism and Christianity. The God of the Old Testament does not speak directly to His people: Moses serves invariably as the intermediary. The words 'the Lord said to Moses "say to" or "speak to" [the Israelites, priests, Aaron . . .]' appear at the beginning of most chapters of Leviticus as well as elsewhere. Likewise in the Gospels the speaker to men is not the Father in Heaven but the son of Man whose place is 'at the right hand of the Mighty One' (Mark xiv.62). In the Qur'an also God speaks through a messenger but the tone of the message is more personal: the Prophet is often addressed with a message affecting himself or his wives, but more generally he is commanded to speak to others, when the intent is to preach, persuade, incite or challenge. Most frequently Allah's words are addressed to a designated audience according to the content of the message. Thus in the Meccan Suras messages begin with the words 'O people', 'O man', 'O sons of Adam', 'O assembly of Jinn and men', 'O unbelievers', the subject being expostulation or warning. In the Medinese Suras (the Moslem community having been formed) Allah calls directly upon believers. The words 'O you who believe', followed by commandments and counsels, occur 85 times, mostly in Suras II to VIII. In the same Suras the 'People of the Book' are addressed 16 times urging on them to understand the true significance of their faith. In particular the 'Children of Israel' are called upon three times to remember their debt of gratitude to their Lord (II.38, 44 and 116).

CHAPTER THREE

THE PROPHET AND THE QUR'AN

This Chapter contains an introduction to the Qur'anic Revelation and a description of the message conveyed and the mission entrusted to the Prophet, as well as the manner in which the Prophet is personally affected by the Revelation. An attempt is made at reproducing the emphasis laid in the Qur'an on its own perfection, majesty and holiness as the very Word of Allah, and reflecting the splendour with which Allah invests His messenger. Reference is also made incidentally to certain particular features of the Qur'anic mode of expression.

The Qur'an

Iqra' (Recite!): the history of the Prophet and of Islam begins with this word. Muhammad is an 'ummi' (this word means either one who cannot read and write or one, in the Arab community of Muhammad's times, who was neither a Jew nor a Christian)[1] to whom a mighty angel (Gabriel) appears during the Night of Power (XCVII.1) to convey the command: Iqra' (Recite!) is the imperative tense from the Arabic root which also provides the substantive word 'Qur'an' meaning 'Recitation'. Muhammad is thus commanded to recite verses which are revealed to him by Allah. These verses which constitute the Qur'an contain a message that Muhammad is commanded to convey to all and in particular to the people of Mecca and the environs. When reciting this Revelation Muhammad sees the angel stationed 'in the highest part of the horizon' whence he approaches and comes close until he is at the distance of two bow-lengths or even nearer (LIII.4). He then utters the Revelation. These utterances continue throughout the life of Muhammad until the Qur'an is concluded, but the appearance of Gabriel to the Prophet is mentioned only once more in the Qur'an. This second descent of the angel (believed by tradition to have happened on the occasion of the Prophet's Mi'raj or ascension to heaven) took place under the 'Lote-tree not far from the Garden of

39

Dwelling', the mysterious border tree beyond which none may pass (LIII.14 and LXXXI.23).

The Qur'an refers to itself also by other titles: Furqan (Criterion), Balagh (Message), Tanzil (Revelation, literally sending down), Zikr (Reminder, literally remembrance), but its essence, of which these terms are tokens, is wahy or revelation. 'The Qur'an', says verse LIII.4, 'is no other than a revelation revealed to him [Muhammad]'. To the same effect is verse VI.19 which directs Muhammad to say: 'This Qur'an is a revelation which I have received by inspiration.' The Qur'an abounds in passages which refer to Muhammad as recipient of revelation. Verse XLI.5 and verse XVIII.110 command the Prophet to say: 'I am but a man like you but revelation has come to me . . .'

In pre-Islamic Arabia the word wahy,[2] which came later to signify revelation in the technical sense, was applied to the communication of a message of especial or mysterious import (blessing, cursing, divination, incantation, spell binding) by voice, sound, sign, and was commonly used in this sense by poets and soothsayers. With the rise of Islam it acquired a sacred meaning representing direct communication from God to man. This meaning finds ample illustration in the Qur'an, of which the following are relevant exampes: revelation, meaning essentially communication in a two-person relationship in that an intermediary (the angel Gabriel) comes between God and the Prophet in the capacity of messenger. This is announced in several verses of the Qur'an: 'The Holy Spirit [the title of Gabriel] has brought the revelation from thy Lord . . .' (XVI.102); 'This Book is certainly a revelation from the Lord of the Worlds: the faithful spirit [i.e. Gabriel] has come down with it upon thy heart . . . (XXVI.193 and II.91)'. Revelation can also be regarded as a four-person relationship since it does not terminate with the communication to the Prophet but goes on to the last stage which is its transmission to the ultimate recipients, i.e. the Meccans and others in the whole world to whom God has commanded the Prophet to convey the message. Finally it should be added that revelation is defined in the Qur'an also in a wider context, namely in relation to the question as to whether and how God speaks to man. 'It is not for man', says verse XLII.50, 'that God should speak to him except by inspiration or from behind a veil or by God ending a messenger to reveal what God wills.'[3]

The Qur'an is a book that God has sent down to guide the virtuous, to bring the good news of salvation to the righteous and the warning of eternal torment to evildoers. It is revealed in clear Arabic: a detailed exposition couched in easily understandable language, illustrated by many parables, and containing intimations of hidden things with an ample discourse on everything great or small, fresh or dry (VI.59). It consists of pure pages recording counsels of wisdom as well as warnings, the latter addressed particularly to the Meccans. None but the pure may touch the Book, God having breathed from His Spirit into its verses. It leads the believer from darkness to light; it increases the faith of believers and the error of the unbelievers. Some of the verses have established meaning and constitute the essence of the Book; others are allegorical and susceptible of interpretation. Only the perverse who desire to spread discord seek the interpretation of the allegorical verses whose interpretation is, however, only known to God. (III.5). If God abrogates a verse or causes it to be forgotten He replaces it by one that is better or similar (II.100). The Qur'an styles itself a Glorious Book inscribed in a (celestial) Preserved Tablet. God, having revealed it, is Himself its preserver. The Qur'an applies various adjectives to itself: glorious, esteemed, free from deviousness; healing, rich alike in glad tidings and in admonition; grand, noble, exalted, awesome to such degree that if it were exposed to a mountain, the mountain would cleave asunder for fear of God (LIX.21); so beautiful in its diction that those who hear it and fear God will find their skins trembling and their hearts softening at the remembrance of Allah. Those who hear the Qur'an fall face downwards and begin to weep and lament. Only the vicious and the impious deny the Qur'an, and call it a fabrication, the utterance of a poet, of a soothsayer or a madman; fables of the ancients, its composition aided by others.[4] Far from being such as its detractors allege, the Qur'an is a revelation from God. If it were not, it would be inconsistent with itself. Let all Jinns and men assemble and help each other to produce ten Suras like those of the Qur'an! This they can never do. Those who object ask in astonishment: why did this revelation not come to us? Why was it not addressed to an eminent member of the community of Mecca, or of Taif? Why was it not revealed all at once? Why was it not accompanied by a descent of angels or by signs from heaven? God says: had We so willed, We would have sent a sign, but in the past whenever We have sent a sign it has been rejected by the people. Had the Qur'an been revealed in an alien tongue, the objectors would have asked why the Arab people have been addressed in a tongue other than their own. If the Qur'an had appeared inscribed on paper, they would have said that this was sheer magic. Beware! The Qur'an is a proof from God. It utters a warning to those who claim that God had a son. It resolves the differences that divide the people of Israel. It confirms the previous Revelations. Containing God's message, it is unchangeable. God says to Muhammad: We have chosen you, an ummi, to receive the Revelation and We will protect you from those who desire to lead you astray. God warns the Prophet against a precipitate recitation. God himself will decide the putting together, the manner of reading, and the exposition of the verses. God's injunction to Muhammad in this respect is emphatic: 'Do not move your tongue too fast in reciting this [revelation] thus making haste with it. We Ourselves shall see to its collection and recital. When We have recited it follow its recitation. We shall Ourselves explain its meaning' (LXXV.16–19). Those who do not reflect on the magnificence of the Qur'an and who do not prostrate themselves on hearing it recited are deaf and dumb. God has sealed their hearts so that they say: all this is nothing but ancient fable.

But what is the purpose of the message contained in this continuous revelation? It can be expressed in these terms: to count God's favours to mankind; to teach wisdom; to bring good news of salvation to believers and the virtuous, and warning of eternal torment to infidels and evildoers; to emphasise that there is only one God and that He has neither associate, consort or offspring, and that both the visible and invisible worlds are in His power and dominion; to explain all mysteries, to prescribe a code of imperative commandments for believers and to condemn those who do not obey them as infidels; to warn against the promptings of Satan, to such an extent that the Prophet himself is commanded to utter a formula for taking refuge with God against Satan at the beginning of all recitations of the Qur'an (XVI.100). Especial emphasis is laid, in the course of numerous verses, on the condition of the Blest in Paradise and of the Doomed in Hell.

On several occasions the Qur'an uses, in relation to itself, the expression 'umm al-kitab' (the mother of the book). This term has been differently interpreted. The opening verses of Sura XLIII quote Allah as announcing that He has made the Qur'an a revelation in the Arabic language. The Qur'an, He says, is 'the Mother of the Book, in Our Presence, sublime, full of wisdom'. These words have given rise, on the one hand, to the well-known controversial belief that the Qur'an is uncreated, and, on the other, to the highly esoteric conception of the Qur'an as the copy of an original (a heavenly archetype) which has existed in heaven from all eternity. Appeal is made, in support of this conception, to the last two verses of Sura LXXXV which say 'This is a Glorious Qur'an [inscribed?] in a Preserved Tablet.' Some commentators have described the Celestial Tablet in material terms, saying that its length is equal to the distance between heaven and earth, and its width to the distance between east and west, and that its leaves are made of pearls and rubies.

These beliefs have been questioned on rational grounds, and the prevailing opinion among exegetes seems to be that by the mother of the book is meant, figuratively, the fountainhead of all Revelation and the essence of God's Eternal Law. This interpretation is borne out by the content of verse III.5 which says that the Holy Book contains, on the one hand, verses of firmly established meaning, and on the other, verses of an allegorical nature, and qualifies the first kind as the 'Mother of the Book'. Likewise it is argued that the expression 'Preserved Tablet' is only intended to emphasise that the Qur'an is protected from all corruption and alteration. Thus Allah says in verse XV.9: 'We have sent down the Message and We will assuredly guard it [from corruption].' In this manner both the expressions in question (the 'Mother of the Book' and the 'Preserved Tablet') are divorced from a literalist interpretation.

The nature of the Prophet's mission and of the duty that God has laid upon him is described in no less than 35 verses. He is a bearer of glad tidings, a warner, a councillor. Again and again it is stressed that this is his only task. He is to call men to God, to preach the pursuit of virtue and the avoidance of vice. Such delimitation of the Prophet's mission is declared with striking repetition. To quote one from among many verses, God addresses the Prophet, referring to the hostility of the pagans, in these words: 'If then they turn away, We have not sent you to act as guard over them. Your duty is but to convey the Message' (XLII.47). That the Prophet is not sent to manage men's affairs has been emphasised in verse LXXXVIII.22 and also in verse VI.107: 'We did not make you one to watch over their doings, nor are you set over them to dispose of their affairs.' If men dispute with him he must argue with them in mild and gracious language, and must say that he is not their guardian; if then they persist in their antagonism he must leave them to God.

If God addresses such frequent messages of comfort, solace and encouragement to the Prophet, it is because the Prophet has many opponents and enemies who persecute him in every way, taunting him and calling him a poet, a soothsayer, a magician, a madman or a liar. They say to him: if you come from God, where is your miracle? Why can you not show us a treasure? Why are you not accompanied by angels? The Prophet replies: miracles are in the hands of Allah; if He so wills they will appear, but the miracles which He sent with His previous messengers did not make men less obdurate. 'I do not tell you that God's treasures are with me; I do not know what is hidden, nor do I tell you that I am an angel. I only follow what is revealed to me.' (VI.50). He emphasises that he is a man like others with this difference: he has received a revelation in the way that previous prophets had also received a revelation. He argues that his coming has been foretold in the Old and New Testaments. God reminds the Prophet that nothing is said to him that had not been said to the apostles before him (XLI.43). In several passages of the Qur'an the Prophet is mentioned alongside the apostles of past times: Noah, Abraham, Ismael, Isaac, Jacob, Job, Jonas, Solomon, David, Moses,

Jesus. In this connection God commands the believers to make no difference between any of them. He consoles the Prophet, by reminding him that past apostles were also rejected by the people. God bestows special favours on Muhammad. He declares him to be the last of the prophets, and a mercy for all creatures. Allegiance to the Prophet is allegiance to God; believers are commanded by God to praise the Prophet day and night.

In a number of verses, God addresses the Prophet with words of personal import, reminding him of the special favours which have been conferred on him. These passages say in essence: We chose you as Our apostle; We sent Gabriel to you with a revelation; We lifted up your heart, removed your burden and gave you high renown; We found you orphaned and gave you shelter; We found you wandering and gave you guidance; We found you poor and enriched you; We granted you a sublime nature; We gave you victory to forgive your past and future sins (XLVIII.2); We gave you light and made you a radiant lamp; We laid low your enemies. God addresses to the Prophet a series of exhortations: not to listen to sinners; to pay no heed to those who deny the truth, to backbiters, slanderers, oath-breakers, evildoers and transgressors; to call people to God and to be the first Moslem; to persevere day and night in the remembrance of God; to seek no aid save from God; to show patience towards those who call him a maker of fables and a madman; not to lose heart because of attacks from his detractors, but to counter their reproof with fair words; to guard against the guiles of hypocrites; not to covet the worldly fortunes of others, remembering that the rewards of the Hereafter are far greater; to utter no verse save what is revealed to him; to rest assured that if Satan prompts spurious verses to him, God will abrogate these and substantiate the true revelation; not to expect from men more than their natural disposition allows; to remember that he cannot cause the deaf to hear nor the blind to see; not to fear those who plot against him, because God is the best of plotters (III.47, VIII.30). If men turn away from him he should say I am but the bearer of a message; I am not sent to be your guardian or to manage your affairs. God assures the Prophet that whoever denies him will be dragged in chains, on the Day of Judgement, to Hell, where boiling water and scorching fire await him.

God commands the faithful to glorify the Prophet. 'God and His angels send blessings on the Prophet. Bless him then, you that are true believers and greet him with a worthy salutation' (XXXIII.56). The comportment of believers in the presence of the Prophet must be especially respectful: they must not precede him, raise their voices above his, shout to him from outside his inner apartments, enter his house without leave, or confer with him without having previously given alms. Again and again the believers are commanded to obey the Prophet, just as they must obey God.

The Qur'an confirms the miracles attributed to Moses and Jesus but claims no miracle for Muhammad save that of having received the Qur'an.

The subject of the 'Night Journey' mentioned in verse 1 of Sura XVII, which has been interpreted as the miracle of Mi'raj or the Prophet's ascension to heaven, is controversial. The verse says: 'Glory be to Him who made His Servant go by night from the Sacred Mosque [Mecca] to the Farthest Mosque [Jerusalem] whose surroundings We have blessed, so that We might show him some of Our Signs.' Most commentators, relying on tradition, stress the apparent meaning of the verse, and go so far as to determine the time of the departure (the night of the 21st Ramadan or of 27 Rajab) and the place from which the ascent began (the house of Umm Hani), but others interpret the verse as a mystical allegory.

God's revelations to the Prophet are not confined to the description of the message which he is to convey to men. In addition to the special favours which are conferred on the Prophet, God intervenes on several occasions in his private life. He aims blows at the Prophet's enemies when a battle is being fought (VIII.17); He curses the Prophet's uncle Abu Lahab for having maltreated his nephew (Sura XCI); He becomes the best of all plotters in order to thwart the machinations of the Prophet's enemies (VIII.30); he also relieves the Prophet of embarrassments which occasionally result from his relations with his wives. As the Qur'an contains a number of indirect references to the Prophet's wives, and as these references have an important bearing not only on some aspects of the Prophet's life and mission but also on Islamic law, it has been deemed necessary to treat this subject at some length in a special section.

No attempt at indicating the particularities of the Qur'anic mode of expression would be complete without a passing reference to two special features of the Qur'an which are generally believed to have an esoteric significance: the appearance of certain initials or abbreviated letters at the beginning of many Suras, to which no perceptible meaning can be attached, and the fact that Allah frequently utters oaths and imprecations. These subjects will be briefly discussed in the following two sections.

The Abbreviated Letters

Twenty-nine Suras of the Qur'an begin with a mysterious combination of letters of the alphabet which have been called 'the Abbreviated

Letters'. There is one single letter in three cases (Qaf, Sad, Nun), two letters in four cases (Ta Ha, Ta Sin, Ya Sin, Ha Mim repeated seven times), three letters in four cases (Alef Lam Mim repeated six times, Alef Lam Ra repeated five times, Te Sin Mim repeated twice and Ain Sin Qaf), four letters in two cases (Alef Lam Mim Sad, Alif Lam Mim Ra), five letters in one case (Kaf Ha Ya Ain Sad). Altogether 14 letters of the Arabic alphabet have been used in these combinations. Various suggestions have been offered as to the meanings of the Abbreviated Letters, but none goes further than conjecture.[5]

A point of importance to be borne in mind in studying this enigma is that these combinations of letters are prefixed (with two exceptions) only to the Meccan Suras, from which it may be inferred that there is a connection between these Letters and the spirit of the Meccan revelations. That the Qur'an has, beyond its literal expression, an esoteric (hidden) sense or rather several layers of sense is a fundamental doctrine vouched for by sayings of the Prophet and Imams. Theologians, Sufis, mystic poets and others have differentiated as many as seven levels of significance corresponding to ascending levels of initiation. The Persian Hurufi sect (late 14th century), an extremist offshoot of Shiism, upheld the belief that in the letters composing the words of the Qur'an lies hidden the most perfect revelation of truth. In this perspective letters are not mere signs of speech sounds, but are symbols of a sacred content, or, to use a term applied to ancient Egypt, hieroglyphs (sacred carvings).

The traditions of Judaism and Christianity testify to the sacredness of letters of the alphabet. In the Book of Revelation (I.8) the Lord says: I am the Alpha and the Omega. The Jewish kabala maintains that the letters of the alphabet represent the name of God by which God reveals His creative acts, and that the letters of the Torah correspond to the forces which operate according to the Creator's plan. As the traditions of Judaism in particular enlarge on the sacred meaning attributed to letters they may be consulted with profit by those who will continue the attempt at unveiling the secret of the Abbreviated Letters. I have received valuable guidance in a personal communication from Mr J. I. Somers under the title of *Note on Hebrew Hieroglyphs* from which a few specimen passages are quoted below:

> According to both the Hebraic and Islamic traditions their respective languages, Hebrew and Arabic, were used by God to convey sacred scripture. As such, man can only aspire to understand the truth contained in the Torah and Koran. Neither can be merely literal and the letters in which they are written are not profane but hieroglyphs ... The true hieroglyph, as a sign or symbol, seeks to transmit meaning beyond the competence of literary language ...

Torah itself is the Word of God and therefore by definition could not communicate through any ordinary language ... There are twenty-two main Hebrew letters, which are all consonants. The vowels, which indicate the vocalisation of the words ... were introduced by a group of scholars in the seventh century ... who also codified the letters into a grammatical framework ... There is, however, another approach to the meaning of the Torah and this is to treat the letters of which it is composed as hieroglyphs ... Tradition tells us that when Moses descended from Mt Sinai he explained the Law three times. Firstly to his brother Aaron, secondly to all the Priests (Cohanim), thirdly to all the children of Israel. Thus, we are told, the oral tradition and the different grades of initiation have existed from the beginning. The letters of the 'Book' are always the same, but in addition to their literal meaning there is the meaning corresponding to all the other grades.

Another and no less fundamental guide to be found in the Kabbalah is the study of the Hebrew script of which the Torah is formed; each separate letter has a meaning and by their combination in the Torah deeper layers of meaning can be found in the sacred text so often accepted at its most simple and exoteric level. The letters form a language more precious than an instrument for contact between men. It contains the fundamental spiritual nature of the Universes. The Hebrew letters are hieroglyphs – sacred ideographs. All the letters as combined in the Torah return with him who is able to read their meaning to the single light of the One. Twenty-two sounds and letters are the foundation of all things.[6]

Oaths Uttered by Allah

Seventy-four verses of the Qur'an consist wholly, and seven verses partly, of the utterance of oaths by Allah. This fact calls for an inquiry into the nature and significance of oaths and imprecations in order to throw light on their use in sacred texts.

An oath is generally defined as an invocation of God or some object or entity held sacred, in witness of the truth of a solemn affirmation or the binding character of a promise or undertaking. The oath is usually sanctioned by an express or implied curse that the person taking it calls down upon himself in the event that his affirmation proves false or his promise fails. It is clear therefore that the oath involves the following components:

(1) A matter of importance which is to form the subject of an affirmation or a promise by a given person; (2) the necessity for such

person to provide an unimpeachable other-worldly witness to the truth of his statement or the validity of his promise; (3) an appeal to God or to some agent believed to be endowed with supreme and occult power to punish perjury and default; (4) occasionally an object specially cherished by the person taking the oath, to the loss of which he condemns himself, by way of self-imprecation, in the event that he commits default.

A curse or imprecation is uttered by a person who desires to harm another, but is powerless to do so, and who therefore appeals to a supernatural power to effect such harm.

The oaths and imprecations which appear in the Qur'an can be examined in the light of the foregoing analysis.

1. *Content* The affirmations and promises that Allah makes on oath concern the following matters: oneness and omnipotence of God; inevitability and certainty of Resurrection and the Last Judgement; warnings having been given to mankind concerning those events; rewards and punishments in the Hereafter; reminder of the calamities sent down in past ages upon those who rejected God's messengers; the eminent station of the Prophet Muhammad as the recipient of God's special favour, bounties and grace, and the assertion that he is neither misled nor 'possessed'; the glory and magnificence of the Qur'an as an utterance of the Supreme Truth; the mystery of the creation of Man and the quality of his soul; Man's ingratitude; men's error in following discordant doctrines; the assurance that every soul has a protecting angel.

2. *Witness* It is of course unthinkable that God should have the need to corroborate His statements and promises in any manner.

3. *Entities invoked* The invocations contained in God's oaths are (a) to Himself as the Lord Creator of Heavens and Earth and all things; (b) to the glorious Qur'an, full of wisdom; (c) to the life of Muhammad; (d) to heavenly bodies, i.e. the firmament, stars, planets, zodiac, sun, moon, earth; (e) to natural phenomena in the evolution of time, i.e. the course of ages, day, night, dawn, sunset; (f) to angels entrusted with various divine missions; (g) to localities, i.e. oceans, Mount Sinai, the city of Mecca; (h) to objects of mysterious significance, i.e. the Pen, the Record, the Scroll, all that can be seen or cannot be seen, the ties of parent and child, panting war-steeds, the fig, the olive, males and females, even and odd numbers. But swearing implies, as already stated, invoking the support of a superior power, whilst it is of course inconceivable that God should need to seek confirmation for His utterances from any object or entity outside of Himself.

It is clear from the foregoing that the Qur'anic oaths and imprecations do not fit into any of the conditions described above and are therefore *sui generis*. But the light in which they are to be regarded and the reasons which make them a necessary part of Revelation do not appear in the Qur'an.

By way of ilustration we will now quote some instance of the oaths uttered by Allah in the Qur'an.

'I swear by those who range themselves [angels?] in ranks, by those who cast out demons, and by those who recite Our Word, that your God is one, the Lord of the heavens and the earth and all that lies between them' (XXXVII.1–5).

'By the Qur'an, full of wisdom, you are indeed one of the Apostles' (XXXVI.1).

'By the declining star, your companion [Muhammad] is not in error' (LIII.1).

'By the light of day and by the fall of night, your Lord has not forsaken you' (XCIII.1).

'By the Pen and what they [the angels] write, you [Muhammad] are not mad' (LXVIII.1).

'By the glorious Qur'an they marvel that a Prophet of their own has arisen among them' (L.1).

'I swear by the setting of the stars: a mighty oath if you but knew! that this is a glorious Qur'an' (LVI.74–75).

'I swear by all that you can see and all that is hidden from your view, that this is the utterance of a noble messenger' (LXIX.38–39).

'I swear by the turning planets and by the stars that rise and set, by the fall of night and the first breath of morning, this is the word of a gracious and mighty messenger, held in honour by the Lord of the Throne, obeyed in heaven, faithful to his trust' (LXXXI.15–17,22).

'By the Fig and by the Olive, by Mount Sinai and this inviolable land, We moulded Man into the most noble image' (XCV.1–3).

'By the panting war-steeds, which strike fire with their hoofs as they gallop to the raid at dawn and with a trail of dust split the foe in two, man is ungrateful to his Lord' (C.1–6).

'By your life, O Prophet, those [the people of Lot] were in wild intoxication' (XV.72).

A few instances of curses and imprecations:

'The Jews say God's hand is tied up; may their own hands be tied up; may they be accursed for the blasphemy which they utter' (V.69).

'May the hands of Abu Lahab perish' (CXI.1).

'We cursed them [the people of Israel] because they broke their covenant' (V.16).

'These are the men whom God has cursed' (IV.50).

'My curse shall be on thee [Satan] till the Day of Judgement' (XXXVIII.79).

Verse IV.55 says: 'For those whom God has cursed, you will find no helper.'

Verse V.65 says that those cursed by God, including the worshippers of Evil, are farthest away from the path of salvation.

A point of importance is that, with only a single marginal exception, all the oaths uttered by Allah occur in the Meccan Suras. Oaths appear in 32 of these, of which no less than 22 begin with the utterance of the oath. Oaths are absent from the Medinese Suras.

The Language of the Qur'an

In verse XIV.4 Allah says: 'We have sent no apostle but with the language of his people so that he might make the revelation clear to them.' This divine norm of the use of the indigenous language of the people addressed, characterised by clarity of expression, is especially emphasised in the Qur'an in relation to itself. No less than 12 verses state that the Qur'an is revealed in the Arabic language, and is couched in the clearest terms. Sura XII begins thus: 'These are the verses of the Perspicuous Book. We have revealed the Qur'an in the Arabic tongue so that you may understand it.' Sura XLIII begins with these words: 'By the Perspicuous Book, We have made it an Arabic Qur'an so that you may understand.' Similarly Sura XLI says: 'This is a Revelation, the verses of which are distinctly explained: an Arabic Qur'an for the instruction of the people who understand.' The quality of clearness as a condition of intelligibility to the people addressed is inseparable from mention of the Qur'an (XXVI.195, XLI.44, XVI.105, XLIV.58, XV.1, XXVII.2, XXXVI.69). Yet the Qur'an questions whether men have benefited from this God-given aid to understanding. Sura LIV repeats four times the refrain: 'We have indeed made the Qur'an easy to understand and remember; is there any one that will receive admonition?' But, paradoxically, Allah Himself has deprived certain men of the faculty of understanding His message. 'But We have cast veils over their hearts and made them hard of hearing lest they understand your words' (VI.25). 'We cast a veil upon their hearts and make them hard of hearing lest they understand it [the Qur'an]' (XVII.48). 'We have cast veils over their hearts lest they should understand Our words, and made them hard of hearing' (XVIII.55). And it is emphasised that no one can enlighten those whose judgement has been darkened by Allah. 'Would you guide those whom Allah has caused to err? He whom Allah has led astray cannot be guided' (IV.90).

The Qur'an strongly implies, and commentators make it explicit, that the Qur'an was dictated verbatim in Arabic by Gabriel to the Prophet. As Gabriel uttered the revelation, the Prophet repeated his message word for word after him. Sometimes he showed undue haste in reproducing the dictated words, and thus risked losing the trend of the revelation, or stumbled through part of the recitation. He was then rebuked by Allah. 'Do not move your tongue too fast in reciting this [revelation] thus making haste with it. We Ourselves shall see to its collection and recital. When We have recited it, follow its recitation; We shall Ourselves explain its meaning' (LXXV.16–19). 'Do not make haste with reciting the Qur'an before its revelation is made complete to you' (XX.113). The Moslem view accordingly is that the Qur'an embodies Allah's speech in Arabic, and should therefore be recited and studied in that language and not in translations. It is also believed, on the authority of traditions, that Arabic is the language of those in Paradise.

That Gabriel brought down the Qur'an to the Prophet is specifically stated in II.91. The Moslem attitude of veneration towards Gabriel was one of the causes of Jewish antagonism towards Islam. The Jews refused to believe in Gabriel as the bringer of good tidings. They held Michael to be their guardian and protector on the strength of a biblical passage (Daniel XII.1) and Gabriel to be their enemy as he had revealed a terrifying anti-Jewish vision to Daniel (Daniel VIII.16–17). In spite of Moslem remonstrances and warnings to the Jews that such hostility towards an angel would bring down God's wrath on them, they persisted in their disbelief in Gabriel, which was condemned by the Prophet in the same verse where Gabriel is mentioned as the transmitter of Revelation to the Prophet: 'Whoever is an enemy to Gabriel (he it was that brought down the Qur'an to your heart) . . . whoever is an enemy to God and His angels and His messengers and Gabriel and Michael, surely God is an enemy to the unbelievers' (II.91–92).

The subject of the Qur'anic language figures prominently among those which constitute the 'Science of the Qur'an'. The linguistic research undertaken during centuries as an important part of this science touches on various aspects of the Qur'anic expression: the dialect in which it is revealed, its stylistic, grammatical, rhetorical and aesthetic qualities, to all of which the experts in the science of the Qur'an attribute a more than earthly excellence, invoking them as proofs of the miraculous inimitability (i'jaz) of the Qur'an. The extensive discussion of the subjects, including that of variations in the writing and articulation of words, is reflected in commentaries and specialised treatises. Some conclusions reached may be briefly outlined: the Qur'an is expressed, not in the dialect of Mecca as was advanced by early commentators but in a perfected form of a poetic idiom which had developed through the centuries over and above the various dialects in use in the peninsula. The Qur'an, as an embodiment of the Word of God, not only provides the most authoritative laws concerning the use of the Arabic language, but constitutes the very perfection of human speech. The eloquence of the Qur'anic language is unsurpassable. This theme has been enlarged upon with especial emphasis. A 13th-century inquirer into literary style, the Syrian as-Sulami, completing the work of two 11th-century predecessors, has compiled a treatise to illustrate all the varieties of parables, allegories and figures of speech (simile, metaphor, metonym, hyperbole, etc.) used in the Qur'an. These evaluations represent the Qur'an as a peerless literary masterpiece possessing the most effective aesthetic appeal, an appeal to which, it is said, even non-Moslems may also respond. Thus the eminent British scholar Sir William Muir in his *Life of Mohammed* finds in the Qur'an 'passages of grand imagery and true poetry'. And the well-known contemporary French translator of the Qur'an, Régis Blachère, says of the aesthetic quality of the Qur'an: 'It can be felt even by a non-Arabic-speaking listener. When recited aloud, the Qur'anic language, thanks to the musical quality of its syllabic arrangements, the rich tonality of its vowels, and the rhyme or assonance of its phrases, strikes us as pure poetry in the strongest sense of the term.' (*Le Coran*, 1947, p. 72.)

In reading and meditating on the Qur'an it must be borne in mind throughout that He who speaks is Allah Himself, the Prophet being His mouthpiece. This is amply clear from the wording of the earliest Suras in which the word of command 'Say', addressed to the Prophet, occurs most frequently. But even when this word is not used, it is obviously implied as, for instance, in the Exordium or the Moslem ritual prayer: 'Praise be to Allah. Thee alone do we worship.' If attention is drawn to this point it is because there are passages in the Qur'an which might suggest that the speaker is the *Prophet*, and in numerous cases Allah appears in the third person, as in the well-known extended doxology in the verse of the 'Throne' (II.25) or in passages like II.82 and II.254 where it is said, respectively, that 'Allah curses them for their blasphemy', and that 'If Allah had so willed, they would not have fought.'

The Prophet: Neither a Madman nor a Soothsayer nor a Poet

In no less than 25 verses the Qur'an condemns those who call Muhammad a madman, a soothsayer, a poet or a man bewitched. The word translated as 'madman' is 'majnun' (possessed by the Jinn). The Jinn, recognised by the Qur'an as real beings half worldly and half other-worldly, occupied a prominent place in pre-Islamic conceptions. They were believed in as heavenly beings related to a divinity (XXXVII.158) who took momentary possession of certain ecstatic persons and uttered through them words and formulas of special import to society: prophecies, blessings, curses, oaths and incantations. These utterances, imagined as descending from on high, were clothed in a para-mystic style (saj') between prose and poetry and were considered to have magic power in themselves and to be other-worldly and occult. The saj' is believed to have been the earliest form of Arab poetry, and the persons who uttered it were called 'poets' who, as mouthpieces of demons, revealed knowledge of the unseen world. In moments of inspiration, the ecstatic person, whether soothsayer or poet (becoming majnun or one with the Jinn) folded himself up in a way that, except for his head, he was almost invisible. The majnun, the kahin (soothsayer), the sha'er (poet) and the mas-hur (bewitched) all belonged to the same family of spiritual mediums. Examples of such mouthpieces of Jinn or other demons of the unseen world exist in pre-Islamic traditions. There is, for instance, mention (in Ibn Hisham's *Sirat al-Rasul*) of a famous soothsayer by the name of Satih who, it is said, foretold the invasion of Yemen by the Ethiopians in the saj' style, corroborating the truth of his prophecy by oaths peculiar to the style of soothsayers: 'by the evening twilight, by the darkness, by the dawn . . .' (cf. the Qur'anic oaths in Sura LXXXI: 'by the planets that recede, go straight or hide, and the night as it dissipates, and the dawn as it breathes away the darkness . . .'). As most of the early Meccan Suras follow the saj' style, including the use of oaths, and also as according to Tradition, Muhammad had himself wrapped up in a special garment in moments of prophetic inspiration (see Suras LXXIII and LXXIV where he is addressed by Gabriel as 'O thou wrapped up' and 'O thou folded up') the Arabs regarded him as just another soothsayer or poet. Muhammad, receiving his revelation from Allah through Gabriel, strongly resented the allegations which placed his recitals, which were unsurpassable in eloquence, on the same level as the utterances of soothsayers and poets. Allah then sent down verses which emphatically belied such imputations. In answer to the unbelievers who said of the Qur'an and of Muhammad 'this is nothing but evident magic' (XXXIV.42), or 'he is but a poet' (XXI.5) or 'you follow none other than a man bewitched' (XX.9, XVII.50), Allah said: 'By the grace of your Lord, you are no soothsayer, nor one possessed' (LII.29). 'You are not, by the grace of your Lord, mad or possessed' (LXVIII.2). 'This is not the word of a poet, nor of a soothsayer' (LXIX.41–42).

The Qur'an taught that all pretended communication from the

unseen world to man by the Jinn or other demons was sheer fabrication and blasphemy. The Jinn have never been a source of revelation;
they have now even lost their ancient false show of authority, i.e. their
habit of eavesdropping at the door of the Celestial Concourse because
they find their access thereto forever barred by flaming meteors
(XV.18, LXXII.8–9). As for the poets, their only prompter was Satan:
'Shall I inform you on whom it is that the evil ones descend? They
descend on every lying, wicked person, into whose ears they pour
hearsay vanities . . . And the poets, it is those straying in evil who follow
them. Do you not see that they wander distracted in every valley and
they say what they do not practise?' (XXVI.221–226). Referring to the
Prophet, the Qur'an says: 'We have not taught him poetry, nor would
it beseem him' (XXXVI.69).

This brings us to the question as to how the Qu'ran views Revelation. 'It is not fit for man', says verse XLII.50, 'that God should speak
to him otherwise than by inspiration' (i.e. according to commentators,
illumination of the heart or vision in a dream) 'or from behind a veil'
(as when God spoke to Moses from behind a veil of flaming fire) 'or
by His sending a messenger to reveal, by His permission, that which
He pleases.' The revelation to Muhammad falls into this last category
(although, according to traditions, he also saw and conversed with God
on the night of his ascension) and involves a four-person relationship
from the initial source to the final recipient, i.e. Allah–Gabriel–
Muhammad–the people.

Some Qur'anic Parables

The fact that parables, similes and metaphors abound in the Qur'an
as well as in the Old and New Testaments may be attributed to a
characteristic of the Semitic peoples who can best approach and
understand the abstract by way of the concrete. A current Arabic
proverb says, 'Metaphor is the bridge to Reality.' Recourse to figurative
ways of expression for the edification of the hearers and the reader is
no reflection on their intelligence. Thus Allah does not disdain to
speak in parables, extracting similitudes from all appropriate things,
even the lowliest such as a gnat. Parables, says the Qur'an, are intended to enlighten and stimulate men's understanding. The faithful
recognise in them the message of truth; only the cynic questions their
instructive import (II.24, XIII.18). 'Allah sets forth parables for men
in order that they may receive admonition' (XIV.29,47, LIX.21).

A study of the Qur'anic rhetoric brings to light the prominent role
played in it by similes used in spiritual and moral contexts. Many of

these have passed into proverbs and are currently used in ordinary speech. A collector of adages can gather a rich harvest from the verses of the Qur'an. A few examples may be chosen by way of illustration from among a very large number:

Unbelievers turn away from admonition like frightened asses fleeing from a lion (LXXIV.51). The heart of the unbeliever is like a rock or even harder, for there are rocks from which rivers gush forth (II.69). Good words are like good trees which send their roots deep into the earth and their branches high up into the air with goodly fruit; evil words are like evil trees which are torn out of the earth and shorn of their roots (XIV.29). The pious build on a solid foundation, while the ungodly build on a sand cliff which is ready to crumble to pieces (IX.110). One simile, echoing a comparison made in the New Testament (Mark IV.27–28), likens the believer to a good seed which sends forth its blade, then makes it strong until it stands on its own stem to the delight of the sower (XLVIII.29). Another figure of speech which corresponds to a well-known simile appearing in the New Testament (Matt. XIX.24) is used in verse VII.38 which says that those who reject Allah's signs will not enter Paradise until the camel can pass through the eye of the needle. The Jew who pretends to follow the Torah but who does not understand it is likened to a donkey, which carries huge tomes (LXII.5).

Many parables are used to illustrate the condition of those who reject faith. Their deeds are deceptive as a mirage (XXIV.39); they are submerged in an ocean of darkness, overwhelmed by billows above and billows beneath (XXIV.40); no sooner do they kindle a fire than Allah extinguishes it (II.16); they are like cattle which when the goat-herd calls out to them, hear only a cry without distinguishing its meaning (II.166); dazzled by dense clouds fraught with thunder and lightning, they press their fingers to their ears to keep out the thunder clap for fear of death (II.18); they limp and stumble when walking while the man of faith walks evenly and securely (LXVII.22); they grope in eternal gloom while the good man walks in a path illumined by divine light (VI.122). The difference between a polytheist and one who believes in the One and Only God is like the difference between a man who serves one master and a man who serves several masters at war with one another.

Many similes are of an exhortatory nature. The believer is often reminded of the transitory nature of life on earth. The cycle of vegetation is used as a simile. There is rainfall, growth of vegetation leading to a promising harvest, but suddenly by Allah's command the harvest is mown down, leaving nothing; it is as if nothing had flourished on the day before (X.24). It is emphasised that charity must be sincere. Thus a distinction is made between charity which is given in all sincerity and charity which is given for ostentation. The first brings a manifold increase like a grain which grows into seven ears, each yielding one hundred grains. The latter is likened to a rock on which there is a little soil; a heavy rain falls, washes the soil away and leaves the rock bare. Prayer must not be regarded as a mere ritual act. One who prays without faith is likened to a thirsty man who stretches forth his hand to bring water to his mouth, but his hand does not reach his mouth. The teaching that faith in God purifies is illustrated by the action of fire on mineral ore which separates the dross and scum from pure metal.

A parable can be the vehicle of an esoteric allegory, lending itself to a mystic interpretation. An outstanding example is the Parable of the Light set forth in verse XXIV.35. Allah is called the Light of the heaven and the earth. The divine Light is represented by a series of symbols: a niche, a lamp, a glass, a brilliant star, an unlocalised Olive Tree yielding a self-luminous oil, the whole forming Light upon Light. The allegory ends with the words: 'Allah sets forth parables for men; Allah knows all things.'

In a number of cases, where the context so requires, parables are expanded into stories.

The Qur'an, using a parable in which polytheists are likened to the spider which builds for itself, and lives in, the flimsiest of all houses, says: 'Such are the parables We set forth for mankind, but only those understand them who have wisdom' (XXIX.42). A few of these parables are quoted below:

In the context of God's power to bring the dead back to life (which was denied by the pagans referring to the Qur'anic doctrine of Resurrection): a parable is given in verse II.261 which is generally regarded as referring to Uzair or Esdras, the priest-reformer. According to the legend, once in the course of his travels, the person referred to arrived at a village in ruins. How, he thought, could God bring this dead village back to life? Thereupon God made him die for a hundred years and then raised him up again. Opening his eyes, he said 'Oh, I have been asleep for a day or part of a day.' It did not take him long, however, to realise that he had been dead for a century. He said: 'I know now that it is in God's power to restore the dead to life when He so wills.'

A warning to those who reject God's Signs: verses VII.174 *et seq.* tell the story of a man to whom God sent His Signs, but he passed them by. He went astray by Satan's temptation and preferred the pursuit of his vain desires to following divine guidance. Commentators suggest that the person meant is Balaam son of Beor, who lived at the time of Moses and was a gifted seer (God's Sign conferred upon him) in the city of Jericho. But he rejected the divine favour: the enemies of Moses seduced him by promise of rewards to put a curse on the people of Israel. The story of Balaam is told at length in the Bible (Numbers XXII *et seq.*). He is also mentioned in 2 Peter II.15 as one 'who loved the wages of wickedness'. In Jude XII, men like Balaam are likened to the 'wild waves of the sea, foaming up their shame'. Likewise the Qur'an likens the subject of its parable to a dog which, whether you attack it or leave it alone, lolls out its tongue and foams at the mouth.

On the commandment that man must give thanks to God for His favours: a parable occurs in verses XVIII.31–34. There were two men (according to commentators, two brothers named Bu-Qatrus and Yehuda) of whom one was blessed with abundant wealth, consisting of gardens, orchards, cornfields, gold, silver and a host of attendants. Every time he visited his garden he said: 'Never will this place perish!' But the other, who was not richly endowed but who attributed to divine favour what he did possess, reproached him for forgetting God when he spoke of his riches. He urged him to utter words of trust in God every time he entered his garden, saying: 'That which God ordains must surely come to pass; there is no strength save in God.' But the proud possessor of fortune did not heed this counsel, and divine retribution descended on him. One day his vineyards tumbled down upon their trellises, and his possessions were all destroyed. He began to grieve and wring his hands, but his remorse brought him no relief. There was no one to help him or to console him in his great loss.

A warning to nations who live in heedlessness: 'Recount to them [to the believers]', says verse XXXVI.13, 'as a parable the story of the city to whose inhabitants We sent Our messengers.' At first two messengers were sent, but they were rejected, and a third joined them. He did not fare any better. The people said to them: 'Your presence among us bodes ill; desist, or we will stone you and inflict a grievous punishment on you!' While the three messengers were being persecuted, a man came from the far side of the city and remonstrated with the people, urging them to listen to the messengers. 'Follow', he pleaded, 'these men who ask no reward of you and who have themselves received guidance ... For me, I have faith in the Lord of you all; listen then to me!' How the people reacted to this exhortation is not stated, but can be implied from the next verse. Evidently he was martyred, for in verse 25 he is addressed by a voice in heaven: 'We said to him: "Come to Paradise", and he exclaimed, "Would that my people knew how gracious my Lord has been to me." ' The end of the story is told in these words: 'But when he was gone We sent down no host from heaven against his people ... one shout was heard, and they fell down lifeless.' It is suggested in the commentaries that the city referred to is Antioch, the first two messengers were Barnabas and Paul, and the third was Simeon. And the common man was one Habib Najjar who was tortured and put to death.

A particularly significant parable is contained in verse XXXIII.72 which says: 'We proposed the Trust to the heavens, the earth and the mountains, but they refused it being afraid thereof, but Man undertook it; indeed he was unjust and foolish.'

What is the Trust which was offered to all creatures, but was only assumed by Man? The essence of the different classical interpretations is that it is the exercise of will, the assumption of the responsibility of choosing between good and evil, and the fulfilment of divine commandments. The physical world, knowing itself powerless to exercise any will of its own, and standing in awe of God's majesty (LIX.21) bowed unreservedly to God's Will ('The sun, the moon and the stars are in subjection to His command' XVI.12, XLI.10, XXII.18). Man, on the contrary, showed temerity by assuming the Trust, unjustly (because part of his progeny would inevitably breach the Trust) and foolishly (because Man did not measure the extent of his powers). The result, stated in verse XXXIII.73, was the divine institution of punishment and reward merited respectively by the faithless and the believers.

A subtler, more spiritual interpretation has, however, been proposed by the mystic poets of Iran. One of the greatest (Hafez of the 14th century) touches on this theme in two of his odes. In his vision the Trust that God proposed to all creation was Love, but all created beings, even angels, flinched before the burden of Love's responsibility. Man alone had the temerity to assume it. In one ode, addressing God, he says: 'At the dawn of eternity Love accompanied Thy appearance and set the whole universe aflame.' In another, Man says: 'The heavens were powerless to bear the burden of the Lord's Trust; it fell to my lot, mad that I am, to bear it.'

The Doctrine of Abrogation

This doctrine has its origin in two verses of the Qur'an: 'We do not abrogate any verse or cause it to be forgotten unless We substitute for it something better or similar; do you know that God has power over all things?' (II.100). 'When we substitute one verse for another – and God knows best what He reveals – they say "You are but a forger" ' (XVI.103).

That there are cases of abrogation in the Qur'an is undisputed, but the authorities differ widely in identifying the abrogated verses, some limiting their number to as few as five, others pointing to as many as 225. The doctrine has been developed in the course of interpreting the Qur'an. The task has not been free from difficulties, as it has required the establishment of two conditions in each case: i.e. that the abrogating verse is posterior to the abrogated verse, which raises the moot problem of the chronology of the Suras of the Qur'an, and that there is no possibility of reconciling the contents of the two verses concerned.

The authorities distinguish three kinds of abrogation: (1) where both the written word and the content are eliminated (as in reported cases where a recorded verse is said to have disappeared mysteriously and its substance to have faded from memory; (2) where the written word somehow vanished but the content remained in force (a once-existing verse ordering the punishment for adultery by stoning is believed to have disappeared, but the commandment has been maintained by tradition); (3) where a still-existing verse is in effect repealed or modified by the introduction of a new text (all references in the commentaries to the doctrine of abrogation fall into this category).

By far the greatest number of verses held to have been abrogated are those which counsel the Prophet to be patient with the unbelievers and to remember that he is no more than a warner, leaving the punishment of recalcitrants to God. The abrogating verses, on the other hand, are those which command the Prophet and the faithful to fight and kill. Below are cited by way of illustration, a few verses of both kinds: the abrogated as well as the abrogating.

The abrogated: 'Say "O men, I am sent to you only to give a clear warning"' (XXII.48). 'If they contend with you, say, "God knows best what you are doing"' (XXII.67). 'Repel evil with that which is best' (XXIII.98). 'Leave them [the unbelievers] in their confused ignorance for a time' (XXIII.56). 'Be patient at what they say' (XX.130, XXXVIII.16). 'All are waiting, so you too wait if you will' (XX.135). 'Have patience with what they say and leave them with dignity' (LXXIII.10). 'Make no haste against them' (XIX.87). 'Warn them of the Day of Distress' (XIX.40). 'Forgive and overlook' (II.103).

The abrogating: 'Fighting is prescribed for you' (II.216). 'Fight those who do not believe' (IX.29). 'Fight the unbelievers whom you find round about you' (IX.124). 'Fight them [the unbelievers] until Allah's faith prevails' (II.189). 'Slay the pagans wherever you find them' (IX.5).

Several inconsistencies exist in the verses of the Qur'an which may be, and by some commentators have occasionally been, brought within the doctrine of abrogation. One important incompatibility is that which exists between the statement in II.256 to the effect that there shall be no compulsion in religion, and that in IX.29 which commands Moslems to fight non-Moslems, including the People of the Book, namely Jews and Christians, until they accept Islam or humbly pay tribute. Similarly the dictum in XLIX.13 to the effect that God's purpose in creating men in nations and tribes is that they shall know each other is contradicted by several verses which forbid Moslems from associating with non-Moslems. Thus verse V.56 enjoins on Moslems not to take Jews and Christians for friends; to the same effect are verses III.27, III.114 and IV.143.

A further reference to abrogation is made in the Qur'an where it states that Allah abrogates the interpolations of Satan into the utterances of Prophets (XXII.51). It is generally believed that reference is made here to the words pronounced by the Prophet when, in the course of reciting Sura LIII, he said (following verses 19 and 20) that the three female idols of Arab paganism were acceptable to Allah as intercessors. These words, having been interjected by Satan, were soon withdrawn.

Islamic theology and jurisprudence give the widest scope to the doctrine of abrogation. One commentary (*Kashf al-asrar* in commenting on verse II.100) says: 'The orthodox view is that abrogation applies both to the Qur'an and to tradition. Thus the Qur'an abrogates the Qur'an, tradition abrogates the Qur'an, tradition abrogates tradition, and the Qur'an abrogates tradition. All this is firmly established and is recognised by jurisprudence.'

An example of an existing verse held to have been abrogated by another is verse XXIV.3 which says: 'An adulterer may only marry an adulteress, and an adulteress only an adulterer,' and which is considered to have been repealed by verse 32 of the same Sura which contains this commandment: 'Marry those among you who are single.' Incidentally the same abrogation is also indirectly deduced from circumstantial evidence furnished by Tradition: the Prophet is reported to have meant the ruling in XXIV.3 to apply only to the case of two men who intended to marry two particular women of easy virtue plying their trade in Mecca, the ruling having lapsed after these cases had been disposed of.

Finally, it does not appear that commentators have discussed the question as to how the doctrine of abrogation stands in relation to the Qur'anic affirmation that Allah's word is unchangeable. 'No change can there be in the Words of Allah' (X.64).

The Qur'an as Seen by Itself

A special characteristic of the Qur'an is that it pronounces its own eulogy as a divine utterance in emphatic and varied terms, spelling out its merits one by one. It is a Glorious Record (XV.87) inscribed in the celestial Preserved Tablet (LXXXV.22) and the Heavenly Archetype (XLIII.4) and is sent down from Allah's Presence to earth by Gabriel (XXVI.194, XVI.104, LIII.10). It consists of exalted, pure and holy pages penned by noble scribes (LXXX.15). No human hand has aided its composition (XVI.105). It epitomises the ancient scriptures of Abraham (?) and Moses (LXXXVII.19). It is the very Word of Allah, not the invention of a poet or a soothsayer (XLIX.40). It brings God's blessing to mankind (VI.92–156, XXI.51, XXXVIII.28). God Himself protects it (XV.9) and will Himself teach the manner of its recital and explain its meaning (LXXV.18–19). It is strictly inimitable (XVII.90, II.21, X.38, XI.15), unchangeable for all time (X.64, XVIII.26, VI.115), free from all crookedness (XVIII.1) and all inconsistency (IV.84). It is a treasury of divine wisdom (XI.1, XIII.37), a healing and a mercy (XVII.84). It is eminently easy to understand (XIX.97, XLIV.58, and four repetitions in Sura LIV). It is awe-inspiring, to such an extent that its recital causes the skin of the faithful to tremble (XXXIX.24) and if it were revealed to a mountain, the mountain would split asunder and collapse for fear of God (LIX.21). The Jinn, half-human, half non-human, on hearing it recited, bowed down before its superiority (LXXII.1). A grievous penalty is in store for those who do not fall prostrate on hearing it recited (LXXXIV.21). Nothing on earth or in heaven is omitted from it (XXXIV.3, VI.59, X.61, XI.7, XXVII.77). Contact with it is forbidden to the impure (LVI.78).

The originality of its revelations is emphasised: many stories are related in it which were unknown to man before their revelation in the Qur'an, such as that of Noah (XI.51), the account of how Zacharias was chosen to take care of Mary (III.39), or the adventures of Joseph (XII.103) which are called 'the most beautiful story' (XII.3). And yet, in spite of all the sublimity and divine virtues of the Qur'an, it is not by itself immune to Satan's influence; Allah Himself has to be called upon to vouchsafe such immunity. When reciting the Qur'an, even the Prophet is commanded to 'seek God's protection from accursed Satan' (XVI.100).

Twice the term 'Mathani' (plural of Mathna meaning two-by-two and repetition) has been used in the Qur'an with reference to itself (XV.87 and XXXIX.24). In XV.87 the word is associated with the figure seven and with the glory of the Qur'an: 'We have bestowed upon thee the seven Mathani and the Grand (Azim) Qur'an.' This has given rise to the most common interpretation, namely that Mathani refers to the Opening Sura with its seven verses which epitomise the Qur'anic message, and which, according to several traditions, were glorified by the Prophet as being equal to the whole of the Qur'an. The original meanings of the term (two-by-two and repetition) are also maintained in this interpretation. There is repetition in that the 'seven verses', constituting the ritual prayer, are repeated more often than any other part of the Qur'an, and the Qur'an has a dual quality in that it is characterised by the oft-repeated and balanced alternation of certain concepts such as amr and nahy, wa'd and wa'id (promise and threat), etc. Another interpretation equates Mathani with the repeated history of past prophets related in the Qur'an. This interpretation is supported by a similar concept in Judaism where repetition in the context of oral tradition of scriptural ordinances is designated by the Hebrew term 'Mishnah' equal to the Aramaic 'Mathnitha'.[7]

The Qur'an and Miracles

Apart from its assertion of inimitability and its reference to the Prophet's ascension (if taken literally) the Qur'an does not attribute any miracles to the Prophet. This does not mean, however, that it is less committed to the reality of miracles than the preceding religions, for it confirms unreservedly the accounts of miracles which are believed to have been performed, and supernatural events to have occurred, in bygone ages. Muhammad was often challenged by the pagans to produce miracles; his reply was that God makes miracles appear when He so wills, but that the miracles which were performed by prophets in the past were powerless to convince the people, who treated them as lies and sorcery.

The pagans' persistent challenge greatly embarrassed the Prophet who, reciting the Qur'an, always laid emphasis on the miracles bestowed by Allah not only on Moses and Jesus but also on lesser figures such as Salih and Solomon. If, asked the pagans, Allah empowered Moses to dry the sea, and Jesus to bring the dead back to life, why did He not send down a miraculous sign to confirm Muhammad such as by enabling him to cause a spring to gush forth from a rock, by giving him a well-watered orchard, or a house adorned with gold, or a treasure, by sending angels to accompany him on earth, by exempting him from the necessity of eating and walking in the market, by permitting him to mount to heaven and bring back written confirmation of his mission, or by causing a piece of the sky to fall upon the unbelievers and crush them? (XVII. 92–95, XX.133).

To all this the Prophet's answer was: I am only a man and a warner; signs are in Allah's hands, and those which were revealed to the former generations did not make men less intransigent. Allah Himself answers: 'If there were on earth angels walking in peace We would certainly have sent down from heaven an angel as an apostle' (XVII.97). 'Former apostles also ate and walked' (XXI.8 and XXV.22).

'Even if We sent down angels to them and caused the dead to speak with them and ranged all things before them, they would still not believe unless Allah willed it' (VI.109–111). 'We refrain from sending signs only because the men of former generations treated them as false' (XVII.61). 'When Our signs came to them, that should have opened their eyes, they said "This is manifest sorcery"' (XXVII.13). 'Never did a single one of the signs of their Lord reach them, but they turned away from it' (VI.4). 'Say, signs are in the hands of Allah, my mission is only to give warning. Is it not enough for them that We have revealed to you the Book for their instruction?' (XXIX.49–50).

Accordingly Muhammad declared that his unquestionable miracle was the revelation of the Qur'an. Nevertheless the pagans' questions troubled his mind, and his bewilderment brought reproaches from Allah: 'In case you are in doubt as to what We have revealed to you', says the Qur'an in X.94, 'perhaps you feel inclined to suppress a part of what has been revealed to you, being distressed at heart lest they say why has not a treasure been sent down to him or why an angel has not come with him; but you are only a warner' (XI.14). 'If you find their aversion hard to bear, seek if you can a tunnel in the earth or a ladder to the sky by which you may bring them a sign' (VI.35).

The Prophet continued to contend with the pagans, but as their attitude did not change he did not reason with them any further but said: 'Allah alone has knowledge of what is hidden. Wait if you will; I too am waiting' (X.20).

The possibility of supernatural occurrences is clearly recognised by the Qur'an, which cites many examples of such phenomena as having taken place in the past. To quote a few from among them: Abraham was saved from Nimrod's blazing surface (XXI.69); God heard Jonah's prayer from inside the body of the fish and caused the fish to cast him safe and unhurt ashore (XXXVII.144); Moses saw his staff change into a serpent (XX.21), divided the sea by striking it with his staff (XXVI.63), caused 12 springs to gush forth from a rock by striking it with his staff (II.57); Solomon caused a Jinn to bring the throne of the queen of Sheba in the twinkling of an eye from Saba to Jerusalem (XXVII.38); after his death his corpse remained standing for a time, propped up against his staff until a worm of the earth gnawed away at it and the corpse fell down (XXXIV.13); Jesus spoke in the cradle (XIX.30), made the figure of a bird out of clay and breathed life into it (V.110) and accomplished other wonders.

Believers accept unconditionally all that is contained in the Qur'an, but a question arises as to the mental faculty which is exercised in such acceptance. It is often argued that the faculty involved is intellect or reason (aql), but the student of the Qur'an soon reaches the conclusion that if reason is at all relevant to belief in supernatural phenom-

ena it is reason in a very special sense, i.e. reason of faith, rather than
that of logic and philosophy. Reason in the latter sense cannot explain
miracles, nor can it authenticate the descriptions of hell, purgatory
and paradise as given at length in the Qur'an. But the Qur'an attributes a transcendental function to reason by asserting that it is the
faculty which leads man to the understanding of God's signs which
pervade all existence (III.114, XXIX.34–63, XXVI.27, II.166). Thus the
Qur'an conceives of reason as the faculty by which one sees the hand
of God in everything and accepts unquestioningly all that is contained
in divine scriptures.

Explanation, Interpretation and Exegesis (Ta'wil)

The Qur'an contains many verses which describe the essential characteristics of the Holy Book. It is an earthly copy of a heavenly original
(The Reserved Tablet: LXXXV.22); it is a Revelation sent down
through the angel Gabriel; it is in pure Arabic,[8] free from crookedness;
it is expressed in a clear, inimitable language; God has made it easy
to understand. This last characteristic is given such prominence that
the verse in which it is expressed ('We have indeed made the Qur'an
easy to understand and remember') is repeated four times in the form
of a refrain in Sura LIV. The description of the Qur'an as 'the Book
that makes all things clear' is repeated seven times (XV.1, XXVI.2,195,
XXVII.2, XXVIII.2, XXXVI.69, XLIII.1).

Nevertheless, a careful study of the Qur'an leads to the conclusion
that the assurance given to the effect that the contents of the Holy
Book are easy to understand does not exclude the necessity of seeking
the explanation or clarification of a number of passages by recourse
to various means, namely literal, historical or mythological interpretation,
or even, in some instances, to esoteric exegesis (ta'wil).

The experience of several centuries has shown that in order to
make the prescriptions of the Qur'an applicable to all eventualities it
is necessary to explain, interpret, develop by the process of deduction, and otherwise amplify and complement its prescriptions. All
these methods have in fact been resorted to in the course of centuries and have largely contributed to the gradual formation of the vast
corpus of the Islamic faith. In this respect no theoretical difficulty has
been experienced. If the Qur'an does not expressly authorise recourse to methods of explanation or logical deduction for the purpose of better understanding the contents of the Holy Book, it does
not anywhere, directly or indirectly forbid the use of such expedients.
On the other hand, where the question is not one of explaining the

meaning of terms used in their ordinary sense, but is one of finding a hidden meaning for an allegorical or ambiguous passage, the Qur'an lays down a definite rule.

Verse III.5 divides the verses of the Qur'an into two categories: those which have a precise and established meaning (constituting the 'Essence of the Book') and those whose meaning is allegorical, ambiguous or vague. The Qur'an forbids any attempt at 'interpreting' passages of the latter kind, because their interpretation (ta'wil) is only known to God; indeed, says the Qur'an, only those whose hearts are diseased would seek to interpret such passages and to follow the interpreted sense thus attributed to them.

Here arises a substantial difficulty. There are several passages in the Qur'an which fall clearly into the category of the allegorical. As examples one might point to: the parable of the Light of God contained in verse XXIV.35; verse XXXIII.72 concerning God's offer of the 'Trust' to the heaven, the earth and the mountain, their refusal and Man's assumption of the 'Trust'; the mysterious journey undertaken by Moses, his meeting with a sage endowed with divine knowledge and all the incidents arising in the course of the journey, such as the coming to life of the dead fish which was to serve as a meal (related in Sura XVIII). Such obviously allegorical themes invite serious reflection in order to make their meaning clear, but as no help can be obtained from the apparent sense of the relevant words, one is inevitably led to search for a hidden meaning but such search might, following the strict letter of the Qur'an, be held to fall within the prohibition expressed in verse III.5. Indeed, on a narrow interpretation of the terms of the Qur'an, it could be maintained that not only the exegesis of allegorical texts, but even the explanation of ordinary passages of the Holy Book pertains exclusively to God. In verse LXXV.17 God, warning the Prophet as to how the verses of the Qur'an should be recited, affirms that He Himself will determine the manner of their recitation, and ends by saying: 'It is for Us to collect them and to *explain* them.'

However, as a study of the numerous classical commentaries[9] on the Qur'an will show, the arguments outlined above have not in fact stood in the way of adopting important interpretations in respect of difficult, including metaphorical, passages of the Qur'an. For instance the verse of Light, already referred to, and which is of a highly allegorical nature, has been frequently interpreted. An outstanding esoteric explanation of it has been proposed in Imam Ghazzali's famous *Meshkat al-anwar*. It appears that this striking attempt at the exegesis of an undoubtedly allegorical verse of the Qur'an has never been challenged on the ground of inconsistency with verse III.5.

Attention may here be drawn to the fact that certain terms in the

Qur'an have been held by some to have an 'allegorical' and by others a 'precise' meaning. The first group have not hesitated to interpret them, and their opponents, while disagreeing with the interpretation, have not condemned it as conflicting with verse III.5. A difference of opinion arose early within the Moslem community as to whether the anthropomorphic expressions used in the Qur'an in referring to God's attributes should be taken literally or interpreted metaphorically. In the language of the Qur'an God sees, hears, sits down, stands up, smiles, etc. He has hands, feet, ears and eyes. At the battle of Badr He throws a handful of dust at the enemy (VIII.17). He fashions His creatures with His hands (XXXVIII.75). His two hands are out-stretched (V.69). Now, as early as the second century of Islam one school (the Mu'tazila) argued that to take such passages literally would bring God almost to the level of Man, and that therefore such passages must be treated as metaphorical. In taking this bold stand in regard to the interpretation of the Qur'an this school met with severe opposition from another school (the Ash'ari) which declined to go into the explanation of such passages as the following: 'The hand of God is above your hands' (XLVIII.10); 'the face of your Lord shall remain in full glory and majesty' (LV.27). However, this school qualified the extreme materialism of its doctrine by affirming that the believer, whilst accepting the passages must not inquire as to 'how' (bila kaif) or in what manner the human-like attributes of God should be conceived. In all this controversy no reference was made to the prohibition contained in verse III.5.

Notes to Chapter Three

1. One verse (III.19) uses the term 'ummi' distinctly in the sense of one who does not belong to the People of the Book, i.e. Jews and Christians. It says: 'Say to the People of the Book and ummis . . .' It is clear therefore that ummi means non-Jew and non-Christian. The verse shows further that 'ummi' does not mean illiterate, for if it did it would follow by implication that all Jews and Christians are illiterate, which of course cannot have been meant. Another instance in which the word 'ummi' clearly means a person outside the People of the Book occurs in verse III.69 where the People of the Book say 'We are not bound to keep faith with the ummis.' However, there is another argument on which the opinion that the Prophet could not read and write is based; Verse XXIX.47 says 'Never have you read a book before this, nor have you ever transcribed one with your right hand. Had you done these the unbelievers might have justly doubted.'

2. A full discussion of the meaning of wahy in all its ramifications is contained in Toshihiko Izutsu, *God and Man in the Koran: Semantics of the Koranic Weltanschauung*, Tokyo, Keio Institute of Philological Studies, 1964, pp. 156–93. One important suggestion made therein brings the word qalam (pen) within the scope of revelation, originating with the attitude of pre-Islamic illiterate Arabs towards the pen and writing, regarding them as mysterious, awe-inspiring objects. This attitude, it is suggested, would seem to lie behind the use of the word pen and the reference to writing in the title and commencement of Sura LXVIII, and also behind the statement in XCVI.4–5 to the effect that Allah taught by the pen.

3. Under this mode (inspiration) can be brought the numerous spiritual visions and auditions which have been recorded in sacred history, such as the voice heard by St Paul on the way to Damascus (the Acts IX.3), by Jeremiah in I.2, by Ezekiel in I.3 and by St John in Revelation I.2, and also related from ordinary human experience, such as the voice heard by Socrates and by Joan of Arc.

4. The Qur'an shows special sensitiveness to the charge that it is nothing but 'fables of the ancients'. This charge is repeated at least nine times (VI.25, VIII.31, XVI.26, XXIII.85, XXV.5, XXVII.70, XLVI.16, LXVIII.15, LXXXIII.13) in order to be strongly refuted. Especially condemned is the allegation that the 'fables of the ancients' are taught or dictated to the Prophet by others' (XXV.5–7). The adversaries of the Prophet refer to him as 'a madman taught by others' (XLIV.13). These charges are specifically answered: 'We know that they say "It is a man that teaches him!" But the man to whom they allude speaks a foreign tongue, while this is clear Arabic . . . It is those who disbelieve the revelations of Allah that forge falsehood; it is they who lie' (XVI.104–107). The 'man to whom they allude' is believed to be Salman the Persian. Others have also been named in this connection, such as Soheil son of Sinan who was a non-Arab.

    The Prophet never forgave those who disparaged the revelations of the Qur'an. One such detractor is referred to in verse XXXI.5 without being named. 'Some there are who would pay for frivolous tales so that in their ignorance they may mislead others from the path of Allah and throw ridicule on it. For these we have prepared a shameful punishment.' It is believed that the person referred to is Nazr ibn Harith, who used to recite romances from Persian history and legends and claim them to be superior to the Prophet's utterances. He met his 'shameful punishment' when he was put to death at the end of the battle of Badr.

5. Nöldeke, the celebrated student of Islam, says: 'It need hardly be said that the Moslems have from old times applied themselves with great assiduity to the decipherment of these initials, and have sometimes found the most profound mysteries in them. Generally, however, they are content with the prudent conclusion that God alone knows the meaning of these letters.' (T. Nöldeke, *Sketches from Eastern History*, Beirut, Khayats, 1963.)

6. As a matter of interest to the reader, a list of the basic idea contained in each letter of the Hebrew alphabet considered as a hieroglyph is given below:

   Aleph: Potentiality; *Beth*: Inwardness, i.e. the esoteric; *Ghimel*: a Channel; *Daleth*: a Gift; *He*: Breath; *Vav*: Conjunction; *Zayin*: Direction; *Cheth*: Polarity; *Teth*: Protection; *Yod*: Creative Spirit; *Kaph*: Assimilation; *Lamed*: Extension; *Mim*: the Matrix; *Nun*: Progeny; *Samekh*: Containment; *Ayin*: Materiality; *Phe*: Expression; *Tsade*: Termination; *Qaf*: Collected energy; *Resch*: Movement; *Shin*: Relationship; *Tav*: Fulfilment.

   References: Fabré d'Olivet, *The Hebraic Tongue Restored* (Reprint), New York, Weiser, 1976.

   Anon, *The Hebrew Letters as Hieroglyphs*, Bray, Private Press, 1976.

   Anon, *A Sacred Script*, Bray, Private Press, 1977.

7. Maxime Rodinson, *Mahomet*, Paris, Edition du Seuil, 1968, p. 151.

8. The fact that the Qur'an has been revealed in Arabic has been emphasised and a reason has been assigned to it. 'This book is revealed . . . that you may give warning in plain Arabic speech . . . If We had revealed it to a non-Arab and he had recited it to them [the Arabs] they would not have believed' (XXVI.192–195). 'Had We revealed the Qur'an in a foreign tongue they would have said . . . "Why in a foreign tongue when the Prophet is Arabian?" ' (XLI.44).

9. To cite only one eminent commentator, Muhammad ibn Jarir al-Tabari (d. AD 929) is the author of a monumental work consisting of 30 volumes entitled *Jami' al-bayan fi tafsir al-Qur'an* (*A Comprehensive Exposition in the Interpretation of the Qur'an*).

CHAPTER FOUR

THE PREVIOUS BEARERS OF THE DIVINE MESSAGE

A most important part of the Qur'an (1,453 verses or about one-fourth of the total number) consists of narratives concerning the prophets, sages and other historical or legendary celebrities of ancient times, particularly of Semitic (Jewish and Arab) origin. These narratives are contained in different Suras and some of them are repeated many times. The longest of them (510 verses) concerns Moses and his people; the shortest (only seven verses) relates to Job. In between, varying in length and detail, are 16 other narratives, beginning with Adam and ending in Christ. In the Sections that follow a summary is given of each of these 18 narratives. It will be obvious that the motive behind these lengthy descriptions is not mere story-telling. What is important is the leitmotiv running through all of them, namely the emphasis on faith in the one and only Creator, and on certain religious and ethical principles which are expressed also in other verses of the Qur'an. Over and over again the Qur'an dwells on the calamities which God caused to descend on the people of past history for believing in polytheism, for discarding the notions of the Hereafter, of resurrection, Paradise and Hell; for not fearing the wrath of God, for yielding to the temptations of Satan, and, in a word, for not obeying the commandments of God and His Apostle.

A clear example of the development of this leitmotiv is found in Sura XXVI, all the verses of which (227) enlarge on this theme. At the beginning of the Sura, God consoles the Prophet and tells him not to fret himself to death because of lack of response from unbelievers; he should recall that the prophets of old received the same treatment. Developing this theme there follows a succession of accounts of the experiences of prophets of ancient times: Noah, Abraham, Hud, Salih, Lot, Shuaib and Moses. In essence the experiences of all of them is the same. Each declares his mission to his people and says that he asks for no reward but only wants to preach to them the truth that there is but one God. However, his people deny him, save a few. They say: 'You are but one of us, in no way superior to us. The cult of our father

69

is best for us.' They threaten to banish or kill him. Thereupon God
sends a calamity which destroys the recalcitrant people and saves the
believers. At the end of the Sura God says to the Prophet: The Qur'an
is not the work of Satan; it is a revelation from Us. We will tell you on
whom the work of the evil ones descends: it descends on lying and
wicked persons, among others on poets who wander aimlessly and who
preach what they do not practise.

Adam

In relating the episode of the creation of the first man, the Qur'an
uses both the proper noun Adam and the common nouns 'man'
(insan) and 'human being' (bashar); consequently, where the text so
requires, the term 'man' may be taken to mean 'humanity' in general,
of which Adam is the progenitor.

God created Adam from clay, breathed of His spirit into him, taught
him 'all names' knowledge of which He had not given to angels,[1] and
announced to the angels that He was placing a vicegerent on earth.
The angels demurred: would God place on earth one who would make
mischief and shed blood in it, whilst they, the angels, never ceased from
singing His praise? God replies: 'I know what you do not know.'[2] He
then commanded the angels to prostrate themselves before Adam.
They all obeyed except Iblis (Satan) who said: 'You created me from
fire and him from clay.' Satan was doomed because of his disobedience,
as has been explained elsewhere in this book. But God turned gra-
ciously to Adam and Eve[3] and bestowed on them the favour of taking
up their abode in the Garden of Paradise, where they could eat of all
its fruits, but must not approach 'this tree'[4] for otherwise they would
be sinners (II.33). He warned them against the temptations of Satan
who would try to deprive them of the blessings of existence in Paradise,
where they would feel no hunger, thirst or excess of heat (XX.115).

Adam and Eve entered Paradise, but Satan appeared to them,
claimed to be their friend and counsellor, and suggested to them that
in bidding them not to approach 'the tree' God had intended to
prevent them from becoming immortal like angels (VII.11). Adam and
Eve fell a prey to the temptations of Satan and ate of the fruit of the
forbidden tree. Thereupon they became aware of their nakedness
which was hidden from them before; a feeling of shame came over
them and they covered their nakedness with leaves from the garden.
For this disobedience Adam and Eve incurred God's wrath and were
expelled from Paradise. Thus Satan achieved his purpose by making
Adam and Eve conscious of their original nudity (VII.19) or, alterna-

tively, by stripping them of their garments to expose their nakedness (VII.26).

When God reproached Adam and Eve for the disobedience they admitted their guilt, repented of their sin, and implored forgiveness. God forgave them (II.35) but relegated them to earthly existence with its attendant evils and hardships.

As in the Bible, where God makes garments of skin for Adam and his wife and clothes them (Genesis III.21) so in the Qur'an Allah bestows on them (and generally on mankind) the gift of clothing to cover their nudity and also to embellish it, accompanying this favour with the counsel that the robe of piety is the most fitting adornment (VII.25)

A point of importance to the development of Islamic theology is that the Qur'an does not interpret the disobedience of Adam and Eve as an 'original sin' affecting all humanity and necessitating a vicarious act of redemption.

The Sons of Adam: Abel and Cain

The story of the two brothers is told in six verses (V.30–35). Each brother presents a sacrifice to God. Abel's offer is accepted; Cain's is rejected. Thereupon Cain, moved by anger, kills Abel, whilst the latter does not move to defend himself, or still less to attack the aggressor. He desists because his soul prompts him to be righteous and to fear God, whilst his brother's soul prompts him to commit the crime of murder. However, Abel does pronounce a curse on Cain, telling him that he is doomed to hell-fire for 'my sin as well as yours'. The difficulty of understanding Abel's reference to himself as a sinner has caused some commentators to interpret the words 'my sin' as meaning 'your sin against me', a far-fetched construction.

A feeling of contrition comes to Cain, not for the crime which he has committed, but for not having thought of hiding the shame (i.e. the corpse) of his brother until a raven appeared and showed him how to do so by scratching the ground.

The Qur'an establishes a link between the commandment not to take life and the Abel–Cain episode. Verse 35, introducing the moral of the narrative, says that 'on that account' it was impressed on the people of Israel that to slay one person is tantamount to slaying the whole of mankind, and to save one life is tantamount to saving the life of all mankind. This verse almost coincides with a passage which occurs in the Mishnah (codification of the Talmudic oral traditions) which says: 'That is why Man was created simply to show that whoever kills someone shall be held responsible as if he had killed the whole of mankind, but whoever saves someone it is as if he had saved the whole of mankind.'

Adam being the progenitor of the human race, the phrase 'sons of Adam' (Bani Adam) signifies humanity as a whole. On creating the universe God took from the whole future progeny of Bani Adam a solemn undertaking that they would recognise Him forever as their creator and attribute no associate or partner to Him. This undertaking (called the Pact Am I not your Lord?) was taken in the name of future generations so that they would have no excuse on Judgement Day if they had violated it (VII.171).

Noah

The story of Noah as it is told in the Qur'an, like the story of other prophets of ancient times, is meant to be taken as a warning. This is clearly stated in two verses: No. 31 of Sura XXIII and No. 15 of Sura LIV; in the latter the statement is followed by the sceptical question: but will anyone take heed?

The point of the story from which the desired lesson is to be drawn will appear from the following summary:

Noah is sent to his own people, who are wicked and ungodly, to preach to them the straight path, with promises of rewards and threats of grievous penalties. In his preaching, Noah stresses the themes that constitute also the mission of the other prophets, i.e. there is only one true God, everything that exists is a sign of His greatness and of His favours to mankind, and whoever will not believe will be doomed to hell-fire.

The people reject Noah scornfully and mock him saying that he is only one like themselves and that nothing will cause them to abandon the worship of their idols. They remind each other of the names of their five principal idols (verses 22 and 23 of Sura LXXI) whose worship they must not neglect.

Noah despairs of his mission and implores God to destroy every one of the unbelievers, for if any are left they will but mislead the believers. Thereupon he receives the divine order to build a ship, to place himself, his kindred and a couple of every species of animals on board and then to set sail. When the ship departs a storm breaks out and the whole earth is submerged by a mounting flood. When everything is destroyed, and the deluge subsides, God causes the ship to come safely to shore. Noah and his retinue of believers and specimen animals are saved.

It will be observed that the above recital conforms substantially to the biblical version, but the Qur'an considers that it bears an original message. Verse 51 of Sura XI addressing the Prophet says: 'Such are some of the stories of the Unseen, which We have revealed to you; before this neither you nor your people knew them.'

Hud and Salih

The 'Ad were a people of Semitic origin having descended from Noah through Shem, and they took their name from their ancestor 'Ad who lived in the fourth generation after Noah. They lived in a tract of country situated between Oman and Yemen in Southern Arabia. As they were idol worshippers God raised up one from among them, named Hud, to bear His message to them and guide them to the worship of the One and Only God. Hud fulfilled his mission and told his people that he did not expect any reward from them but only desired to make them realise that their idols were man-made objects lacking any reality or power. He appealed to them to abandon their beliefs and to fear the true God and the Last Judgement. But they reacted to his counsel and warnings with denial, contempt and mockery. They said: 'You are one of us and yet you try to alienate us from the traditions and creed of our forefathers; we look upon you as a madman who has been visited by a demon by order of our gods.' They challenged him to show that the message which he bore brought them any advantage. 'What can you give us', they asked, 'that we do not already possess? Our capital city Iram with its superb palaces and monuments is without parallel in the whole world.' Hud said in reply that as they refused God's message their cities would crumble to dust and all they possessed would perish together with themselves. Misfortunes then began to befall the people, but they took no heed; at last a furious wind arose which lasted seven days and nights, and wholly destroyed the city and its people except Hud and his loyal followers.

According to the legends concerning the ancient people of Arabia, a people named Thamud succeeded the 'Ad, to whom they were related by blood, having descended like them from Noah, but through a different ancestor whose name they bore. They lived in the north-eastern corner of Arabia in an area situated between Medina and Syria. They were skilful builders and used to carve houses, fortresses, temples and mausoleums out of the rocky mountains which surrounded them. Like the 'Ad, they were idol-worshippers, and God raised up from among them one called Salih to teach them the true faith. He fulfilled his mission, but his people, like the 'Ad before them, rejected his teachings and maltreated him for attempting to undermine their traditional cult. They challenged him to produce proof of his alleged divine mission, and he pointed to a she-camel which he declared to be a sign or symbol from God. He pleaded with the people to inflict no harm on her, to leave her to graze freely and to let her drink at the common source to which men and beasts had access each at an appointed time. But the people turned a deaf ear to Salih's recommendations as to his teachings, and instead of treating the she-camel humanely, hamstrung her. They then laid a plot against Salih himself. Nine men swore an oath to make a secret night attack on him and his kinsfolk. But before they could put their plan into execution God's plan was fulfilled. An earthquake, accompanied by a mighty blast, overtook the people of Thamud overnight. In the morning they all lay prostrate in their homes, except Salih and his followers.

Abraham

Abraham lived among Chaldeans who worshipped the heavenly bodies. Practising their cult, he used to meditate on the stars, the sun and the moon, but God chose to inspire him. Once when he was engaged in his meditations the thought struck him that bodies which fluctuate between rising and setting cannot be worthy of adoration. How, he asked himself, can men worship such bodies? How can they deify images which they have hewn with their own hands out of the rocks? Remonstrating with his father, he said: 'The idols that you worship can neither hear, nor see, nor speak, nor benefit you in any way; cease worshipping them and I will teach you to worship the true God, the unique Creator.' Infuriated by these words, the father said: 'Do you dare renounce the cult of our forefathers? If you do not desist I will have you stoned to death.'[5] Abraham remonstrated also with the people, saying that their gods were false and powerless, and that the true God was the unique Lord, master of all creation, but they also turned a deaf ear to his words. He then went to their temple at a time when there were no witnesses and broke all the idols to pieces with the exception of the chief idol. When the people saw what had happened they suspected that he was the culprit. They asked him who had destroyed the idols, and he replied that it was the chief idol, and that if they wanted confirmation they could ask the stricken idols. They said: 'But they cannot speak,' and this was the answer that he expected in order to bring home to them the helplessness of their gods. But the people persisted in their opposition and resolved to put Abraham to death by burning him at the stake. But God said to the fire: be cool to Abraham and keep him safe. He was thus saved and was chosen by God as His friend (IV.124). God said to him: submit, and he answered: I have submitted to the Lord of the Universe (II.125). God then said that He had appointed him a leader of mankind and would bestow prophecy and wisdom on his descendants. He then directed him to emigrate to a 'land blessed for all mankind', and he thus betook himself, together with his nephew Lot, to Palestine.[6]

Time passed and Abraham grew old. One day he received a strange visit from unexpected and unknown guests. These were angels who appeared to announce to him the glad tidings that a son endowed with wisdom would be born to him. Abraham's wife on hearing this beat her face and said: how can I bear a child when I am old and barren? But the angels said that all was possible to God. Their announcement was fulfilled, for a son was duly born and Abraham became the fountain-head of generations of apostles.

The Qur'an calls Abraham's faith 'Hanif' (true, upright). One verse makes it clear that at the time of the Prophet the creed of monotheism was not confined to Judaism and Christianity; it existed also in the Hanif faith which went back to Abraham. Verse II.129, contradicting the then current belief that if one was neither a Jew nor a Christian one was necessarily a polytheist, says: 'They say: "Become a Jew or a Christian if you wish to be guided aright." Say: "By no means, ours is the faith of Abraham, the true [Hanif] faith." ' In this context the Qur'an mentions several times Isaac, Ismael, Jacob and others of the progeny of Abraham. In particular the name of Ismael is joined to that of Abraham in connection with what can be regarded as the earliest foundation of Islam. Verse III.90 says: 'The first temple ever to be built for men was that at Becca (Mecca), a blessed place, a beacon for the nations. In it is the spot where Abraham stood.' The House of Ka'ba was built by Abraham and Ismael.

After Palestine Abraham had proceeded to Mecca, settling part of his family there (in a 'valley without cultivation'). There Abraham and Ismael raised the foundation of the House, praying thus: 'Lord, make us submissive to You [Moslems]; make of our descendants a nation that will submit to You [Moslem].' Verse II.125 says: 'We enjoined Abraham and Ismael to sanctify Our House for those who walk round it, who meditate in it, and who kneel and prostrate themselves.'

One other feature in the life of Abraham, which is given special prominence in the Qur'an, constitutes the origin of one of the characteristic rituals of Islam. Abraham is quoted to have had a vision in which God commanded him to sacrifice his son (it is not stated whether Isaac or Ismael is meant). Father and son surrendered to God's will but when Abraham made ready to fulfil the act of immolation God called out to him and said: 'You have already fulfilled the vision,' and sent down a 'noble sacrifice' (a ram) to serve as a ransom for the son. The commemoration of this event is celebrated annually in the course of the pilgrimage to the House of Ka'ba.

The importance of the personality of Abraham and of the concept of the 'Hanif faith' as the precursor of Islam emerges more particularly from verse XXII.77 which says, speaking of the religion of Islam, 'It is the cult of your father Abraham. It is he who had named you Moslems, both before and in this Revelation.' Among the numerous references in the Qur'an to Abraham and his progeny not the least important in the context of enjoining tolerance is verse 130 of Sura II which says: 'Say: we believe in what was revealed to Abraham, Ismael, Isaac, Jacob and the tribes, to Moses and Jesus and the other Prophets. We make no distinction between any of them, and to Allah we have surrendered ourselves [Muslimun].'

Lot

Lot, Abraham's nephew, was at first an idol-worshipper, but later he embraced the faith of his uncle, whom he accompanied on his emigration. His conversion was blessed; God looked with favour upon him and sent him as an apostle to a people who lived on the coast of the Dead Sea. He tried to fulfil his mission, but was thwarted in his endeavours. He found that the people to whom he had been sent, in addition to being idol-worshippers, were morally corrupt and incurably addicted to unnatural practices. He said to them: 'Will you not have fear of Allah? I am indeed your true apostle. Fear Allah then and follow me . . . Will you fornicate with males and leave your wives whom Allah has created for you?' But they replied: 'Bring down Allah's scourge upon us if what you say be true.' When they said, 'Desist or you shall be banished,' Lot cried out in despair: 'Lord, deliver me from these degenerate men!'

Now, when unknown messengers (angels) visited Abraham, he asked them: 'What is your errand?' They replied that they had been sent to destroy the wicked people who had rejected Lot. But, seeing that Abraham was concerned for the safety of his nephew, they added that Lot and his household would be saved except his wife who was condemned to stay behind and perish with the rest.

The angels then visited Lot. The people of the city, learning of the arrival of handsome youths, came running to Lot's house. Lot, ashamed of their conduct, said to them: 'Here are my daughters, they are more lawful to you. Have fear of Allah and do not humiliate me by wronging my guests. But they only said in answer: 'You know full well what we are seeking.' The angels consoled Lot, told him what would happen to the city and its dwellers at daybreak and urged on him to depart with his kinsfolk in the dead of night, but not to try to save his wife, who was condemned to suffer the fate of the others. The fate of the city is described as follows: 'And when Our judgement came to pass, We laid their town in ruins, and let loose upon it a shower of clay-stones bearing the tokens of your Lord. The punishment of the unjust was not far off' (XI.84).

Joseph

Sura XII (entitled the Sura of Joseph), containing 111 verses, is principally a narrative concerning the life and experiences of Joseph. In fact this part of the Qur'an, more than any, has the characteristics of a pure narrative, a particularity to which reference is made at the beginning of the Sura in these words: 'We will recount to you the most beautiful of stories.' Only in a few verses does the Sura strike a note of general other-worldly counsel and guidance, where appropriate in the context of the events described.

God bestows special favours on Joseph and on the house of Jacob. Joseph is chosen by the Lord, is given knowledge and vision, and in particular is taught the science of interpreting dreams.

The story of Joseph begins with the description of a dream in which he saw that eleven stars, together with the sun and the moon, prostrated themselves before him. The interpretation of this dream comes at the end of the Sura, where it is shown to have been a prediction that Joseph would be venerated by his eleven brothers and his parents and would attain to a high degree of dignity, glory and power after a series of untoward incidents.

The first of these incidents was the hatching of a plot by his brothers (except the youngest) who, moved by a strong feeling of jealousy because of their father's preference for Joseph, contrived to bring about his death. They persuaded their father, by giving false assurances, to let them take Joseph with them on an outing. Arrived at a far-off place in the desert, they cast him into a well and left him to his fate; then they returned home, mournfully informing their father that Joseph had been devoured by a wolf. In the meantime a caravan of merchants passed by. Their waterman, sent ahead to search for water, let down his bucket into the well in the hope of bringing up water, but the well was dry and instead of water Joseph came up in the bucket to the joyful surprise of the waterman who exclaimed: 'Rejoice, here is a boy.' In due course the merchants sold the boy as a slave. He was bought by an Egyptian nobleman who took him to his house and recommended him to his wife, saying that they might adopt him as a son. The boy grew to full manhood in the Egyptian's house and became so strikingly beautiful that whoever saw him said: this is no mortal but a gracious angel! The Egyptian's wife conceived a strong passion for him and sought to seduce him. One day she bolted the door and invited him to embrace her, but Joseph's virtue and piety made him repel her advances. Thus, as she was clinging to him and he was trying to break away, his shirt was torn at the back. At this juncture the master of the house arrived. His wife accused Joseph of having assaulted her, but as the evidence of the torn shirt spoke in Joseph's favour, the master of the house was convinced of his innocence. Nevertheless, as his wife persisted in her accusation, he caused Joseph to be imprisoned.

Two young men went to prison at the same time as Joseph, and shared his cell. Each had a dream and was anxious to know its meaning. They consulted Joseph who explained what each dream foretold. The interpretations came true: one of the two was executed and the other liberated. Several years passed; then it happened that the king had a dream in which he saw that seven fatted cows were devoured by seven lean ones, and seven green ears of corn by seven dry ones. The king consulted many wise men, but no one was able to interpret the dream. At last the man who had been liberated from jail bethought himself of the interpretation of his own dream and hastened to the prison to consult Joseph, who, reflecting on the dream, said: 'If during the next seven years which will be years of plenty the farmers will sow abundantly and will save as much of the harvest as will be surplus to current needs, then the hoarded crops will serve to feed the people during the ensuing seven years which will be years of drought. Then will follow a year of abundance.'

The king, having been informed of this interpretation, had Joseph brought before him after ascertaining that the accusation which had led to his imprisonment was false, and gave him the charge of the granaries of the realm. Thus Joseph became the most important officer of the court. When the years of plenty came to an end and the seven-year period of drought began, men came from all parts of the land to appeal to Joseph for help. Among them were Joseph's brothers, but not accompanied by the youngest, whom Joseph specially cherished and who shared with Joseph their father's preference. Joseph recognised them, but they did not recognise him. He gave them the provisions which they had come to seek, but told them that when they came next they must bring their youngest brother with them, failing which they would be given no corn. He also ordered secretly that the money which they had paid should be put back in their saddle-bags. When the party returned home and Joseph's generosity was discovered, Joseph's father, pressed by his sons, consented, though with hesitation, that his youngest son should accompany the others on their next trip in search of corn. When the brothers presented themselves for the second time before Joseph, he rejoiced to see his favourite brother, and succeeded, by employing a ruse, in retaining him when the others returned with the supply of provisions. On the return of the party, the father's grief when he saw that his youngest son was missing knew no bounds. He did not, however, lose hope and he sent his sons back again saying: 'Go, my sons, and seek news of Joseph and his brother. Do not despair of Allah's mercy.' On this third encounter Joseph felt that the time had come for him to reveal his identity. The disclosure had the effect which was to be expected. The guilty brothers, responding to a mild reproof from Joseph, confessed their misdeed, expressed remorse and implored their brother's forgiveness. Joseph replied: 'None shall reproach you this day. May Allah forgive you; He is most merciful.' Then at his request the party returned home to bring the rest of the family. When the happy reunion took place, and Joseph had embraced his parents, they all prostrated themselves before him and he said: 'This is the meaning of my old dream; my Lord has fulfilled it. He has been gracious to me . . . My Lord is gracious to whom He will.'

As stated at the beginning of this section there are in the Sura of Joseph a few verses which contain precepts of other-worldly wisdom. Apart from incidental references which occur in the narrative verses, there are some independent verses which dwell on faith and reliance on God's mercy. The contents of these verses can be summarised as follows: God is one, He has power over all things; He hears all and knows all; He is the best of guardians and the best of judges; He is most merciful; He rewards the righteous and the charitable. Man's soul is prone to evil; man can only avoid evil if God so wills; God's grace is conferred upon those who adopt the true faith, which is the faith of Abraham who destroyed idols and preached 'Islam' (submission to the One God). God inspires His messengers to reveal the signs of His grace and His mercy to mankind. Such is the essence of the Qur'an which is no invented tale but is a vehicle of divine wisdom.

Elias

Elias, to whom reference is made in Sura XXXVII as an apostle, was sent to the people of Samaria (in the northern kingdom of Israel) to dissuade them from the worship of Baal and to guide them to faith in the one true God. But the people rejected him and incurred God's wrath. Elias is the same as Elijah of the Old Testament, who lived in the 9th century BC and whose story is told in 1 Kings XVII–XIX and 2 Kings I-II. According to this story it is believed that Elias was taken up to heaven and was granted immortality. Indeed he reappears in the New Testament where he is once mistaken for John the Baptist and again is said to have been present at the transfiguration of Jesus (Matt 9–14 and Matt 17. 3). It is no doubt by way of an echo of this last account that the Qur'an refers to Elias in another Sura (VI.85) where he figures as one of a group of 'righteous ones' with Zacharias, John and Jesus.

Jonah (Jonas)

Jonah is mentioned in the Qur'an as one of the apostles. He was sent by God on a mission to the city of Nineveh, capital of Assyria, to guide its wicked people to the straight path. The people treated him with contempt and rejected him. Frustrated in his mission, he gave up all hope, called down the wrath of the Lord on the people, left the city and boarded a ship. But the ship was already overloaded; soon after it set sail a violent storm broke out and the captain, either supposing superstitiously that a man of ill omen was on board, or simply judging it necessary to lighten the ship, cast lots to determine whom to unload. The lot fell on Jonah, who was thrown overboard, but was at once swallowed by a big fish or whale. Now Jonah called on God from the depths of the darkness in which he found himself, and repented of his sin of deserting his mission. God answered his prayer, commanded the whale to cast him ashore, and caused a fruit-tree to grow over his head so as to nourish him and give him shelter. Jonah's repentance being sincere, God entrusted him once more with the same mission. He then returned to Nineveh, which was under the curse of destruction, but this time his preaching to the people of the city, numbering over 100,000, bore fruit. The people believed and were given a new lease of life 'for a while' (verse 148 of Sura XXXVII), from which it would appear to follow that they later reverted to wickedness and forfeited God's favour.

Job

Cited in the Sura entitled 'The Prophets', as 'Our Servant', Job is a faithful, god-fearing man, but he suffers from a number of ills which are not described in the Qur'an, but are related at length in the Old Testament. In the face of the evils that befall him, he shows patience, but he calls out to God against Satan, whom he believes to be the cause of his torments. Two facts may be deduced from the Qur'an, without their having been clearly expressed. One is that Job is covered with loathsome sores from head to foot. This is inferred from the fact that God tells him to stamp his feet on the ground so that a cool spring will gush forth, and he can wash and refresh himself with its water. The other is that his wife had been blaming him for his long-suffering attitude and for holding fast to his faith in God, and that Job, in a moment of anger caused by his wife's revolt, had taken an oath to beat her. This is inferred from the passage in which God counsels Job not to break his oath but to beat his wife with only a bunch of twigs (verse 43 of Sura XXXVIII).

Job's patience pays in the end. God removes all the causes of distress which had afflicted him, restores his people and his possessions as 'a grace from Ourselves and an admonition for our worshippers'.

Shuaib

Shuaib (popularly identified with Jethro, priest of Midian and father-in-law of Moses) belongs to the fourth generation after Abraham. He was charged with a mission by God to a people of Arab origin who led a nomadic life in the desert of Midian in the north-eastern region of Sinai. Communicating his divine mission, he urged them to worship God, to desist from corrupt practices, to give just measure in dealing with others, and generally to fear God and not to hinder others from following the straight path. But most of the people rejected him and blamed him for trying to turn them away from the cult of their fathers. Thereupon God caused a terrible calamity to befall them, from which only Shuaib and his followers were saved.

Moses and the Israelites

The Qur'an tells the story of Moses and the Israelites at greater length than that of any other Prophet or people. No less than 26 Suras contain recitals relating to the history of the Jewish people from the time when Moses conceived the plan of delivering them from their Egyptian bondage to the time when they were settled in the Promised Land. The Qur'anic accounts are broadly similar to the contents of the Old Testament as well as the Talmud or the official commentary thereon compiled by the doctors of Jewish theology.

Moses was born during the time when the Egyptians, acting on Pharaoh's decree, were killing all male infants born to Israelites. His mother hid him for a short while, but when it was no longer possible to hide him, God directed her, through an inspiration, to put him inside a chest and set the chest afloat on the river. She was assured that the river would cast the chest on the bank, and that the infant would be saved and returned to her and would in time be made an apostle. The mother did as she was told. The chest flowed down the river until it reached opposite Pharaoh's palace. It was seen from the bank by Pharaoh's attendants who pulled it ashore and took it to the palace. When it was opened, Pharaoh's wife on seeing the child felt a strong affection for him and pleaded with her husband not to kill him (which shows that the child was recognised to be of Israelite origin) but to let her bring him up in the palace and adopt him into the family. Pharaoh having consented, it became necessary to search for a nurse to take care of the child. At this point Moses' sister, who had been ordered by her mother to keep an eye on what was happening to the child, appeared and said that she knew of a house in which there were people who could provide a trustworthy and affectionate nurse. She pointed out the place where her mother lived. In this way the mother was chosen as nurse, and was given custody of the child. She was known to be an Israelite, and Moses became aware, as he grew up, of his Israelite origin.

The years passed, and Moses grew up under his mother's tender care, and was cherished by Pharaoh and his wife. When he reached the age of manhood, God bestowed wisdom and insight on him, and prepared him for the great mission which he was destined to embark upon.

One day Moses left the palace secretly and ventured into the heart of the city. There he happened to come upon two men who were fighting. One was a Egyptian and the other an Israelite. The latter having appealed to Moses for help against his adversary (the Egyptians were in the habit of persecuting the Israelites) Moses intervened, struck the Egyptian with his fist and killed him. He forthwith regretted his act, which he attributed to a Satanic temptation, and he turned to God for forgiveness and was forgiven. However, on the following morning he came upon the same Israelite who was now engaged in a fight with another Egyptian. Before he could intervene, another arrived on the scene and warned Moses to be prudent, for the chiefs of the city were taking counsel to punish him for the misadventure of the day before. Hearing this, Moses became fearful and decided to flee from Egypt. He arrived safely in Midian situated in the Sinai Peninsula. There he found a large crowd of shepherds gathered round a well, watering their flock, and behind them were two girls waiting to water theirs. As they were weary of waiting and helpless against the shepherds who blocked the approach to the well, Moses took it upon himself to water their flock. For this act of kindness the girls invited him to visit their home and meet their aged father. The latter yielded to his daughters' suggestion that he should hire Moses to serve him and he promised Moses to give him one of his daughters in marriage if he would serve him for eight years. Moses accepted the offer, entered the old man's service in which he remained for the stipulated eight years and then married one of the girls and raised a family.

One day when he was travelling in the desert with his family he reached a valley below Mount Sinai. There in the distance he saw a flame burning bright. He said to his people to tarry while he would go near and perhaps fetch a burning brand. When he drew near to the flame, a voice called out to him: 'Moses, I am your Lord. Take off your sandals for you are in the sacred valley of Tuwa, and know that I have chosen you' (XX.8 *et seq.*). God's plan for the fulfilment of which Moses was chosen was then revealed to him. He was to go to Pharaoh to warn him with gentle words to believe in the true God and to mend his ways. As Moses would need a sign to prove the divine origin of his mission, God gave him power to perform two miracles. One was that the staff which he was carrying would turn into a serpent on being thrown down. The other was that if he put his hand under his armpit, and drew it out it would come out white and shining. Moses did not feel confident of the success of his mission: the charge of murder was still outstanding against him in Egypt; Pharaoh was a ruthless tyrant, while he himself was weak and helpless and in particular suffered from an impediment of speech. He therefore prayed to God to allow him to take his brother Aaron with him as his lieutenant. Granting this prayer, God said: 'Go, you and your brother with My signs ... have no fear, for I will be with you ... Go to him and say "We are the messengers of your Lord. Let the Israelites depart with us and oppress them no more. It is revealed to us that His scourge will fall on those who deny Him." '

When Moses and Aaron appeared before Pharaoh, he rejected their mission and ridiculed the miracles performed by Moses as witchcraft. He said that there were among his own people magicians who could confront Moses with acts of jugglery more dazzling than his. To prove this he sent heralds to all parts of the kingdom to assemble the best magicians and bring them to the palace on a given day to meet Moses in a trial of skill. The contest took place in Pharaoh's presence. The sorcerers threw down their cords and rods, which turned to serpents.

Then Moses cast down his staff, and it also became a serpent, but so much more formidable than the sorcerers' reptiles that it devoured them all. Thereupon the sorcerers prostrated themselves and much to Pharaoh's displeasure acknowledged the God of Moses. Their conviction was so firm that even Pharaoh's threat of having their arms and legs amputated did not make them recant.

This incident infuriated the Egyptians still more. They demanded Pharaoh exterminate the Israelites as mischief-makers in the land. The time was now ripe for divine intervention. Calamities began to befall Pharaoh's people: they were plagued in turn with floods, locusts, lice, frogs and blood. After each calamity the Egyptians entreated Moses to intercede with his Lord on their behalf, promising that if the scourge were removed, they would believe in him and let him take his people out of Egypt, but no sooner was relief granted than they broke their word.

Finally Moses received God's command to depart with his people in the night without fearing that they would be pursued and overtaken. Pharaoh and his people did pursue them, but when the Israelites arrived at the sea, Moses struck the sea with his staff and a dry path opened up for the Israelites to cross in safety. Then when the pursuing legions arrived, the water rolled back into the dry path and they were all drowned.

The Israelites crossed from Egypt into the Sinai Peninsula. There Moses numbered and organised his people and instituted the priesthood, and then the party marched south in the direction of Mount Sinai. Then came the celebrated forty-nights' communion of Moses with God on the Mount, by God's command. The Qur'an, mentioning the divine summons (verses II.48 and VII.138) dwells on Moses' prayer that the Lord should show Himself to him, and the Lord's answer: 'You shall not see me, but look at the mountain; if it remains firm on its base then only shall you see me.' But when the Lord revealed Himself to the mountain, He crushed it to dust, and Moses fell down in a swoon. When he recovered, God announced to him that He had chosen him of all mankind to receive His mission and commandments. Thereupon the Tablets containing the Ten Divine Commandments were given to him as the record of the law ordained for his people. Now, Moses, when he was called for the forty-nights' communion, had entrusted the care of his people to his brother Aaron, but when he returned bearing the Tablets he found that in his absence they had given up the worship of God and, led astray by a magician named Samiri, were worshipping a calf that they had fashioned out of gold ornaments. On seeing what had happened, Moses threw the Tablets to the ground, and his fury did not abate until he had commanded his people to kill one another (verse II.51) so that God would forgive them. Then the effigy of the calf was re-melted, destroyed and its pieces thrown into the sea, and the magician's punishment was announced: in this life he would be an outcast, and in the next his torment would be eternal.

His anger appeased, Moses took up the Tablets, and chose seventy men from among the leaders of his people to go up to the Mount with him to be present, at some distance, when he would ask God for forgiveness.

The Israelites as a people were essentially intransigent and querulous, and the seventy elders proved to be no exception to the rule. Moses had intended them to be silent witnesses to the repentance of their people, but they acted otherwise. They said to Moses: 'We will not believe in you until we see God with our own eyes.' For this insolence they were struck down by a thunderbolt and lightning, but God revived them in answer to Moses' entreaty so that they might repent.

The Israelites then resumed their wandering northwards in the Peninsula. During this wandering they caused Moses frequent vexation. It is probably to his experience during this period that Moses refers when he addresses his people in these words: 'O my people, why do you vex and insult me when you know that I am the apostle of God?' (verse LXI.5). They constantly showed signs of discontent, although God sent clouds to protect them from the scorching rays of the sun, made food descend upon them from the sky in the shape of Manna and quails, and caused ten springs to gush forth from the rocks to quench their thirst. Yet they found cause for ceaseless murmuring. They complained of the monotony of the food that they found in the desert, and said to Moses: pray to the Lord to give us some of the varied produce of the earth: green herbs, cucumbers, garlic, lentils and onions. When they approached a city (probably east of the Jordan) which they might have inhabited in peace, Moses bade them enter it and eat of its plenty on condition of making their way reverently through the gates and uttering a formula of repentance. Instead of which they 'transgressed' by changing the word that was dictated to them, and by infringing God's commands, because of which a plague descended on them from heaven.

There is another outstanding instance of the vexatious attitude of the Israelites towards Moses. It is important to mention it, if only because it has provided the title of the second Sura of the Qur'an: 'The Cow'. In the course of seven verses (68–71) the Sura relates how Moses communicated to his people God's command that they should sacrifice a cow, and how they quibbled and vexed him with questions regarding the kind, the colour and the peculiarities of the animal before obeying the command.

To continue the tale of the Israelites' wanderings: when they reached the southern borders of Canaan, they camped there and 12 men were sent to spy out the land. They proceeded north until they reached a country which was very rich in the produce of the earth. They went back to the camp heavily laden with samples of the fruits they had found in the city, but much reduced the attractiveness of their description when they said that the city was inhabited by a people of excessive strength. Although Moses, Aaron and two of the pioneers pleaded with the people saying that if they entered the city they would be victorious, for it was the land that God had promised them, their answer was that they would not enter the city until its strong inhabitants were driven out. 'O Moses', they said, 'we will not go in so long as *they* are in it. Go, you and your Lord, and fight them; we will stay here' (verse V.27). Frustrated and despairing, Moses turned to God and said: I have no power except over myself and my brother, so separate us from this rebellious people. God then pronounced the punishment to which the people of Israel were condemned because of their rebellion: 'Therefore this land shall be out of their reach for forty years, during which time they shall wander homeless on the earth; do not grieve for this rebellious people' (verse V.29). To quote from a footnote to this verse written by A. Yusuf Ali in his English translation of the Qur'an: 'Forty years afterwards they crossed the Jordan opposite what is now Jericho, but by that time Moses, Aaron and the whole of the elder generation had died.'

The Qur'an repeatedly reprobates the Jews for 'altering words from their proper places', falsifying the scriptures and disregarding the prophecies contained in them. These reproaches stem principally from the Prophet's disappointment at the Jews' refusal to recognise him as the prophet promised in the Old Testament (Deut. XVIII.18). But there is also mention of violations of Mosaic law by the Jews, such as eating forbidden food and in particular breaking the Sabbath. Reference is twice made to a particular instance of such violation, for which a whole group of Sabbath-breakers (identified by commentators with the Jewish community of Eliath on the Red Sea during the time of David) was transformed into apes (II.61 and V.65).

This section will not be complete without a reference to a passage of the Qur'an concerning the people of Israel, which sounds a note of general disapproval of their comportment, a note which can be detected in several other passages as well. Verses 4 to 6 of Sura XVII say: 'In the Scriptures We solemnly declared to the Israelites "Twice you will commit evil in this land, you shall become great transgressors." ' It is then stated that on both occasions the punishment with which the Israelites had been threatened was inflicted on them, the first being the destruction of the Temple by Nebuchadnezzar and the ensuing Babylonian captivity (588 BC), and the second being the destruction of Jerusalem by Titus in AD 70.

Among the Qur'anic narratives concerning Moses there appears a mysterious episode (described in 23 verses of Sura XVIII) which has given rise to speculation as to whether it has an occult meaning.

Accompanied by a young attendant (Joshua according to tradition) Moses started one day on a journey whose destination was 'the land where the two seas meet'. They reached journey's end and passed beyond. Then Moses, worn out with fatigue, called on his attendant to bring them their early meal. Now, the only food that they had brought with them was one fish; but the attendant was not able to serve it because, he said with regret, when they reached their destination the fish, which Satan caused him to forget, made its way into the sea and miraculously swam away. Thereupon Moses said, 'That is what we were seeking.' They made their way back to the junction of the two seas where they encountered a mysterious being (identified in tradition with the legendary Khidr, the immortal sage on whom God has bestowed divine wisdom). Moses asked to be permitted to travel in his company, but the sage only agreed reluctantly because he foresaw that what was going to occur in the course of the journey would be beyond the understanding of Moses who would be unable to restrain himself from asking questions. However, as Moses promised to be patient and not to ask questions the journey began. Soon afterwards the enigmatic behaviour of the sage manifested itself. First, on setting sail he bored a hole in the bottom of the boat causing many passengers to drown. Secondly, they came upon a young man, to all appearance harmless, and the sage killed him. Thirdly, they came to a city whose inhabitants refused to offer them any hospitality. Now, in that city there was a wall which was on the point of falling down, and the sage took it upon himself to restore it without asking for a reward. After the first two events Moses, forgetting his promise, had asked a question and then requested to be forgiven. But on the third occasion when he showed curiosity, the sage said that the time had come for them to part company. However, he was willing to give an explanation of his strange deeds before parting. He had scuttled the boat because if he had not done so, it would have been captured by a tyrant who was following close behind. He had killed the youth because had he lived, he would have brought suffering to his parents, whereas now that he was dead God would give his parents a worthier son. Finally he had repaired the wall because beneath it was hidden a treasure which an honest man had buried for his sons to dig up in due time, and this they would have been unable to do if the wall had collapsed.

David and Solomon

Several verses of the Qur'an speak of David and Solomon and relate how God bestowed abundant favours on them and exalted them above others. He made David master in the land, gave him wisdom and sound judgement and inspired him with the Psalms. He made the mountains and the birds join with him in chanting the praise of the Lord. He made hard iron pliant to him so that he could make coats of mail and armours. He made him, though weak and unaided, victorious over the hosts of Goliath. Yet David, in spite of all his wisdom, was not immune to the temptations of the flesh and constantly added to the number of his concubines until he was cured of this blemish by a subtle lesson that he received from two common men. These unknown individuals broke into his private chamber one day by climbing over the wall and explained their strange behaviour by saying that they had come to ask him to arbitrate in a dispute which had arisen between them. One of the two, stating the case, said that the other had 99 ewes while he himself had only one, but the other was intent on laying hands on his single ewe. David gave judgement for the wronged one, but realised that he himself had been tried in this pretended dispute, asked forgiveness of God and was forgiven.

Solomon received, in addition to the gifts of prophecy, wisdom and sound judgement, untold other favours: the raging wind was subdued to him, he was taught the language of birds, he was given a spring flowing with molten brass, jinns and demons were assigned to his service. They fought in his army, dived into the sea for him, built him palaces, shrines and statues, and rendered him any service that he required of them. Solomon acquired magical and unusual powers. He sent his lapwing on a mission to the Queen of Sheba, to take a message to her and to bring back an answer. He caused the Queen's throne to be brought to him in the twinkling of an eye and performed other prodigious acts when the Queen arrived in his presence, with the result that she abandoned her pagan cult and became a believer in the one true God. From the text of one verse (XXXVIII.33) it is inferred that Solomon became conceited because of his power, for the verse says: 'We put Solomon to the proof and placed a counterfeit upon his throne, so that he at length repented and said "Forgive me, Lord." ' According to commentaries the counterfeit was a demon who impersonated Solomon but whose simulation was finally detected. Another abnormal event occurs when Solomon dies; since knowledge of his death would have caused the jinn workers to stop their work, the corpse was made to stand up leaning on a staff, thus causing the illusion that Solomon was alive, and it was not till a long time later when earthworms had eaten away the staff causing the corpse to fall down that the jinns realised that Solomon had died, but by then their task had been completed (XXXIV.13).

The Qur'an deprecates the inconstancy of some of the People of the Book who break their covenant with God's revelation, and in this context mentions their adherence to false suggestions concerning the nature of Solomon's power. These suggestions come from the devils who pretended to have read in 'Solomon's books of magic', alleged to have been unearthed after his death from under his throne, that he knew and practised sorcery. But the accusation is false. It was the devils who taught witchcraft and what had been revealed to the two angels Harut and Marut in Babylon. These two, however, never imparted their knowledge to others without adding the warning: 'We are only a temptation, so do not renounce your faith.' What the devils learn from them and teach to others is an art which breeds discord between man and wife, and brings harm to men though only within the limits permitted by God. Those who credit such false opinions sell their soul for a vile price and forfeit the happiness of the Hereafter (II.95–96).

Zacharias, John, Mary, Jesus

The Qur'anic version of Christ's mission begins with a reference to Mary's mother. Finding herself pregnant and hoping for a son, she vows to dedicate the fruit of her womb to the service of God. But she gives birth to a girl, whom she names Mary. Then she prays to God to accept the dedication of her daughter to His service. God grants her prayer and entrusts the care of the child to the prophet Zacharias. At the same time Zacharias who is old and childless turns to God and, though knowing that his wife is barren, entreats Him to grant them a child to become heir to the house of Jacob and his own. Answering his prayer, God gives him the good news that a son will be born to him, to be named John, who will rank among the prophets and confirm the Word of God. Zacharias asks for a sign in confirmation of this promise, and is told that he will be bereft of speech for the space of three days and three nights. In due course John is born, and God grants him wisdom, virtue and the gift of prophecy.

Reference should here be made to a difficulty which arises in respect of the appellations used in certain verses of the Qur'an in mentioning Mary and her mother. Mary is referred to as 'Imran's daughter' and 'Aaron's sister', and her mother is designated as 'Imran's wife'. Thus Imran (Arabicised form of the Biblical Amram, the father of Moses, Aaron and Miriam) becomes Mary's father and the husband of her mother. Historically, of course, this is a serious inexactitude, Mary's father being Joachim, who was separated by an interval of over 15 centuries from Amram. Commenting on this striking anachronism, critics have suggested that it arises from an error, i.e. confusing Mary mother of Christ with Miriam, daughter of Amram and sister of Aaron, both names being Maryam in Arabic. It is possible, however, that the Qur'anic appellations have been used metaphorically. There is indeed an example of such usage in the New Testament, where Elizabeth, Zacharias' wife and John the Baptist's mother, is referred to as one of the daughters of Aaron (Luke I.5), obviously on the ground that she was a descendant of the priestly family going back to Aaron. Similarly, as Mary and her mother belonged to the progeny of Amram, the terms 'daughter' and 'wife' of Imran may be held to mean 'descendants of Imran'.

To quote the verses which contain the appellations referred to: 'God sets forth the example of Mary, Imran's daughter who guarded her chastity; We breathed of Our Spirit into her womb, she put her trust in the words of her Lord and His scriptures and was truly devout' (LXVI.12). 'O sister of Aaron, your father was not a man of evil, nor was your mother unchaste' (XIX.29). 'Remember the words of Imran's wife "O Lord", she said, "I dedicate to Your service that which is in my womb; accept it from me, You alone hear all and know all" ' (III.33).

Mary grows under the special care of Zacharias. Every time Zacharias visits her in the temple he finds, stretched out before her, food which he had not provided. Asked where this comes from, she says that it is sent by God. One day an angel in human shape appears to Mary and commands her to prostrate herself because he has come to her with a message from on high. The message is that God's Word will be incarnated in her in the person of a son whose name will be Christ Jesus son of Mary (III.41) and who will be honoured in this world and in the next. Mary, untouched by man, is taken aback at this announcement, but the angel reassures her and says: 'God creates what He wills by saying "Be" and it is.' The angel also announces that Jesus will speak to men in infancy and in maturity.[7]

Mary finds herself with child and decides to leave her people and retire to a far-off place.[8] When she feels the throes of approaching childbirth she cries out in despair to God, Who causes a spring to gush forth beneath her and makes ripe dates fall on her lap. She eats and drinks and is delivered of a son (XIX.22–26). Her people then arrive and begin to reproach her. For all reply she points to the child; but her people say 'What are we to do with a babe in the cradle?' Thereupon the child speaks up and says: 'I am a servant of God, who has bestowed revelation on me, made me a prophet, given me His blessing and commanded me to be devout, charitable, upright and virtuous.'

The name of Jesus Christ as an apostle, but not the son, of God, and mention of the Gospel as a divine revelation jointly with the Old Testament and the Qur'an, appear frequently in the Qur'an. 'We gave Jesus the son of Mary clear signs and strengthened him with the holy spirit' (II.81). 'Jesus the son of Mary was an apostle of God' (IV.169). 'God will teach him the Book and Wisdom, the Law and the Gospel, and appoint him an apostle to the Children of Israel' (III.43). 'We sent him the Gospel: therein was guidance and light' (V.50). 'Allah . . . sent down to thee [Muhammad] in truth the Book . . . [and sent down] the Law [of Moses] and the Gospel [of Jesus] before this' (III.1–3). 'The promises made by Allah are binding on Him in truth through the Law, the Gospel and the Qur'an'(IX.112).

In speaking of Jesus, the Qur'an dwells on a number of points: his birth, his relation to the divinity, his mission, ministry and death.

Birth and relation to the divinity

The Qur'an affirms that Jesus had no human father. The mystery of the immaculate conception is referred to in verse XXI.91 which says: 'And remember her who guarded her chastity; We breathed into her of Our Spirit and made her and her son a sign to all men,' and also in IV.171 where it is said that Jesus was 'God's Word which He cast into Mary as a spirit proceeding from Him'. Verse III.52 points out that Jesus' relation to God is the same as Adam's. 'He created Adam from dust and then said to him "Be" and he was.' In other words Jesus was no more God's son than Adam was; they were both His creatures.

In most cases where the Qur'an mentions Christ, it refers to him as 'Jesus son of Mary' in order, obviously, to emphasise its rejection of the Christian doctrine of Christ's divinity and of the belief in him as the son of God. Verse III.54 refers to a disputation which occurred in 630 between the Moslems and a Christian delegation from Najran on the subject of the Christian belief in the divinity of Jesus. It was agreed that the two parties would summon not only their men, but also their children and women, to a solemn gathering at which they would call down God's curse on the party which was 'lying'. The outcome of the invocation is not mentioned, but the Qur'anic position is conclusively declared in verse III.55: 'This is the whole truth, there is no God but Allah.'

The Qur'an's condemnation of any theory which derogates, in any manner whatsoever, from its fundamental conception of the 'oneness' of Allah, is absolute. Verse XXI.26 says: 'They [the Christians] say that God most Gracious has begotten offspring. Glory be to Him: they [the Prophets] are but servants raised to honour.' Other passages in the same Sura (XXI 'the Prophets') emphasise the rejection of the

doctrine of Sonship. Allah, referring to the Apostles whom He has sent
to mankind, dooms to hell-fire any of them who should say, 'I am god
beside Him' (XXI.30). In another passage (XXI.98) God, addressing
the polytheists, consigns them, as well as the gods they worship, to
hell-fire. This condemnation gave the polytheists a chance to contend,
mockingly, that Jesus must also share the fate of their gods. They
facetiously brought together the contents of the three verses quoted
above, and made merry at the conclusion which they drew from them,
namely that according to the Qur'an the 'son of God' would share the
same fate as the 'daughters of God', i.e. their divinities. In this spirit
they asked (XLIII.58): 'Are our gods better or he?' The answer comes
in verses 59 to 64: 'Jesus was no divinity but an Apostle of God.'

The dogma maintaining that Jesus is the son of God, and the dogma
of the trinity are treated by the Qur'an as fabrications, sheer blasphemy and unpardonable polytheism. Jesus, says verse V.116, taught
nothing but the worship of God and devotion to what would meet with
God's approval. God, addressing Jesus, asks whether he told the people
that he and his mother were divinities, and Jesus answers: 'Never did
I say anything but what You had commanded me' (V.116). It has been
suggested that the wording of God's question addressed to Jesus
implies that Muhammad assumed the members of the Christian Trinity to be God, Jesus and Mary. But the Qur'anic refutation of the
Trinity, whatever its import, is categorical. 'In blasphemy indeed', says
verse V.76, 'are those who say that God is one of three in a Trinity,
for there is no god but one God.' And verse IV.169 is strikingly
imperative: 'Say not "Trinity"; desist, it will be better for you, for God
is one God, far exalted is He above having a son.'

Mission and ministry
Verses XLIII.59 *et seq.* say of Jesus: 'He was no more than a mortal to
whom We granted Our favour and We made him an example to the
children of Israel . . . He shall be a sign for the coming of the Hour
of Judgement . . . When Jesus came with clear signs he said "Now have
I come to you with wisdom and in order to make clear to you some
of the points about which you differ; therefore fear God and obey me,
for He is my Lord and your Lord; worship Him, that is the straight
path." ' That Christ was no more than an apostle of God and one
whom God has strengthened with the holy spirit has also been declared in other verses such as IV.171, II.81, V.109 and III.40. Also
(verse LXI.6) Jesus says to the Israelites that he has been sent to them
by God as an apostle to confirm the Law and to announce that another
apostle would come after him whose name would be Ahmad.[9]

Christ's ministry is briefly mentioned in the Qur'an. God says that

He sent Jesus as a messenger to the children of Israel, confirmed him with the Holy Spirit, with revelation, the Torah and the Gospels, and commanded him to reaffirm the Old Testament and to manifest himself as the Sign of God (II.81, V.109). Jesus declared to the children of Israel that he was God's messenger to them, and performed miracles such as curing the blind, the leprous and the sick, and raising up the dead[10] (III.43). Some believed in him but the majority denied and slandered him. Some attributed to him the teaching of monasticism whereas he had brought no such commandment from God (LVII.27). His insistence on his divine mission fell on deaf ears, and his appeals for understanding and support received no response except from his apostles. However, after his short-lived ministry God regarded his mission as having been accomplished and raised him up to Himself.

Death and ascension

On the subject of Christ's death the Qur'an denies the Jews' claim to have killed him. It says: 'They did not kill him or crucify him but so it was made to appear to them ... assuredly they did not kill him' (IV.156). The words 'so it was made to appear to them' have been taken by some commentators to mean that a person other than Christ (Judas, according to one conjecture) was given his appearance by God and was crucified in his stead.[11] Here, it has been suggested, lies the explanation of verse III.47 which, after mentioning the Jews' refusal to recognise Jesus, says that they devised a stratagem, but God also devised a stratagem which was better than theirs. The Jews' stratagem is held to have been a plot to kill Jesus, while God's stratagem was to put another person in the place of Jesus, thus deluding the Jews into thinking that they had crucified him.

Verse IV.156 presents a difficulty in respect of the concordance of the Qur'an with the Gospel. According to the four Gospels, Jesus was crucified and died on the cross. The event is described circumstantially and in terms which cannot be taken in any but the literal sense. The Qur'an on the other hand, refers to the crucifixion as an illusory appearance. This interpretation existed previously in the form of a doctrine adopted by certain heretical Christian sects, to which Rodwell's translation of the Qur'an refers in a footnote under verse IV.156. But a point arises in relation to the Qur'anic version: how can its dissent from the Gospels be reconciled with the clear recognition of the Gospel by the Qur'an as a book containing guidance and light? This point has not received in the commentaries the attention it deserves.

Christ's ascent to heaven has been mentioned twice in the Qur'an.

Verse III.48 says: 'God says "O Jesus, I will cause you to die and will take you up to Myself." ' Again verse IV.157, after denying the crucifixion of Christ, says: 'God raised him up to Himself.' According to this quotation Jesus was raised up without dying, but the first quotation clearly makes his ascension follow death. In other words, the ascension is a resurrection from death, which was indeed foretold by Jesus himself when speaking in the cradle: 'Peace was on me on the day I was born; peace will be on me the day I die, and peace will be on me the day I shall be raised up again' (XIX.34).

Some Minor Prophets

The Qur'an mentions some of the Biblical prophets along with the major prophets, but appears to refer to all of them in verses XIX.54–59 where, after applying the term prophet to Aaron, Ismael and Idris, it says that these were some of the prophets whom God guided and chose from among the posterity of Adam, Noah, Abraham and Jacob, and on whom He bestowed His Grace. It is thus implied that the other prophets belonging to the same progeny also form part of the Company of the Elect. Of Ismael the Qur'an says that he was an apostle, a seer and a man of his word, submissive to the will of his Lord. God was pleased with him because he enjoined on his people prayer and charity. Aaron was also made a prophet to help Moses fulfil his mission. Idris, commonly identified with the Biblical Enoch, is commemorated as a saint and a prophet whom God raised to a lofty station. Ismael and Idris are also referred to in the Sura of the Prophets, together with Zulkifl (believed to be an Arabicised form of Ezekiel). They are qualified as men of constancy and patience, whom God admitted to His mercy for they were among the righteous. Ismael and Zulkifl are again referred to together with Elisha in verse XXXVIII.48 as being of the Company of the Good. (The story of Elisha who succeeded to the prophethood of Elijah, is told in the Bible: 1 Kings, XIX.19–21.)

Some Legendary Figures

In the course of developing its teachings, the Qur'an frequently cites the example not only of prophets and sages of ancient times, but also of some legendary, mythical or even fictitious persons. Chief among these is Khidr, the Evergreen who, though not mentioned by name, is recognised as the mysterious person (the possessor of divinely-inspired knowledge of the secret sources of life) whom Moses met on his allegorical journey. This episode has been referred to in the section on Moses and the Israelites. Another legend prominently described in the Qur'an is that of the 'seven sleepers' or the 'Companions of the Cave' also mentioned in another section of this book. Sura II (verses 100 *et seq.*) reprimands the People of the Book for neglecting their scriptures and giving credence to the suggestions of demons who attributed magical powers to Solomon. In this connection mention is made of the angels Harut and Marut who taught magic at Babylon, but warned the people that the teaching was imparted to them only to try them. In the commentaries of the Qur'an Harut and Marut have been identified with the two fallen angels of Jewish tradition who, having sinned on earth, were hung by their feet over a well for punishment.

A summary is given below of the contents of the Qur'an relating to three legendary figures: Dhulqarnain, Luqman, Qarun. A section is also included on Pharaoh who, although a historical person, often appears in the Qur'an as an archetype for autocracy. The experiences or characteristics of these mythical or semi-mythical figures are intended to serve as a salutary example or as a dissuasive lesson to believers.

Pharaoh

Pharaoh and his people have been mentioned often in the Qur'an, mostly in connection with what happened to the people of Israel, as described in the section on Moses and his people. But there are also references to Pharaoh which are not connected with the history of the Israelites and which refer to him as an evil-doer and as a tyrant who impaled his victims upon the stake. Because of his having disobeyed God's messenger, the scourge of God fell on his people and he was doomed to stand, on the Day of Resurrection, at the head of his people to lead them into the fire of Hell. There is, however, mention in the Qur'an of Pharaoh having repented at the end of his life. He is quoted to have said: 'Now I believe that there is no god save the God in whom the Israelites believe; to Him I give myself up.' In response to this repentance God reminds Pharaoh of his past misdeeds, but grants him nevertheless the favour of saving his body from the sea, so that he may become a sign to all posterity (verses 90–92 of Sura X).

At the end of Sura LXVI mention is made of Pharaoh's wife as an exemplary woman because she had turned to God and had said: 'Lord, build me a house with You in Paradise and deliver me frpm Pharaoh and his misdeeds.'

Luqman

Luqman, the legendary Arab sage, reputed according to the oldest traditions for his longevity and wisdom, is mentioned in the Qur'an. Nothing is said about when and where he lived or what happened to him, but he is held up as an example to all. He is specially endowed with wisdom by God. His attributes, which place him almost on the same level as the Prophets, appear from the counsels of wisdom which he gives to his son. He urges on him to beware of the company of polytheists, to revere his father and mother, to observe the ritual prayer, to incite others to do good and to avoid evil, to guard against arrogance, to show humility and patience in all circumstances, and to be at all times mindful of the fact that nothing can be hidden from God.

Dhulqarnain

Sixteen verses in Sura XVIII tell the story of Dhulqarnain, who is generally identified with Alexander the Great. The Qur'anic account of Dhulqarnain conforms to the legend of Alexander to the extent that it shows him mainly as a traveller with benevolent intentions. Specially endowed by God with power and the means of doing good, he sets out on travels eastwards and westwards and performs outstanding exploits. Somewhere in the west he comes upon a spring of murky water. Near the spring he finds a certain people, and God tells him that he may either torment them or treat them kindly. Dhulqarnain, in his wisdom and justice, awards punishment to evildoers and deals indulgently with those who have faith and do good works. Then he undertakes two expeditions eastwards. In one place he finds a people living in a state of nature, exposed to the sun, and he feels it to be wise to leave them in that state, and God confirms his judgement. Next he arrives at a place between two mountains, inhabited by a primitive people who complain to him that their land is constantly ravaged by the tribe of Gog and Magog. They implore him to build a rampart between the two mountains, and say that they will pay him tribute if he will thus protect them from further incursions. Dhulqarnain says: 'The power that my Lord has given me is better than any tribute.' He then instructs them to help him, and using molten lead and blocks of iron he erects a dam which effectively stops the gap between the two mountains and constitutes a wall so strong that the Gog and Magog are unable to scale it or dig through it.

Qarun

Qarun (the Korah of the Bible), a contemporary adversary of Moses, was a man of boundless wealth. He defied God, was arrogantly blasphemous, rejoiced in his possessions which he regarded as the fruit of his knowledge and enterprise and in no way due to God's favour. He acted insolently towards the people of Moses and treated them with contempt when they remonstrated with him and advised him to show gratefulness to God by doing good works with the treasures that God had bestowed on him. He persisted so long in his self-conceit that God caused the earth to open and to swallow him together with his house and his treasures. His fate became a salutary lesson to those who had envied his great wealth.

Notes to Chapter Four

1. The word Adam is taken from Hebrew, in which it means 'man' and Adamah means 'ground'. On the subject of giving names to things, cf. the Bible (Genesis II.19) according to which God brought before Man all the beasts and birds that He had formed out of the ground, to see what he would name them, and Man gave names to all of them.

2. In connection with Allah's announcement to the angels, an example may be given of painstaking efforts which have been made by commentators to elucidate apparent obscurities in certain passages of the Qur'an. In verse II.29 Allah announces to the angels that He is going to place a vicegerent on earth (in the person of Adam). The angels ask: 'Will You place there one that will do evil and shed blood?' This question implies that the angels knew beforehand what would happen if Allah did what He intended. But, unable to admit such foreknowledge on the part of the angels, certain commentators suggest that there is an ellipsis here: after Allah's announcement, the angels must have asked, 'And what will the vicegerent do?', to which Allah's answer would be: 'He will do evil and shed blood.' Thus the angels' question does not imply knowledge on their part; it only repeats Allah's words. A further point needs elucidating: Allah refers to His vicegerent in the singular: he is *one* who will do evil and shed blood. But as no misdeed can be imputed to Adam, the word 'one', suggest the commentators, must be taken to include the 'many', i.e. Adam's descendants. Stated more logically, the word Man in this context does not mean Adam but refers to his progeny or humanity as a whole.

3. According to the Qur'an Eve must have been created at the same time as Adam for God sends *both of them* to Paradise. But according to the Bible Adam went to Paradise alone and Eve was created afterwards. The Qur'an, like the Bible, refers to Eve as having been made from the body of Adam though no mention is made of her having been taken from Adam's rib (IV.1, VII.189, XXXIX.8).

4. The Qur'an does not identify the forbidden tree, but according to the Bible it is the tree of knowledge of good and evil. The Qur'an does not mention the other tree in the garden, i.e. the Tree of Life (Genesis II.9), nor does it state why God forbade the approach to the tree. The Bible throws light on this interdiction: after the disobedience of Adam and Eve God says: man has now become one of us knowing good and evil. In order to preclude man from becoming immortal by tasting the fruit of the Tree of Life, God banishes the couple from the Garden, and sets armed cherubim to guard the approach to the Tree of Life.

5. Abraham responds to the threat by promising to pray for his father's forgiveness (XIX.49) but when it becomes clear to him that his father is an enemy to God he renounces his promise and disowns him. This is referred to in verse IX.114 which follows the verse in which the Prophet and believers are forbidden from praying for forgiveness on behalf of idolaters.

6. Verses LXXXVII.14–19, emphasising that the blest are those who purify themselves, glorify the name of the Lord and pray to Him, say that this exhortation is also contained in earlier scriptures including 'The Book of Abraham'. The Old Testament refers to Abraham as a prophet but attributes no book to him. Attempts at clarifying the Qur'anic reference to the 'Book of Abraham' have brought to light an apocryphal book called

the 'Testament of Abraham', which is believed to have been written in Hebrew in the second or third century AD and of which translations exist in Greek and Arabic. It has been pointed out that certain conceptions of the Qur'an, in particular that of the Balance in which the deeds of men are weighed in the Hereafter, appear in great detail in the description of Abraham's visions contained in this book. For a detailed discussion of this subject see *The Original Sources of the Qur'an* by St Clair Tisdall, London, Society for Promoting Christian Knowledge, 1911, pp. 200 *et seq.*

7. A debate has arisen around the term 'maturity' which occurs in the angel's announcement. It is a translation of the Arabic adverb 'Kahlan', i.e. between the ages of 32 or 34 and 51. Since Jesus is believed to have lived no longer than 33 years, a question has arisen as to how the inclusion of 'maturity' in his life span as predicted by the angel according to the Qur'an should be regarded. The following two interpretations have been suggested by commentators: according to one the Qur'an shows that Jesus lived to a sufficiently old age, and according to the other the prediction refers to Christ's second coming when he will live to an old age.

8. Some commentators have identified this 'far-off' place with 'the peaceful hillside watered by a spring' mentioned in XXIII.52 as the place in which God 'gave Jesus and Mary secure shelter'. As the circumstances which made it necessary to provide a refuge for mother and child are not mentioned in this verse, those commentators who do not follow the interpretation that the occasion was that of Mary's delivery and the place was that mentioned in XIX.22–26, incline to the hypothesis that Jesus and Mary, having been delivered from the hands of their enemies, travelled to a distant land which has been differently identified with Jerusalem, Damascus or Egypt.

9. Commentators have argued (a) that the word 'Ahmad' is synonymous with 'Muhammad', both meaning 'the praised one', (b) that both words are accurate translations of the word 'paraclete' of Greek origin used in the New Testament and translated in the English versions as 'counsellor' or 'comforter', and (c) that Jesus was predicting the advent of Muhammad when he told his disciples that he would ask the Father to give them another counsellor (John: XIV.16). For a comment on this subject, in which it is pointed out that the translation of the Greek word as 'the praised one' is an error, see Tisdall, op. cit.

10. The Qur'an confirms specifically the miracles attributed to Jesus in the New Testament, and adds to them two which do not appear in the canonical gospels, namely preaching in the cradle, and making the likeness of a bird from clay and giving it life by breathing into it (V.110 and III.43). As for the 'table spread with food' (mentioned in verse V.114) which God sends down in answer to Jesus' entreaty on behalf of his disciples who desire to hold a feast, it has been suggested by some commentators that it may be an allusion to the Last Supper.

11. For the theory of crucifixion in effigy and conjectures as to the person supposed to have been substituted for Jesus, see George Sale, *The Koran*, London, Frederick Warne, 1877 footnote to verse III.47.

CHAPTER FIVE

SOME HISTORICAL EVENTS

Description of Past Events

Many verses of the Qur'an mention historical events which took place during the life of the Prophet. All expeditions, raids, battles and invasions have been referred to, including the measures taken against the Jewish communities of Medina. These events are described with the intention of demonstrating the fulfilment of God's promises and warnings, glorifying the Prophet, encouraging and praising the faithful, threatening the unbelievers, condemning the polytheists and censuring the hypocrites. The principal incidents thus dealt with are the following:

The episode of Nakhla

Verse 214 of Sura II provides justification for an act which was taboo by the traditional standards of Arab society. The act, i.e. a raid on a Meccan caravan during the sacred month of Rajab in the second year of the Hijra at Nakhla, on the road from Taif to Mecca, constituted a breach of the sanctity of the 'prohibited months'. In the course of the raid, one pagan was killed and two were taken captive. When the booty and the captives arrived in Medina, the Quraish at Mecca raised an outcry because a holy truce had been infringed. The justification came in a revelation which declared that though fighting in the prohibited months was a grave offence, acts such as those that had been committed by the Meccans (preventing access to the Holy Mosque, and driving out the faithful) were still graver. In this manner the Nakhla raid was in effect legitimised by recourse to the principle of talion. Thereupon the booty taken was divided and the captives were set free against payment of ransom amounting to 1,600 dirhams for each. The celebrated historian Ibn Hisham, commenting on this incident, points out that it was the first occasion on which Moslems took booty of war, captured prisoners and shed blood.[1]

101

The battle of Badr

The battle of Badr, fought in the second year of the Hijra (624) in the plain of Badr about 50 miles southwest of Medina between Medinese troops numbering some 300 led by the Prophet, and a Meccan army of some 1,000 men, ended in victory for the Moslems. The Medinese had expected to attack a richly-laden caravan from Syria bound for Mecca, but the leader of the caravan, having been warned of the plan, saved the caravan by changing its route. However, a Meccan army which had been sent to the aid of the caravan in answer to the leader's appeal found itself confronted with the Medinese expedition, fought a battle and lost. In the course of this encounter certain Quraish notables including Abu Jahl, the Prophet's principal enemy, were killed and some booty was taken. This episode is referred to in Sura VIII (Booty) which contains passages fixing the general rules as to the distribution of booty of war (verses 1 and 42), describing the course of the battle and the circumstances of victory achieved (verses 7, 17, 19, 43–46, and also verse 11 of Sura III), and encouraging the believers to fight in the path of Allah (verses 4 and 7).

The Qur'an commends the strategy which was adopted by the Moslem army in attacking, not the main caravan which was heavily laden with goods and insufficiently escorted (which would have been safer and more rewarding), but the well-equipped army of 1,000 men which had marched out of Mecca. By this bold action the taking of booty was made secondary to the annihilation of the enemy and the triumph of Truth. Referring to the victory of the lesser over the greater forces, the Qur'an says that God had made it known, in answer to the Moslems' prayer, that He was sending 1,000 angels to their aid, had cast terror into the hearts of the unbelievers, made the army of the enemy appear smaller than it was, in the eyes of the Moslems, sent down water from the sky and commanded the angels to strike off the heads and the fingertips of the unbelievers. Verse 17 attributes to Allah all the acts of warfare which defeated the enemy. 'It was not you, but Allah who slew them, it was not you (O Muhammad) but Allah who threw (a handful of dust at the enemy).' Victory over the enemy was accompanied by capture of booty, including ransom taken for captives at the price of between 1,000 and 4,000 dirhams per head, which was divided in accordance with the prescriptions of the Sura.

The expulsion of the Jewish tribe of Qainoqa'

Less than two years after his arrival in Medina the Prophet had reason to doubt the good faith of the Jewish population (the three tribes of Qainoqa', Banu Nadhir and Qoraiza) in carrying out the terms of the pact of co-existence which had been concluded with them. They are said to have spoken of him in mockery and to have secretly entered into a coalition with the Meccan pagans. The Prophet decided therefore that there must be a clear rupture between the Moslems and the Jewish communities. He proceeded first to abrogate certain ritual practices of the Moslem community which had until then followed the Jewish pattern due to the fact that both religions were founded on the conception of monotheism and had a common source in the Abrahamic cult. The most important step was the change of the Qibla (direction of prayer) from Jerusalem to Mecca (verses 136 *et seq.* of Sura II). 'The foolish will ask', says the Qur'an, 'What has made them change their Qibla? . . . we decreed your former Qibla [Jerusalem] only in order that We might know the Apostle's true adherents and those who were to disown him . . . Many a time We have seen you turn your face towards heaven. We will make you turn towards a Qibla that will please you. Turn towards the Holy Mosque; wherever you be, face towards it!' The next change was in respect of the observance of the fast, which until then had followed the Jewish tenth-day ritual known as the Ashura, but was now altered to the month of Ramadan (verses 179 *et seq.* of Sura II).

But politically the most far-reaching decision taken by the Prophet was to expel the Jews from Medina. This plan which was successfully carried out in the space of three years, began with ousting the smallest of the three tribes, the Qainoqa', mainly artisans and jewellers. Shortly after the battle of Badr, an incident occurred which gave rise to open hostilities between the Arabs and the Jews. A practical joke played by a young Jew on an Arab woman ended in bloodshed. The anger of the Arabs having been aroused, the Jews took refuge in their quarters, expecting their Arab allies to come to their aid. This did not materialise, however; the Moslems besieged them and when they surrendered proposed to kill them, but one of their allies, the chief 'hypocrite' of whom more will be said shortly, interceded effectively with the Prophet, and they were allowed to leave in peace, but on condition that they should leave their possessions behind and depart to the north in the direction of Syria, where some of their co-religionists dwelt.

The battle of Uhud

Several verses of Sura III (verses 117 *et seq.*) refer to the battle of Uhud, a battle fought in January 625 at the foot of Mount Uhud, some three miles north of Medina, between a strong army sent from Mecca by the Quraish and a less numerous and not too disciplined army from Medina, headed by the Prophet. This battle proved disastrous for the Moslems who suffered defeat and the loss of several companions of the Prophet, including his uncle Hamza. The Prophet himself received wounds in his head and his face, and lost a front tooth. The verses in question are in part an elegy on this disaster. They attribute it to various causes: indiscipline and lack of courage on the part of the fighters who fled in panic without heeding the Prophet's orders; discord among the men as to how the battle should be fought, and the fact that some of the warriors were motivated more by the desire for booty than the desire for victory. At the same time there are passages of consolation, pointing out that if God had allowed the Medinese to be defeated, it was in order to put their faith to the proof, and also that if the Medinese had suffered, so had the Meccans. In short the faithful are counselled not to lose heart, not to yield to infidels, not to forget that many a time godly men had fought by the side of their Prophets and had not lost heart in the face of disaster, nor had weakened or given in, for God loves those who are firm and steadfast.

The expulsion of the Bani Nadhir
No single event has been commented on in the Qur'an at such length as that of the expulsion of the Jewish tribe of Bani Nadhir from Medina. Shortly after the battle of Uhud, in June 625, Muhammad found it necessary to raise funds to meet some pressing obligation to settle a blood feud. For this purpose he paid a visit to the Jews of Bani Nadhir. During the conference with the council of the tribe he suddenly felt a suspicion that they were hatching a plot to kill him. He abruptly left the meeting, and lost no time in sending an ultimatum to the tribe to leave Medina within ten days. The tribe demurred at first, expecting their allies to come to their help. But as this did not happen, and as the Moslems laid siege to their stronghold and started burning or uprooting their palm trees, they decided to surrender. Within a few days they vacated their dwellings and their lands, loaded their goods and chattels on 600 camels and departed northwards, some proceeding to Syria and others stopping at Khaibar. The substance of some of the verses of Sura LIX which throw light on this episode is given below.

On divine help in causing the surrender of the Jews: 'It was He that drove the unbelievers from among the People of the Book out of their dwellings . . . You did not think that they would go; and they, for their part, fancied that their strongholds would protect them from Allah. But Allah's scourge fell upon them whence they did not expect it, casting such terror into their hearts that they destroyed their dwellings by their own hands.' On permission to destroy the palm-groves: 'It was Allah who gave you leave to cut down or spare their palm-trees, so that

He might humiliate the evil-doers.' On the Prophet's liberty to distribute the booty as he willed: 'The spoils taken from the town-dwellers and assigned by Allah to His Apostle belong to Allah, the Apostle and his kinsmen, the orphans, the poor and the wayfarers; they shall not become the property of the rich among you. Whatever the Apostle gives you, accept it, and whatever he forbids you, forbear from it.' On the vain hope of the besieged to receive help from the hypocrites: 'Have you not seen the hypocrites? They say to their fellow-unbelievers among the People of the Book: "If they drive you out, we will go with you. We will never obey any one who seeks to harm you. If you are attacked we will certainly help you", Allah bears witness that they are lying. If they are driven out they will not go with them, nor, if they are attacked will they help them.'

The raid on the Bani Mustaliq Tribe
In December 626 news reached the Prophet to the effect that the tribe of Bani Mustaliq who inhabited an area near the sea some marches short of Mecca, were preparing to join forces with the Quraish for an attack on Medina. He decided to make an inroad on the tribe in anticipation of their design. He left with a number of troops for the dwelling-place of the tribe, arrived there after eight days, surrounded the tribe and after a short fight overpowered them and took many prisoners with their families and flocks. He then ordered a hasty return to Medina, the unusual haste being due to a quarrel which had arisen among his followers and had been exploited by one Abdullah ibn Obay, an influential and ambitious man whose comportment in the past and specially at Uhud had caused the Prophet to doubt his loyalty. The raid on Bani Mustaliq, although in itself not important enough to be mentioned in the Qur'an, involved two incidents of sufficient moment to be referred to in the Qur'an. One is the episode of Ayesha and Safwan ibn al-Muattal, of which an important echo is found in Sura XXIV. The other is the conduct of Ibn Obay during the expedition, which came very close to causing serious disaffection in the camp. This incident is reflected in one whole Sura, i.e. Sura LXIII ('The Hypocrites'). The term 'hypocrite' refers specially to Ibn Obay and generally to those (mainly influenced by him) who were outwardly members of the Moslem community, but inwardly lukewarm if not actually hostile to Muhammad's cause. The Sura begins with these words: 'When the hypocrites come to you they say: "We bear witness that you are Allah's Apostle." Allah knows that you are indeed His Apostle, and bears witness that the hypocrites are lying. They use their faith as a disguise and debar others from the path of Allah. Evil is what they do!' Special mention is made in one

verse of words that were uttered by Ibn Obay when one of the
quarrelling men openly expressed feelings of disloyalty. He clearly
incited the men to rise up, on their return to Medina, in opposition
to the prophet, and hinted that by such rising, the stronger element
(i.e. the hypocrites) would overcome the weaker (i.e. the Prophet's
followers). This is what verse 8 refers to when it says: 'They say, Wait
till we return to Medina, then the mightier shall surely expel the
meaner.' By the precipitate return of the Bani Mustaliq expedition
the Prophet prevented the disaffection from developing into a con-
spiracy.

The battle of the Confederates
Verses 9 to 25 of Sura XXXIII ('The Confederates') refer to the battle
of the Confederates, or the Siege of Medina, which occurred early in
627. The besiegers were a coalition of the Meccan Quraish with
members of the Jewish communities and a Bedouin Arab tribe. The
purpose of the invasion was to crush the Moslem community of
Medina. The siege lasted over two weeks, but although the besieging
forces were more numerous than the defenders, and although within
the ranks of the latter there were (to use the terms of the Qur'an)
'hypocrites' who, taking a defeatist attitude, sowed discord and disaffection among the Medinese and encouraged many to desert, yet the
siege ended in the discomfiture of the invaders. This was mainly due
to the use of an unusual defensive device executed by Salman the
Persian, namely the digging of a trench round the vulnerable parts of
the city, because of which the battle is also known as the Battle of the
Trench (Khandaq), and also because on the crucial day a piercing
blast of cold wind arose which terrified the besiegers and made them
beat a hasty retreat.

Some of the verses of the Sura refer to this battle: 'Believers,
remember Allah's goodness to you when you were attacked by your
enemy's army. We unleashed against them a violent wind and invisible
warriors . . . They attacked you from above and from below, so that
your eyes were blurred, your hearts leapt to your throats, and your
faith in Allah was shaken. There the faithful were put to the proof:
there they were severely afflicted . . . A party among them (the hypocrites) said: O people of Medina, you cannot stand much longer; go
back to your city. Yet others sought the Prophet's leave, saying: "our
homes are defenceless" whereas they were not. They only wanted to
flee . . . Say "nothing will your flight avail you. If you escaped from
death or slaughter you would enjoy this world only for a little while".
Say "who can protect you from Allah if it is His will to scourge you?"
. . . Allah well knows those of you who prevent others from following

the Apostle; who say to their comrades "join our side" ... They thought the confederate tribes would never raise the siege. Indeed, if they should come again, they would sooner be in the desert among the wandering Arabs. There they would ask news of you, but were they with you they would take but little part in the fighting.'

The extermination of the Jewish tribe of Bani Qoraiza

Verses 26 and 27 of Sura XXXIII refer to the extermination of the Jewish tribe of Bani Qoraiza. They appear as a sequel to the verses relating to the battle of the Confederates, because during that battle the Jews of the said tribe behaved in a way that led to their being accused of conspiring with the enemy. Because of this accusation they took fright and on the same day that the siege was lifted shut themselves up in their strongholds some three miles to the east of Medina. The Prophet ordered a siege of the community which lasted 25 days, after which the Jews surrendered. They asked to be allowed to depart in peace, but the Prophet did not consent, and ruled that their fate should be determined by an arbitrator. The latter, the chief of the Aus tribe which was in alliance with the Jews, gave his verdict on the basis of the Old Testament law laid down in Deuteronomy XX 13 and 14.[2] This meant the extermination of the tribe. In verses 26 and 27 of Sura XXXIII the Qur'an says: 'God cast terror into their hearts so that you slew some of them and took captive others. He made you masters of their land, their houses and their goods and yet another land on which you had never set foot before.' The reference to 'some' who were killed is a euphemism; all historians agree that all the male members of the tribe, numbering at least 600, were put to the sword, their women and children were sold as slaves and all their property was seized.

The pact of Hudaybiya

In February 628 (during one of the traditional sacred months) the Prophet set out for Mecca, accompanied by a large number of his followers, to perform the lesser pilgrimage. By Arab tradition and usage, every Arab had a right to make such pilgrimage. But the pagan Quraish took alarm at the party's approach, made the party halt at a place called Hudaybiya some 10 miles northwest of Mecca, and tried to prevent their entry into the city. In the meantime as it was feared that the Quraish might do violence to the pilgrims, the party had entered into a pact of fealty evidencing their devotion to the Prophet (the famous Pact of Hudaybiya concluded under a tree). The Pact is mentioned in verses 10 and 18 of Sura XLVIII. Verse 10 says: 'Those that swear fealty to you swear fealty to Allah. The hand of Allah is above their hands. He that breaks his oath breaks it at his own peril, but he that keeps his pledge to Allah shall be richly rewarded.' Verse 18 says: 'Allah was well pleased with the faithful when they swore allegiance to you under the tree. He knew what was in their hearts. Therefore He sent down tranquillity upon them and rewarded them with a speedy victory and with the many spoils which they will take.' Eventually a treaty was concluded between the Prophet and the Quraish by which there was to be a truce for ten years and it was agreed that the intended pilgrimage would take place, not that year, but in the next. It was further provided that if any inhabitant of Mecca went to Medina without his or her guardian's permission, the Medina Moslems would return such person to Mecca. The Sura in which the Hudaybiya episode is mentioned is entitled 'Victory'. Although the intended pilgrimage did not take place until 629 and the conquest of Mecca until 630, nevertheless the pact of Hudaybiya was regarded as a precursor of that final victory.

The conquest of Khaibar
It is related that, on his return from Hudaybiya the Prophet, feeling that his followers, somewhat frustrated by the experience of that expedition, needed some encouragement, foretold a 'speedy victory and abundant spoils elsewhere'. The promise was amply fulfilled a few months later (September 628) when the Prophet led an expedition, with the same number of followers as in the Hudaybiya venture, to the Jewish settlement of Khaibar, a fertile district some 90 miles due north of Medina. There appears no special reason for the invasion of this settlement except expectation of the 'abundant spoils' promised by the Prophet. The expedition as such is not referred to in the Qur'an, but the phrase 'and yet another land on which you had never set foot before' (verse 27 of Sura XXXIII) already quoted in connection with the expulsion of the Jewish tribe of Bani Qoraiza, refers to the well-watered valley of Khaibar.

An abortive expedition to the north
The lesser pilgrimage to Mecca planned in 628 and postponed to 629 (according to the Hudaybiya treaty) duly took place in February 629, when Muhammad and 2,000 followers performed that rite uneventfully during the stipulated three days. In the course of some months after his return to Medina, the Prophet embarked on several minor expeditions, some of which ended in disaster. One of these was an expedition of 3,000 men under the command of his adopted son Zaid,

which was sent in September 629 in the direction of the border districts of Syria. The purpose of this expedition is believed to have been revenge for the treachery of a petty chieftain who had murdered a messenger sent by the Prophet, but the expedition proved a total failure. As soon as the party set foot on Syrian territory, the chieftain sent a large army against it, and a battle took place in the village of Mot'a in which many of the Moslems including Zaid were killed. What was left of the party then retreated in broken ranks and great confusion, and returned to Medina. This incident has not been mentioned in the Qur'an; its inclusion in this Section is due to the fact that the Tobouk expedition of the following year, to be mentioned shortly, is considered to have been conceived as a revenge for the death of Zaid and the defeat of his troops.

The conquest of Mecca

The conquest of Mecca, achieved in January 630, is not mentioned as such in the Qur'an, but it is believed that Sura CX ('Help'), one of the very last, which says: 'When God's help and victory come, and you see men enter God's religion in multitudes . . .' refers to this event. It is also related that when the Prophet struck down the principal idol which was placed in front of the Ka'ba, he recited the following passage from the Qur'an: 'Truth has come and falsehood has perished.'

The battle of Hunain

Almost immediately after the conquest of Mecca, a battle was fought in Hunain, 14 miles to the east of Mecca, between the forces assembled there by the tribe of Bani Hawazin and an army headed by the Prophet. The tribes dwelling in that region were idol-worshippers closely allied to the Quraish. At the news of the Prophet's victory in Mecca they became fearful lest his next blow should be aimed at them and their idols. They therefore proceeded to prepare an expedition against Muhammad to be sent to Mecca. When the news of their design reached the Prophet, he cut short his stay in Mecca and set out for Hunain (28 January 630). He took a strong army with him, but when it neared the valley of Hunain its vanguard was caught in an ambush laid by the enemy. The enemy fell upon the Moslem army with fury, killed many and put others to flight. The Prophet succeeded, however, in rallying the deserters by reminding them of their oath of fealty. A severe conflict followed, and the Prophet's army finally defeated the enemy, who fled leaving behind an abundant booty.[3] The prisoners taken numbered as many as 6,000. The changing fortunes of the battle and the final victory (attributed to divine intervention) are referred to in the Qur'an in these words: 'Allah has been with you on many a battlefield. In the battle of Hunain you set great store by your numbers, but they availed you nothing; the earth, for all its vastness, seemed to close in upon you and you turned your backs and fled. Then Allah caused His Peace to descend upon His Apostle and the faithful: He sent to your aid invisible warriors and sternly punished the unbelievers. Thus were the infidels rewarded' (IX.25).

A sequel to the battle of Hunain needs to be mentioned. When the time came for the distribution of the abundant booty of war, some members of the expedition became discontented because they felt that the Prophet gave too great a part of the booty to the new converts to Islam, neglecting the original believers. These objections were silenced by a revelation, but the feeling of discontent seems to have rankled in the minds of some, and to have somewhat affected their enthusiasm and even loyalty on subsequent occasions. The text of the revelation, addressed to the Prophet, is as follows: 'There are some among them who blame you concerning the distribution of alms. If a share is given to them they are contented, but if they receive nothing they are indignant. Would that they were satisfied with what Allah and His Apostle have given them and would say "Allah is all sufficient for us; He will provide for us from His own abundance and so will His Apostle; to Allah we will submit." Alms are for the poor and the needy, for those employed in collecting the alms, for those whose hearts are to be gained over, and for ransom of captives, for debtors, for the cause of God and for the wayfarer. That is a duty enjoined by Allah' (IX.58).

The Tobouk expedition

In September 630 the Prophet embarked on a great expedition northwards in the direction of the Byzantine empire. It had been persistently rumoured that the Byzantines were collecting a huge army to invade Arabia, and it seems that the Prophet's intention was to lead an expedition in defence of the northern provinces. He collected an army of considerable size, numbering some 30,000, though not as large as he had expected, because many of his followers refrained from joining the expedition on various pretexts. The army proceeded on its way under very difficult conditions, i.e. excessive heat and shortage of foodstuffs, fodder and water. It eventually reached the village of Tobouk about 360 miles north of Medina, close to the Syrian border. There it halted for some 20 days, but as news arrived that no invasion was being prepared by the Byzantines, the expedition went no further. Some minor pacts were concluded with Christian and Jewish chiefs of the surrounding areas by which they undertook to pay tribute, and the army then returned to Medina.

Although no spectacular result was achieved by this expedition, on the whole it enhanced the Prophet's prestige in the outlying districts. At the same time, however, the opposition at home had not died down. During the Prophet's absence, the 'hypocrites' had continued to play a double game. The manner of distribution of the booty of war from the Hunain expedition had embittered several of the original believers who felt that the Prophet had given too great a share to the new converts in order to win their affection, while somewhat neglecting his old and true friends. It was in fact partly due to this feeling that a number of the believers held back when the Prophet called on them to join his expedition. It was even rumoured that some of these malcontents actually joined the expedition to make mischief and went so far as to plot against the Prophet's life on the way back to Medina.

A number of verses in Sura IX relate to circumstances connected with this expedition. Words of strong censure are addressed to those who, advancing lame excuses, had failed to respond to the Prophet's call to arms when preparing for the expedition (verses 38–45). It is pointed out that in fact their failure to join the ranks was an advantage, for they would only have brought an element of discord into the enterprise (46–48). Hypocrites are severely condemned (54 *et seq.*). Special mention is made of a situation which developed out of the Prophet's suspicion that certain hypocrites were planning to provide themselves with a safe place in which they could gather to conspire against him. When the Prophet was on the point of departure for the expedition, some believers stated that they had built a second mosque in Qoba', a suburb of Medina, and requested him to consecrate it. The Prophet replied that he would attend to the matter on his return. But in the course of the expedition news reached him to the effect that the builders had been actuated by a treacherous motive. Accordingly, immediately on his return to Medina, the Prophet sent men to destroy the mosque. In verses 108 to 111 God tells the Prophet that the mosque had been built in preparation for warring against God, and that he (the Prophet) must never set foot in it, but must pray in the mosque which had been built on the foundation of piety (i.e. the first mosque at Qoba'). Finally, verse 58 gives the Prophet full liberty in the matter of distribution of alms, thus silencing those who criticised the Prophet's action in dividing the booty of war, as already explained.

The Qur'an refers briefly to a few other historical events unconnected with Islam, as well as ancient fables, in the obvious expectation that the faithful would derive salutary lessons from them.

The 'Elephant' expedition[4]

Sura CV relates how an expedition to Medina which was led by Abraha, the Abyssinian viceroy of Yaman, came to grief. The expedition set out in 570 to destroy the Ka'ba but God caused stones to rain upon the large army, in which there were some elephants, and it was totally destroyed.

The diggers of the pit

Verses 4 to 8 of Sura LXXXV hint at the persecution of Christians at Najran by the Jewish ruler of Yaman. He was reputed to have dug a pit in which he burned the Christians. The Sura condemns to eternal hell-fire the 'diggers of the pit' and all who persecute the votaries of God.

The defeat of the Roman Empire

The first 5 verses of Sura XXX declare that the Roman (Byzantine) Empire has been defeated, but that in a few years its defeat will change to victory and the believers shall rejoice.

During the first two decades of the 7th century, the Byzantine Empire suffered several defeats, when Persia conquered parts of the Empire: in Syria, in Asia Minor and in Africa. But the major defeat of the Empire came when in 615 it lost Jerusalem to Persia. The Prophet did not look with favour on Persia's victories. The pagan Quraish were pro-Persian, and so were the Jewish communities on the whole. The Lakhmide dynasty of north-eastern Arabia was a vassal of Persia, Persia enjoyed an important sphere of influence all along the southern coast of Arabia, and in particular had for two centuries treated Yaman as a protectorate. For all these reasons the Prophet hoped for a reversal of the fortunes of war and actually predicted that the Byzantine Empire would become victorious within a few years. In the event this prophecy came true in 628 when Persia was defeated by Heraclius.

The companions of the Cave

This is the Qur'anic equivalent of the story of the Seven Sleepers which forms part of Christian legends. This legend, going back to the 3rd century, affirms that in the time of the Roman emperor Decius (AD 249–251) who persecuted the Christians, seven Christian youths of Ephesus fled from the town and hid themselves in a cave. There they went to sleep and did not wake up until some generations or centuries later. The Qur'an refers to this legend in 18 verses of Sura XVIII named after it (al-Kahf: the Cave). God calls the phenomenon of the sleepers a 'wonder among Our Signs' (verse 8) and announces that He is going to relate their story in all truth (verse 12). They were worshippers of the One and Only God, rose up in opposition to the idol-worshippers and fleeing the city took refuge in the cave where they went to sleep. But the Qur'anic version does not settle any of the moot points of the legend. How many were the fugitives? How long did they remain asleep? When and how were they saved? The answer to these questions is: only God knows. In this connection mention should be made of two passages which come between verses relating to the number of the sleepers and those relating to the period of their sleep, without having any apparent relation to those subjects. Verses 22 and 23 of the Sura: 'Do not say of anything: "I will do it tomorrow" without adding "If Allah wills". When you forget, remember your Lord and say: "May Allah guide me and bring me nearer to the truth". ' These parenthetical verses have been explained as follows: The Jews asked the Prophet to tell them more about the sleepers (following the context of verse 21 concerning their number) and the Prophet said he would do so on the following day. However, he forgot to add the imperative reservation 'If Allah wills' and as a result God withheld His revelations for a few days by way of punishment, and in this way the Jews' questions remained unanswered.

The lesson to be drawn from the story of the Companions of the Cave seems to be that whoever perseveres in the worship of the One God will be saved. It is stressed that the men received divine guidance, which is a grace that God bestows on whom He will and withhold from whom He will (verse 16). God's purpose in relating the story appears in the words of verse 20: 'Thus We revealed their secret so that men might know that Allah's promise was true.'

Saul and Goliath[5]

In the context of encouraging the believers to fight in the cause of Allah, the Qur'an cites the story of Saul and Goliath. Verse 245 of Sura II says: 'Fight for the cause of Allah and bear in mind that He hears all and knows all.' There then follows a reference to the episode of the miraculous victory over the giant Goliath. The Israelites asked their Prophet (Samuel) to nominate a king to lead them in war against their enemies. The Prophet nominated Saul, who marched out with his army, and when they came face to face with the enemy and Goliath came forth challenging the Israelites, God came to the aid of the latter and David slew the giant. The salient point of the narrative seems to lie in verse 250 which says: 'Many a small band has by Allah's grace vanquished a mighty army.'

There are in addition numerous references in the Qur'an to historical and mythical persons and even to invisible beings whose deeds, sayings and experiences lend support to the themes developed in the Qur'an. These have been mentioned in other Chapters of this book.

The Destruction of Past Generations

A close study of the narratives contained in the Qur'an concerning the experiences of the prophets and apostles of ancient times shows clearly that these elaborate recitals, emphasising the calamities that God has at all times sent down upon those people who refused to recognise His messengers, were meant to warn the existing and future generations that the same disasters would befall them if they failed to recognise the Prophet of Allah. Numerous verses describe in vivid terms the punishments that were inflicted on recalcitrant peoples of past generations: those of Noah, of Israel, Pharaoh, 'Ad, Thamud, Lot, Aikeh, Madyan and Tubba'. The following quotations indicate the general trend of these narratives. 'How many cities have We laid in ruin! In the night Our scourge fell upon them or at midday when they were drowsing' (VII.3). 'We plagued them with floods and locusts, with lice and frogs and with blood . . . We took vengeance on them and drowned them in the sea' (VII.130–132). 'How many generations have We destroyed before them! Can you find one of them alive or hear so much as a whisper from them?' (XIX.98). 'There is no nation but shall be destroyed or sternly punished before the Day of Resurrection. That is decreed in the Eternal Book' (XVII.60). 'Over a few ill-omened days We let loose on them a howling gale that they might taste a dire punishment in this life' (XLI.15). 'Against some We sent a violent tornado with showers of stones, some were caught by a mighty blast, some We caused the earth to swallow up, and some We drowned in the waters' (XXIX.39). 'How many nations have We destroyed who once flourished in wanton ease! Their dwellings are deserted, all but a few, and We are their heirs' (XXVIII.58). 'How many generations, far greater in power, have We destroyed before them! They searched the entire land, but was there any refuge for them?' (L.35).

These quotations, and others like them, raise a difficult problem, to which reference is made in the section headed Responsibility in Chapter 7, namely that of reconciling the idea of divine vengeance on generations which go astray with the repeated assertion in the Qur'an to the effect that it is by God's own will that men go astray. Among the verses which have been quoted in this context in the section on Responsibility is the following: 'None can guide those whom God has led astray. They shall be punished in this life, but more painful is the punishment in the life to come. None shall protect them from God' (XIII.33–34). In the face of these utterances the difficulty is not altogether removed by invoking the verses (e.g. XXVIII.59) which say that Allah had previously warned the people but they had nevertheless gone astray.

Notes to Chapter Five

1. Sir William Muir, *Life of Mohammed*, Edinburgh, J Grant, 1912, p. 203.
2. 'When the Lord your God delivers it into your hand, put to the sword all the men in it. As for the women, the children, the livestock and everything else in the city, you may take these as plunder for yourselves. And you may use the plunder the Lord your God gives you from your enemies.'
3. It is related that the spoils consisted of 24,000 camels, 4,000 sheep and goats, and heaps of gold and silver. Many stories are told pointing to the abundance of the spoils taken. One of these provides an interpretation of a passage in the Sura 'The Booty of War'. Verse 71 says: 'Prophet, say to those you have taken captive: "If Allah finds goodness in your hearts, He will give you that which is better than what has been taken from you".' This verse finds application in the context of the generous share which Abbas, the Prophet's uncle, was allowed to take in the spoils. Three times, it is said, he spread his mantle and gathered up gold and silver pieces, and still there was more to pick up. The Prophet, looking on, was reminded of an episode in the battle of Badr when, Abbas being in the ranks of the enemy, his possessions were taken from him as booty of war. The Prophet now turned to his uncle and said: 'God is now returning to you what you lost at the battle of Badr, because He has found goodness in your heart.'
4. Different reasons have been assigned to this expedition. One is that a Meccan caravan had shortly before taken shelter from the cold in an Abyssinian temple, which caught fire after the caravan's departure. The people contended that the fire was no accident, but had been wilfully caused by the caravan. They therefore incited their king to send an expedition to Mecca to avenge the sacrilege.
5. Here, as in most cases where the Qur'an refers to historical events, no explanation is given of the actual circumstances, the emphasis being on the spiritual and moral lessons envisaged. For the historical details in each case it is necessary to consult extra-Qur'anic sources. In this case reference must be made to the Bible (Chapters 8 *et seq.* of 1 Samuel). The story of Saul (called Talut in the Qur'an), Goliath (called Jalut) and David is told at length. Saul is made king by Samuel the prophet. He engages in different expeditions, and is now on the point of facing Israel's greatest enemies: the Philistines. But God is not pleased with him, because he had failed to carry out His orders. He is visited by evil spirits and seeks the means of delivering himself from them. He is advised to take into his service a player on the harp who would drive out the evil spirits by his music. Such a player he finds in a handsome, brave and well-spoken youth. This is David, who eventually performs the miracle of slaying Goliath. Goliath is a colossal giant who fights on the side of the Philistines. When the battle lines are drawn up, and the giant challenges the Israelites no one dares enter into single combat with him. But to the great surprise of everyone, especially Goliath, David comes forward, puts a stone in his sling and hurls it at the giant. The stone sinks into Goliath's forehead, and the giant falls face down on the ground. The moral of the Qur'anic reference to this story is foreshadowed in the Biblical version. In the face of Goliath's mockery on seeing an unarmed youth approaching him, David says: 'You come against me with sword and spear and javelin, but I come against you in the name of the Lord' (1 Samuel XVII.45).

CHAPTER SIX

FAITH AND RELIGION

The Words Islam and Moslem

A brief reference is made below to the meaning of the word 'Islam' in the section headed 'Attitude towards other Religions'. In the present section an attempt is made at illustrating the meaning of the terms 'Islam' and 'Moslem' by reference to some of the instances in which these words are used in the Qur'an. It should be noted that the Qur'an gives to these terms the exact meaning that they have in common usage: Islam means resignation, submission, and Moslem means a person who is resigned or who submits.

The Qur'an points persistently to a prefiguration of Islam in the faith of Abraham, which was known in Arabia from ancient times as the 'true [hanif] faith'[1] meaning the faith of submission to the one and only God. The Qur'an says (verse 29 of Sura XXX) that this faith is the immutable pattern according to which God has created mankind. Islam is presented in the Qur'an as identical with the Abrahamic or 'hanif' faith. In fact the words Moslem and Hanif are synonymous. Verse 60 of Sura III says Abraham was 'true in faith' (hanif) and not a polytheist. Verse 77 of Sura XXII, addressing the believers, says of Abraham: '. . . your father Abraham; it is he who named you Moslems both before and after this revelation.'

In verse 122 of Sura II Abraham and Ismael, praying to God, beseech Him to make them and their children 'Moslems'. Jacob on h is deathbed asks his children whom they will worship after him, and they reply: we will be 'Moslems' to the one and only God according to the cult of our father Abraham (verse 127 of Sura II). Joseph, praying to God, entreats Him to make him die a 'Moslem' so that he can join the ranks of the blessed (verse 102 of Sura XII).

In these and also other passages the word 'Moslem' is used in a sense which obviously precedes its current meaning of one who believes in the religion of Muhammad. It means clearly one who submits to God. The same meaning would seem to underlie the term 'Moslem' as applied in the Qur'an to the Prophet himself. In three verses (VI.14,

VI.163 and XXXIX.14) God commands him to be, and to declare himself to all as being, the first of Moslems.

The word 'Islam' as a noun of action bears a double meaning: originally that of submission, and secondarily that of adherence to the religion of Muhammad. Other derivatives from the grammatical root of 'Salama', notably the participle Moslem, are similarly ambivalent. Thus the dictionary definition of the term Moslem is given as (a) one who resigns himself to God, and (b) one who professes the faith of Islam.[2] The question therefore arises as to which of these meanings underlies the different passages in which the words Islam and Moslem appear in the Qur'an.

The matter is one of interpretation in each separate case. Some texts are specially appropriate for examination in this connection. One is that of verses III.17 *et seq.* in which God tells the Prophet how to confront the People of the Book. 'The (only true) faith in Allah's sight is Islam ... If they [the People of the Book] argue with you, say "I have surrendered myself to Allah and so have those that follow me" ... Say to the People of the Book and the Gentiles "Do you also surrender yourselves to Allah?" If they submit themselves [aslama] they are rightly guided.' This is one translation, but because of the double meaning of the word 'aslama', another translation has been proposed which reads: '*If they become Moslems* they are rightly guided.'

Another text which is generally invoked by those who maintain strictly that Islam means everywhere the religion founded by Muhammad, is that of verse III.79 which says: 'He that chooses a religion other than Islam it will not be accepted of him, and in the Hereafter he will be one of the lost.' Here if the two verses which immediately precede the text are carefully examined it will become clear that the word Islam and other derivatives of Salama are used in the wider sense of submission to God. Verse III.77 says that all creatures in heaven and earth have submitted (aslama) to Him willingly or by compulsion. Obviously here the word aslama cannot mean 'have become Moslems'. More particularly verse III.78 commands the faithful to say: 'We believe in God, in what had been revealed to us and to Abraham, Isaac, Jacob and the tribes, and in that which Allah gave to Moses, Jesus and the prophets. We make no distinction between one and another among them and to God do we submit our will [Muslimun].' Accordingly the word Islam used in verse III.79 as the only acceptable religion can only mean any faith which teaches submission to God and recognises the prophets of the past.

Two verses (VI.125 and XXXIX.23) say that if Allah wills to guide a man He opens his heart (breast, bosom) to Islam. This expression has been interpreted to mean that those whom God favours become the recipient of God's grace. One commentator suggests that this expression has a meaning similar to that of the words of Jesus quoted in John VI.65: 'No one can come to me unless the Father has enabled him.'

Finally in one of the last verses to be revealed (the occasion was the Prophet's last pilgrimage to Mecca) is described in one word the perfected form of the religion which God, in His Munificence, bequeaths to those who have listened to His message: *Resignation.* Verse V.5 says: 'This day I have perfected your religion for you, completed My favour upon you, and chosen for you *Islam* as your religion.'

Faith (Belief)

Many verses of the Qur'an containing counsels of wisdom, commandments or admonitions begin with the phrase, 'O you who believe!' But who are believers, and what characteristics distinguish them from non-believers?

Contrary to the terms 'unbeliever', 'polytheist' and 'hypocrite' which have not been defined as such in the Qur'an, the definition of a 'believer' can be found in many verses. The Qur'anic conception of faith and its contrary, 'unbelief', shows clearly that the Qur'anic morality addresses itself to all aspects of human behaviour. But faith (iman) as deduced from the verses of the Qur'an has essentially a transcendental meaning. The first requisite of faith is that man should attain to a state of perception and reflection in which he sees the world and all that is in it, not as natural phenomena, but as signs (ayat) symbolising God and making manifest His favours to mankind. The man of faith is he whose intellect (aql) leads him to the recognition of everything as a sign of God. The heavens, the earth, night, day, lightning, rain, the variety of races and tongues are all such signs (XXX.21–23, XVI.69). The word ayat (signs) as used in the Qur'an applies as much to the Word of God (the verses of the Qur'an) as to material objects. Nothing exists which is not first and foremost a sign of God. Sura XXVI, referring to the ruin and destruction which Allah visited in the past upon the people who denied His messengers, repeats seven times (once in respect of each messenger) the words 'surely in this there is a *sign*, but most people do not *believe*.' Intellect (aql) is only the handmaid of faith. Verse XXIX.34, recalling the scourge which was brought down upon the people who rejected Lot, says: 'Surely the ruins of that city are a veritable *sign* for those who have *understanding.*'

The ethical implications of faith, always with a religious connotation, can be deduced from a large number of verses. In the last analysis faith means belief in one God, in His apostle, in Resurrection, in God's signs, in fear of God and thankfulness for His bounties, and in obedience to His commandments. Verses VIII. 2–3 describe the believer in these terms: 'Believers are those who, when God is mentioned, feel a tremor in their hearts, and when they hear His signs recited find their faith strengthened and put their trust in their Lord; who establish regular prayers and distribute alms from the gifts We have given them for sustenance.' Likewise verse IX.113 defines believers as those 'who repent, those who serve Allah and praise Him, those who kneel and prostrate themselves before Him; those who enjoin justice, forbid evil, and observe the commandments of Allah.' Verses XXV.64 *et seq.* cite the qualities of a believer in different contexts; he is (in the religious context) one who passes the night standing and on his knees in adoration of his Lord, who prays to his Lord to ward off from him the punishment of Hell, who invokes no other god besides Allah; (in the moral context) who walks humbly, does good works and guards his chastity; (in the social context) who is neither extravagant nor niggardly but keeps the golden mean, who says 'Peace' to the ignorant who accost him; (in the legal context) who does not bear false witness, who does not kill except for just cause, and who does not commit adultery.

In the verses quoted above we have the essential attributes of a believer in Islam. But is everyone who submits to Islam a 'believer' in the true sense? The Qur'an gives a negative answer to this question: verse XLIX.14 says: 'The Arabs of the desert declare "We are true believers". Say "You are not, but say rather we profess Islam, for faith has not yet found its way into your heart".' It then defines the believer in these words: 'True believers are those that have faith in Allah and His apostle, and never doubt, and who fight for His Cause with their wealth and persons; such are those whose faith is true.'

In short, all good actions and the avoidance of all evil are by themselves contained in the connotation of faith. The Qur'an says that a nation that has faith and guides men to the right path is the best nation in the world. The reward of the believer is prosperity and happiness in this world and the joys of Paradise in the next. Verse XLVII.13 says: 'Allah will admit those who embrace the true faith and do good works to gardens watered by running streams. The unbelievers take their fill of pleasure and eat as the beasts eat; but Hell shall be their home.'

The Qur'an establishes a close connection between faith (iman) and good works (salihat). To the question what are the 'good works' which characterise the man of faith, specific and detailed answers can be found in many verses of the Qur'an. Some of these have been quoted above; another text which gives a summary description of good works occurs in verses II.76 and 77 which say: 'Those who believe and do good works shall be the inhabitants of Paradise to dwell therein for ever. Remember that We took a covenant from the Children of Israel to worship none but God; to be kind to parents, kindred, orphans and the needy; to speak fair to all; to be steadfast in prayer and to practise regular charity.'

The fact that the phrase 'those who believe and do good works' occurs most frequently in the Qur'an has given rise to a theological question as to whether the two concepts must not be regarded as inseparable. In other words, should faith which is not accompanied by good works be considered as 'faith' in accordance with the letter and spirit of the Qur'an? This question has received extensive treatment in post-Qur'anic doctrinal development. The strictest school defines faith in terms of three requisites: assent by heart, verbal confession and observance of the religious commandments. Another school lays down two conditions, namely confession and action; still another requires only confession, and finally the least exacting school defines faith as consisting only of knowledge of God.

Rejection of faith after submission is a deadly sin. Allah is drastically severe with apostates, whom He dooms to eternal hell-fire unless their recantation has been due to compulsion, their hearts having remained loyal to the faith (XVI.108, II.25, XLVII.34, III.84).[3] He who dies a renegade is irretrievably lost (II.214, IV.115). The apostate from Islamic faith incurs Allah's curse unless he repents and makes amends (III.80 and 83). But remorse and repentance may in fact be rare because Allah sets a seal on the apostate's heart (LXIII.3). In any event repentance will not bring forgiveness if defection is repeated (IV.136). Believers are commanded to fight those who break their oaths after having committed themselves to faith (IX.12). Temptation to turn back from guidance comes from Satan; those who succumb to such temptation will receive severe treatment from angels. 'Because they follow what has called forth Allah's wrath and abhor what pleases Him', angels will strike them on their faces and backs when taking their souls at death (XLVII.27 *et seq.*). In one instance (verse V.59) mention of those who turn back from their faith is followed, not by warning of punishment, but by a statement suggestive of indifference. If one generation defects, Allah will bring into being a loyal generation in its place. 'If any of you renounce their faith, Allah will replace them by a people whom He will love as they will love Him, humble towards the faithful and stern towards unbelievers, zealous for Allah's cause and fearless of men's censure.' Commentators suggest that this pronouncement is a reference to the defections which happened during the latter days of the Prophet or an anticipation of the defections which occurred after his death, when a number of Arabs renounced Islam in favour of Judaism or Christianity, went back to paganism, or embraced the cause of 'false prophets' like al-Aswad, Toleiha and Musailama.[4]

Apart from the question of recantation of one's faith there is the not dissimilar question of dissimulating one's faith, on grounds of expediency, by acting in a way which contradicts the principles of that faith. Two instances of such action are mentioned in the Qur'an: making friends with infidels (III.27) and denying God (XVI.108). In both verses the dissimulator is saved from the wrath of God and is pardoned because he has acted under duress or in the face of threatening injury or damage, and that his heart has remained steadfast in faith in spite of the dissimulation. Yet another prescription of the Qur'an can be invoked in connection with the matter under discussion: verse VI.108 enjoins on believers to refrain from any abusive language respecting the idols which are worshipped by the infidels lest the latter should retaliate by reviling Allah. These rules taken together have given rise to the general principle known as Taqiyya (from the wording of verse III.27) or caution induced by fear of imminent danger. This principle, although incorporated in Shiite doctrine, is not considered as a universal tenet of Islam, being in fact regarded as out of date. An authoritative commentary of the Qur'an[5] comments on it as follows: 'A group of eminent doctors maintain that Taqiyya was valid only during the early days when Islam had not yet gained strength. Today [i.e. the 12th century AD.], Heaven be praised, Islam is all-powerful and triumphant, and infidels hold no sway over it.'

The reward promised in the Qur'an to the believer is entry to Paradise and enjoyment of celestial delights for all eternity as described in numerous verses. But by far the greatest privilege of the believer is that he will meet God in the Hereafter. God commands the Prophet to give the believers the assurance that such meeting is in store for them: 'Give these glad tidings to those who believe' (II.223), and the Prophet does not fail to convey the message: 'Know that you shall meet Him.' Preaching the divine message to hesitant Jews, he exhorts them to believe in the revelation which he brings in confirmation of their own faith, and to bear in mind the certainty that they will meet their Lord (II.43). Already in ancient times Noah had announced the same promise to his people by God's command: 'O my people . . . I will not drive away those who believe, for truly they shall meet their Lord' (XI.31).

Contrary to the believer, who will be rewarded by the sublime vision of the Lord, the unbeliever will be denied that gift, as also every other gift of divine favour. Instead of meeting the Lord, he will meet with His wrath and will be forever consigned to hell-fire. 'They are lost indeed, those who deny that they will ever meet Allah' (VI.31, XXXII.10, XLI.54). 'God will not address them on the Day of

Resurrection' (II.169). 'Vain are the works of those who deny that they will ever meet Him' (XVIII.105).

One last point may be mentioned to complete what has been said concerning the Qur'anic description of the characteristics of faith. Loyalty to faith is of course primarily enjoined on Moslems but faith may be recanted in especial circumstances. 'Anyone who after accepting faith utters unbelief, incurs God's wrath 'unless he does so under compulsion, his heart remaining firm' (XVI.108). Commentators have been at pains to explain this dispensation, which may appear at first sight to be contrary to the spirit of self-sacrifice and heroism. They argue that the triumph of the cause of God is the final goal towards which the efforts of believers must-tend under all conditions. In circumscribing the cases of permitted recantation, they add one further condition to those of 'duress ' and 'loyalty of the heart' laid down in the Qur'an. The permission does not extend to cases in which there is danger to the life or property of Moslems. One commentary relates the case of two Moslems who fell into the hands of the false prophet Musailama. He called on them to recant their faith. One did, and so saved himself; the other did not and was put to death. The Prophet, on hearing what had occurred, said: 'He who remained steadfast was received into God's grace; the other who availed himself of the permission granted by God, was forgiven.' That such recantation is not peculiar to Islam is pointed out by one writer. Muir, in his *Life of Mohammed*, says: 'Deception, in the current theology, is under certain circumstances allowable ... The case of our own religion ... shows that pious fabrications of this description easily commend themselves to the conscience, wherever there is the inclination and the opportunity for their perpetration.'

Unbelief

From the point of view of the Qur'an unbelief (kufr) is a great sin, which entails the most grievous retribution in this life and the next. But what is the meaning of kufr?

This word has been used in a variety of senses in the Qur'an, but the two principal meanings of it are ingratitude and lack of belief in God. The sole meaning of the term in pre-Islamic usage was ingratitude, but the Qur'an used this concept in a special context, i.e. that of man's ingratitude towards the favours and bounties bestowed on him by God. It contrasted the believer who perceives everything in this world as a sign of God and who feels thankful every moment of his life for God's favours, with the unbeliever who denies God and is devoid of any sense of gratefulness towards his Creator. Just as thankfulness is a symbol of 'iman' (faith), so ingratitude is proof of kufr (unbelief): the meaning of kufr as ingratitude moves by natural development into the sphere of lack of faith. Numerous verses of the Qur'an illustrate both meanings of the terms. In the following quotations the operative words are derivatives from the root kufr.

Ingratitude

'He grants you all that you ask Him. If you reckoned up Allah's favours you could not count them. Truly man is unjust and ungrateful' (XIV.37). Speaking of those saved from a tempest at sea: 'When He brings you back safe to land you turn away from Him, most ungratefully' (XVII.69). 'Man shows himself to be most ungrateful' (XLII.47).

Unbelief

'There came to them apostles with clear signs . . . but they rejected the message and turned away' (LXIV.6, XL.23). 'O People of the Book, why do you disbelieve in the signs of God when you yourselves bear witness to them?' (III.63). 'Those who reject God and hinder men from the path of God, for them We will add penalty to penalty' (XVI.90). 'That is their recompense because they rejected His signs' (XVII.100).

In both senses: 'Remember Me, I will remember you; be thankful to Me and do not reject faith' (II.147).

In addition to the concepts of ingratitude and unbelief, certain other qualities are currently associated in the Qur'an with kufr: disputing about the signs of God, haughtiness, self-conceit, injustice, corruption, insubordination, giving the lie to God's words. 'None can dispute about the signs of God but the unbelievers' (XL.4). 'Those who wrangle concerning the signs of God . . . are hateful in the sight of God. God puts a seal on every insolent and arrogant heart' (XL.37). The worst unbelievers are those who sneer at God and make a mockery of His words: 'When the unbelievers see you they treat you only with ridicule . . . they blaspheme at the mention of God Most Gracious' (XXI.37). 'Hell-fire is their reward because they rejected faith and made a mockery of My signs and My messengers' (XVIII.106). A humiliating penalty is in store for those who throw ridicule on the path of God (XXXI.5).

The Qur'an gives the widest range to the term 'unbeliever' (kafir). In addition to the uses already pointed out, it applies to those who maltreat God's messengers and the faithful; who stubbornly refuse to accept guidance, relying on the habits of their ancestors; who follow the ways of Satan; who prohibit others from obeying the commandments of the Qur'an; who hypocritically show themselves desirous of dialogue with believers, but who in reality endeavour to lead them astray; who return to unbelief after having been converted. In short kufr is the most comprehensive term which covers all negative values in the Qur'anic ethical system and world view.

The kafirs are warned again and again that eternal damnation awaits them in afterlife. 'Allah has laid His curse upon the unbelievers and prepared for them a blazing fire' (XXXIII.64). 'Those who reject faith and die rejecting, on them is God's curse and the curse of angels and of all mankind' (II.156). If an unbeliever repents promptly after his error his repentance will be accepted, but if he repents on the point of death he will receive no response (IV.21,22).

Polytheism

The greatest sin, the one sin that is absolutely unpardonable is that of believing that Allah has equals or associates.[6] When the Prophet declared his mission, his greatest opponents were the polytheists of Mecca and other cities of Arabia, i.e. those who worshipped idols and minor deities who were called God's daughters, partners or companions. Three of these, the principal idols of Mecca, namely Allat, Uzza and Manat, are referred to in the Qur'an (Sura LIII) and declared to be mere names. The Qur'an calls polytheists 'unclean' and prohibits them from approaching the Sacred Mosque (verse 28 of Sura IX). The term 'unclean' was no doubt originally used in a ritual context, and the injunction was intended to deprive the pagans of Mecca of the right, previously enjoyed by them, of practising their cult in the Ka'ba (Sacred Mosque of Islam). As stated in the Introduction to this book, this commandment must be read with care, bearing in mind the circumstances which gave rise to it. The term polytheist referred to a particular group of people; the ban on their admission to Ka'ba had a historical, local and political significance. It may therefore be doubted whether certain conclusions which have been drawn from this commandment are in fact warranted. These are: attributing to the term unclean a literal meaning, which necessitates the avoidance of physical contact with polytheists; equating the term polytheist (mushrik) with the term unbeliever (kafir); and extending the prohibition of admission to the Ka'ba to include Islamic places of worship in all places and at all times.

It should be admitted, however, that it is difficult to draw a distinction between the term polytheism (shirk) and unbelief (kufr) in the Qur'an. Indeed there are passages which equate the two terms. Verse VI.1 quotes unbelievers (kuffar) as attributing equals to their God (thus identifying them with polytheists). Verse XL.12 addressing unbelievers, says: 'Whenever God was invoked, you disbelieved, but if others were associated with Him you believed.' The Christian doctrines of Trinity and deification of Jesus are pronounced to be sheer polytheism, and in this context polytheists are called unbelievers (kafir) and their error is termed 'kufr' (verses V.76 and 77).

The utter incompatibility of Islam with any form of polytheism is reflected with especial emphasis in Sura CIX in which Allah commands the Prophet to say to the unbelievers (the polytheists or pagans of Quraish): 'You have your religion and I have mine.' To neutralise the possible interpretation that these words imply tolerance, the commentators maintain that the verse in question has been abrogated by the verses which command the Prophet and the faithful to fight the unbelievers.

Finally, the Qur'an affirms that polytheists incur Allah's wrath more than any other sinners; unclean in this world, they are bereft of the possibility of repentance in this world and pardon in the next, and are irretrievably doomed to hell-fire.

Idols

Idols or images of false gods worshipped by different peoples at different times are frequently mentioned in the Qur'an. They are of course implied in all cases where reference is made to polytheism, but they also appear under proper names. The earliest mentioned are idols which are stated in the Qur'an to have existed in the time of Noah who tried in vain to dissuade his people from worshipping them. Verse LXXI.22 names five such idols, each of which, as explained in the commentaries, represented a special symbol and thereby denoted a special quality: Wadd, in the shape of Man, stood for affection; Suwa, in that of Woman, for beauty; Yaguth, in the form of Lion, for physical strength; Ya'uq, in the shape of Horse, for swiftness; and Nisr (Eagle) for keen vision. But as idols bearing these names were worshipped in Arabia, discussions have arisen around the Qur'anic representation of these Arabian objects of worship as antediluvian idols. These discussions are aimed at refuting the views of critics who regard the attribution of the worship of these false gods to Noah's people as an anachronism.

The history of Abraham begins with an episode relating to idolatry. Abraham appears in the Qur'an in the heroic role of breaker of idols. By the use of subtle arguments and recourse to a clever ruse, he proves the powerlessness of idols and discredits the worship of heavenly bodies (XXI.58–67, XXVI.70–74, XI.76–78).

Idolatry penetrated even the monotheistic Jewish community during its emigration from Egypt and its wanderings in the Sinai Peninsula. Barely landed in safety after crossing the sea, the Israelites asked Moses to fashion idols for them like those worshipped by a people that they encountered (VII.134), and later, during Moses' absence, they made and worshipped a golden calf (XX.90–93) for which they were commanded by God to slay one another in retribution but were pardoned in the end (II.51).

The Qur'an, with its uncompromising emphasis on the oneness of God, reclaimed the Arab peoples from their ancient custom of worshipping certain angels or deities inferior to the greatest god Allah Ta'ala, or certain stars to which they attributed divine powers. Three such angels, namely Lat, Uzza and Manat, considered to be daughters of God, and each represented by an idol or image of that name in Mecca, are specially mentioned in verse LIII.19 in circumstances which recall the withdrawal by Muhammad of a verse in which he had recommended, under a prompting by Satan,[7] recourse to them as intercessors with Allah. Being rebuked by Gabriel for his error, but consoled by a message from Allah (XXII.51) which said that prophets had at all times suffered from satanic promptings, he withdrew the offending verse. Verses 20–23 went on to ridicule the idea that God should have only daughters when men had sons, and that the so-called angels were nothing but words invented by man. The satanic verse referring to the three female angels said: 'These are exalted females whose intercession is to be sought after.' The consoling message ran thus: 'Never before have We sent a prophet or apostle but Satan tampered with his recital, but Allah annuls Satan's interpolations and confirms His own revelation.' Reference is also made in the same Sura (LIII) to Sirius or the Dog Star which was worshipped by certain tribes: verse 50 declares that Allah was the Lord of Sirius as He was the Lord of all creation.

The Qur'an mentions stone altars or columns which were objects of worship and on which animals were sacrificed in the name of different idols. It prohibited the eating of the flesh of animals slaughtered on such stones (verse V.4) and also the performance of any act of devotion before such stones (V.92).

The Qur'an reproved specifically certain Arab practices which symbolised dedication of cattle to their idols, and also the custom of setting aside part of their food for their gods.

The Qur'an contains numerous passages expressing reprobation of idolaters as worshippers of false deities who can create nothing but are themselves created, who have no control of hurt or good to themselves or others, nor any control over life, death or resurrection (e.g. verse XXV.3). Several verses repudiate the pagans' claim that they can approach the divine being through the mediation of their idols (X.18, XXXIX.4).

Two words used in the Qur'an (Jibt once and Taghut several times) are believed to be the names of particular idols. Verse IV.54 says that those (believed to be two chiefs of the Jewish community of Medina who conspired with the Quraish against Muhammad) who bowed down before Jibt and Taghut as a token of their sincerity were irretrievably cursed by God.

The word Taghut has been taken by some to be a synonym of idol. Indeed in some instances it is used in the sense of any object of worship other than the one and true God. Thus verse II.257 mentions among the blest 'whoever rejects Taghut and believes in Allah'. Verse XXXIX.19 brings good news to those who eschew the worship of Taghut. Verse XVI.38 says that apostles have been sent to all peoples with the command to 'serve God and eschew Taghut'. Verse IV.78 says that those who believe fight in the path of God, and those who disbelieve fight in that of Taghut. In one case Taghut is used as a synonym of Satan and his associates: 'Those who reject faith, their patrons are the Taghut' (II.259).

To conclude: as Abraham inaugurated his mission by breaking the idols of his people, so Muhammad inaugurated his conquest of Medina by breaking the time-honoured idols of the Quraish. Tradition says that there were 360 of them ranged round the Ka'ba, and as Muhammad proceeded to the Ka'ba in triumph he ordered them to be hewn down one by one. As the central image of the principal deity Hobal fell with a crash Muhammad recited the words of the Qur'an 'Truth is come and falsehood is vanished' (XVII.82).

The Hypocrites

From the examination of the verses in which the terms 'munafiq' (approximate translation: hypocrite) and 'nifaq' (hypocrisy) occur, the following definition can be given for the word 'munafiq': 'munafiq' is a person who, in matters of faith, says with his tongue what does not exist in his heart. This statement actually appears in the Qur'an. Verse 161 of Sura III, referring to the behaviour of the hypocrites during the battle of Uhud, says that they said with their lips what was not in their hearts. This description also elucidates another point, namely that hypocrisy is an intermediate condition between belief and unbelief and not (as some commentators have argued) a species of unbelief. There is no hypocrisy in either a believer or an unbeliever. In the case of the former his tongue and his heart are at one in acknowledging God's signs and His apostle; and in the case of the latter his tongue and his heart are at one in rejecting them. The verse cited says that on that day (i.e. on the day of the battle) the hypocrites were nearer to unbelief than they were to belief.

The Qur'an mentions hypocrisy mostly in the context of special historical events or persons. Among such events are the battle of Uhud, the expulsion of the Jews of Bani Nadhir from Medina, and the attack on the tribe of Bani Mustaliq. But the term hypocrisy has also been applied to special groups of people. Thus verse 98 of Sura IX refers to the Arab bedouins as specially given to hypocrisy, and a similar statement is made in the same Sura (verse 102) about the people of Medina.

From the verses of the Qur'an it is evident that the Prophet entertained particularly bitter feelings towards the hypocrites. This is because in matters of vital importance they proved themselves to be false. On occasions when the Prophet led campaigns against his opponents, the hypocrites, while outwardly professing faith, in actual fact behaved in a hostile manner. Not only did they not cooperate; they worked against the Prophet's plans. They avoided participating in the expeditions, and if they did participate they were the first to desert. They cautioned others to stand aloof; they tried to cause disaffection among the believers; they conspired in secret or tried to come to terms with the enemy; they made promises on oath and broke them. No wonder then that the Prophet should have treated them as no different from unbelievers and polytheists. Verses 15–18 of Sura LVIII say: 'God has prepared for them a severe penalty; evil indeed are their deeds. They have made their oaths a screen for their misdeeds: thus they obstruct men from the path of God: therefore shall they have a humiliating penalty. Of no profit whatever to them, against God, will be their riches or their sons. They will be companions of the Fire to dwell therein for ever.' Verses 102 to 104 of Sura IX say: 'Certain of the desert Arabs round about you are hypocrites, as well as among the Medina folk; they are obstinate in hypocrisy ... they shall be sent to a grievous penalty.' Verse 9 of Sura LXVI, addressing the Prophet, says: 'Strive hard against the unbelievers and the hypocrites and be firm against them. Their abode is hell.' But in verse 104 of Sura IX the Prophet receives this injunction: 'Take alms from their goods so as to purify and sanctify them. Pray on their behalf, for your prayers are a source of security for them, and God is One who hears and knows.'

Hypocrites are again and again referred to in the Qur'an and placed on the same footing as unbelievers. Their characteristics are described, *inter alia*, in Sura IV which was revealed shortly after the battle of Uhud, the battle in which the hypocrites showed their true colours more openly. It is pointed out that they change constantly from one side to another, that they try to lead the believers astray, that they aim at deceiving God, and if they pray it is only for the sake of ostentation. The whole subject of the hypocrites, namely how they betray themselves, how they should be treated by the believers, and what Allah has in store for them comes up with emphasis in the said Sura. It appears that the conduct of the hypocrites during the battle of Uhud gave rise to a controversy among the Prophet's followers. There were two schools of opinion. One maintained that they should be put to death, while the other was in favour of leaving them alone. The Qur'an decreed a middle course between the two extremes. It laid down that they should not be admitted to the circle of the faithful, that they should be given a chance to set out (fight) in the path of God, but if they turned back they should be put to death wherever found; that if they deserted and took refuge with a tribe with which the Moslems had a pact of non-aggression they should not be molested; that if they came to the believers and declared themselves unwilling to take part in any fighting, while giving guarantees of peace they should be given quarter; but that if they persisted in their ways they should be seized and slain wherever found (IV.90 to 93). The fate of the hypocrites in the life to come is to be consigned for ever to hell-fire (verses IV.139,144) unless they repent and mend their ways, becoming wholehearted believers (IV.145). But here again one is reminded of the mystery of Allah's plans. 'Would you guide those whom Allah has caused to err? He whom Allah has led astray cannot be guided' (IV.90,142).

The People of the Book

The word 'Kitab' (Book) or scripture is used in the Qur'an both in a universal and a particular sense. In the universal sense the Book is the foundation of all Revelation, the fountain-head of God's eternal law, and it consists of 'Kalimat' (Words) which are its unchangeable decrees. It exists from all eternity in a Preserved Tablet as a divine and all-embracing archetypal plan. Its core and essence are referred to in the Qur'an as 'the Mother of the Book'. From this fountain-head have sprung streams in different ages as partial revelations, called 'portions of the Book'. Thus, in the particular sense, the word 'Book' is applied to the Old and New Testaments as well as to the Qur'an, but the Qur'an also refers to itself as the complete revelation, 'the whole of the Book', in harmony with verse XXXIII.40 which says: 'Muhammad is ... Allah's Apostle and the Seal of the Prophets.' Although the phrase 'the People of the Book' means generally nations which believe in the scriptures of a particular religion, as used in the Qur'an it refers more particularly to the Jews and the Christians. But the word 'Book' should not be taken too literally, for it is used in the Qur'an in a sense which is equal to revelation without scriptures: verses VI.83–86 mention a succession of prophets beginning with Noah and including such minor figures as Aaron, Elias and Elisha, and verse 89 says: 'These were the men to whom we gave the "*Book*" and authority and prophethood.'

The term the 'People of the Book' occurs in many verses of the Qur'an. Its meaning is clear: it denotes the followers of religions endowed with Scriptures, principally the Jews and the Christians. But two verses (Sura II.59 and Sura V.73) bring Sabaeans within the group of the 'People of the Book' and extend the meaning of the term to cover all those who believe in God and the Hereafter and who do what is right. A clearer definition can be found in verse 17 of Sura XXII, where all people are divided into three groups as follows: those who believe (in the Qur'an), those who follow the Jewish, the Sabaean, the Christian and the Magian faiths, and those who adhere to polytheism. Some commentators have linked the words 'Magian faith' to the words 'who adhere to polytheism' thus trying to place Magians in the third group. But this is obviously an error, because these two phrases are separated by the words 'and those', which show that Magians properly belong to the second group and count therefore among the People of the Book.

But belonging to the group of the People of the Book is not by itself a sufficient guarantee of salvation. In addition to fulfilling the exterior conditions of belonging to a religion, the believer must have 'true faith' and must do good works. But some People of the Book are not devout and pious; they are unfaithful, untruthful and hypocritical. they entertain polytheistic fallacies and try to lead the believers astray. Several verses of the Qur'an (e.g. verses 67 *et seq.* of Sura V) emphasise that the beliefs, actions and sayings of some of the People of the Book run counter to God's commandments, and that Jews do not stand firm upon the Old Testament any more than Christians stand firm upon the New. The Prophet's mission is to warn them that they must observe the precepts of the Books according to their true import.

The judgement of the Qur'an concerning the People of the Book is expressed in verses 109–111 of Sura III in the following terms: 'Not all of them are alike; of the People of the Book some are steadfast;

they recite the signs of God all night long, and prostrate themselves in adoration. They believe in God and the Last Day; they enjoin what is right and forbid what is wrong; they hasten to do good deeds. These are in the ranks of the righteous; of the good that they do nothing will be rejected, for God knows well those that do right. But those who reject faith ... will be companions of the Fire, dwelling therein forever.'

The Qur'an does not forbid the People of the Book to act according to the commandments of their faith. On the contrary (particularly in the case of the Jews) it confirms some of the basic precepts of their religion, such as observance of the Sabbath, the law of talion, and the rules concerning lawful and unlawful food. Verse 7 of Sura V, addressing the Moslems, says: 'The food of the People of the Book is lawful for you[8] and yours is lawful for them.' What the Qur'an reproaches them for is that they exceed the proper bounds in their religion (verse 81 of Sura V); that they interpret wrongfully the teachings of their faith (e.g. the subjects of the Trinity and of monasticism in Christianity); that they displace words from their right places and practise prevarication (verse 48 of Sura IV); or that they neglect God's commandments and try to lead others astray. Against such People of the Book the Qur'an places the believers on their guard.

Verse 29 of Sura IX sounds an effective note of warning in this sense. Addressing the believers, it says: 'Fight those who do not believe in God and the Last Day and who do not hold forbidden what has been forbidden by God and His Apostle, and who do not acknowledge the religion of truth, even if they are of the People of the Book, until they pay tribute with willing submission and feel themselves subdued.' Verse 106 of Sura III, addressing Moslems, says: 'You are the best of Peoples evolved for Mankind, enjoining what is wrong and believing in God. If only the People of the Book would believe, it would be best for them; among them some have faith but most of them are perverted transgressors.'

Several verses say that the Qur'an is sent to confirm the previous Scriptures, but this does not mean that the believers in pre-existing religions do not need to embrace Islam. In other words the People of the Book are not, by the mere fact of having such faith, equal to Moslems. Though certain verses seem to imply that belief in Judaism, Christianity and the other stated religions by itself entitles the believer to heavenly rewards, yet other verses (e.g. verses 198 and 199 of Sura III) state clearly that among the People of the Book only those who acknowledge all divine revelations (i.e. those of past ages as well as those made to the Prophet of Islam) merit God's favours. Indeed verse 50 of Sura IV addresses the People of the Book in these terms: 'Believe in what We have now revealed, confirming what was already with you, before we obliterate your faces and turn them backwards or lay our curse on you as We did on the Sabbath-breakers.'

Attitude towards other Religions

Certain verses of the Qur'an clearly confirm former monotheistic religions, command the faithful not to discriminate between them and promise God's grace and mercy to the followers of those religions and to all who do good deeds. But there are other verses which reflect the opposite, so that it is difficult to reconcile their content with the principle of tolerance. The contradiction is so obvious that some commentators have, by way of explanation, invoked the Qur'anic concept of 'abrogation'[9] concluding thereby that one group should be held to have abrogated the other. This section illustrates this duality by summarising under one heading the content of the verses which recommend tolerance, and under a second heading the content of the verses which contradict that principle.

The first group

In order to understand in what sense the Qur'an requires Moslems to show tolerance towards non-Moslems it is necessary to examine carefully the meaning of the word Islam, for if this term is taken to mean exclusively the religion of Muhammad in the specific sense, then there can be no question of tolerance towards other religions. Verse 17 of Sura III says: 'The only true faith in Allah's sight is Islam.' Verse 79 of the same Sura says: 'If anyone chooses a religion other than Islam, never will it be accepted of him, and in the Hereafter he will be one of the lost.' However, it is not clear whether in these texts the term 'Islam' means the religion of Muhammad or any religion which teaches 'Islam' (submission to God). From the passages which precede verse 79 it becomes quite clear that in this particular context 'Islam' does not apply exclusively to the religion of Muhammad, but covers also the past monotheistic faiths. Verse 77 defines the term 'religion of Allah' as being that of everyone who submits to him, and the verse that follows makes the point entirely clear. It says: 'Say: We believe in Allah, in what has been revealed to us; in that which was revealed to Abraham, Ismael, Jacob and the tribes; and in that which Allah gave to Moses, Jesus and the Prophets. We make no distinction between any of them, and we surrender [lahu Muslimun] to God' The same point is made in other verses. Verse 62 of Sura II says: 'Believers [in the Qur'an], Jews, Christians and Sabaeans and whoever believes in Allah and the Last

Day and does what is right, shall be rewarded by their Lord; they shall have no fear nor shall they grieve.' Verse 73 of Sura V conveys the same meaning. Verse 45 of Sura XXIX says to the faithful: 'Be courteous when you argue with the People of the Book, except with those among them who do evil, and say: "We believe in that which has been revealed to us and which was revealed to you; our Lord and yours is one, to Him we surrender ourselves [lahu Muslimun]".' Verse 21 of Sura XXXI says: 'He that surrenders himself [yuslim] to Allah and leads a righteous life stands on the firmest ground.' Verses 3 and 4 of Sura II say: 'Those who trust what has been revealed to you and to others before you and firmly believe in the life to come, these are rightly guided by their Lord; these shall surely triumph.' Verse 257 of Sura II is categorical: 'There shall be no compulsion in religion.' Finally in Sura CIX God commands the Prophet to say to the unbelievers: you have your religion, and I have mine!

The second group
The logical conclusion to be drawn from the foregoing is that since the followers of the other religions also worship the God of Islam, since God's mercy and the rewards of the Hereafter are assured, not only to them, but to the righteous in general, and since it is enjoined on the Moslems not to discriminate among the religions, it is therefore incumbent on Moslems to regard the followers of other religions as their equals, and to treat them with affection or at least with tolerance. It is specially required of them, in the event of disputes, to 'argue in ways that are best and most gracious' (XVI.126). Verses LX.8 and 9 say: 'God does not forbid you from dealing kindly and justly with those who do not fight you for your faith and do not drive you out of your homes . . . He only forbids you from befriending those who fight you for your faith and drive you out of your homes and support others in driving you out.' But there are verses which clearly contradict this rule. Verse 57 of Sura V says: 'Believers, do not take Jews and Christians for your friends. They are friends with one another. Whoever of you seeks their friendship is one of them.' Verse 114 of Sura III says: 'Believers, do not make friends with any men other than your own people. They will spare no pains to corrupt you.' Verse 143 of Sura IV says: 'Believers, do not take unbelievers rather than believers for friends. Do you wish to give God an open proof against yourselves?'

Clearly the injunction against taking non-Moslems (even if they are among the People of the Book) for friends is inconsistent with the verses of the first group which affirm that the followers of all religions are equal in the sight of God. Moreover, in so far as those outside the category of the People of the Book are concerned there is no recommendation that they should be treated with tolerance; indeed, on the contrary, the Moslem is ordered to avoid, to oppose and to fight them. The phrase 'not in the category of the People of the Book' of course means polytheists and non-believers in general, two groups whom the Qur'an treats throughout as irretrievable outcasts. The polytheist is 'unclean' (IX.28). All sinners may be pardoned except polytheists (IV.51 and 116). The believers are commanded to seize, bind and kill polytheists wherever they find them. It is forbidden to implore pardon for polytheists; even the Prophet's intercession in their favour would be vain. As for unbelievers in general, they are beyond the pale of the community; they are destined to Hell, as the faithful are destined to Paradise. Believers must not take them for friends and associates. Verse 27 of Sura III says: 'Let not the believers take for friends unbelievers rather than believers; he that does this has nothing to hope for from Allah.' The verse makes an exception in these words: 'unless you fear any danger from them', but adds directly, 'but Allah warns you to beware of Himself.' Verses 3 and 4 of Sura XLVII say: 'The unbelievers follow falsehood while the faithful follow the truth . . . when you meet the unbelievers strike off their heads, and when you have laid them low, bind them firmly.' The injunction to fight the unbelievers (jihad) until they embrace the religion of Islam is contained in numerous verses as explained in the section on fighting in Chapter 8.

The contents of the verses of the second group lead to the inevitable conclusion that if the commandments contained in them are strictly complied with, there can be no relations of friendship, association and even peaceful co-existence between Moslem and non-Moslem communities. Furthermore, within the Moslem community also whoever turns back from his faith becomes an outlaw and incurs the penalty of death; his works shall come to nothing in this world and the next, and he shall be doomed to hell-fire (verse II.214).[10]

There is an obvious contradiction between the verses of the first and second groups. Those of the first group enjoin an attitude of tolerance towards the People of the Book. They even place those who do good deeds on an equal footing with the People of the Book, and it is evident that doers of good deeds may exist also among polytheists and unbelievers. It is even enjoined on the Prophet that if the unbelievers defy him he must reason with them in all gentleness and must leave them to God if they persist in their opposition. On the other hand, the verses of the second group close the door to any possibility of understanding and good fellowship with unbelievers, and commands Moslems to fight them.[11] The Qur'an itself provides no criterion for preferring one group to the other, nor does it point to any method of reconciling them. Consequently if the view is adopted that the verses of the second category were meant to apply only to the particular conditions which existed during the early years of Islam, when it was necessary for Moslems to combat their opponents it can be maintained that the overriding principle is that which is enunciated in the first group of verses. On the other hand, if it is held that both groups are independent of time and circumstances and are to be regarded as binding at all times and in all places, then the contradiction existing between them will exclude any possibility of an attitude of tolerance on the part of Islam towards other religions, philosophies and creeds.

This section does not deal with the kind of tolerance which was 'purchased' in the past by non-Moslems living in a Moslem State in return for payment of a tribute (Jizya) to the State. Tolerance which is obtained in exchange for a payment (whether called poll-tax, protection tax, or compensation for exemption from military service), while undoubtedly valuable is not tolerance in the real sense. Indeed, absence of tolerance is indicated in Verse IX.29 which commands Moslems to fight non-Moslems (even the People of the Book who do not respect the ordinances of Islam) until they pay tribute as a sign of humble submission.

The Prophet's attitude towards the Jewish and Christian communities

The attitude of the Prophet towards these communities was not constant, but changed from the expectation of a mutual understanding on the basis of the monotheistic belief common to those religions and his own, to a state of disappointment and misgiving, and ended in complete rupture.

As far as the Jews were concerned, while the Prophet was in Mecca and for some time after he moved to Medina, some learned men among them showed an intellectual interest in his revelations, and the Moslems hoped that an attitude of unbiased research would lead them to a recognition of Muhammad as the prophet promised in the Old Testament (Deut. XVIII.18). Already in Mecca, their optimism diminished (XLVI.9), but they still entertained hope when the Prophet first came into contact with the Jewish communities of Medina, as is shown by his several pronouncements in the early Medinese Suras, in which the Jews were counselled to embrace Islam as a confirmation of their own faith (e.g. in verses II.38 and 39). But shortly afterwards the Moslems were disillusioned because of their bigotry and their dubious behaviour, with the result that the Qur'an accused them of distorting their scriptures (II.70–IV.48) and thereafter the Prophet treated them generally as enemies. The decision to alter the Qibla from Jerusalem to Mecca (verses II.136 *et seq.*) was not unconnected with this change of attitude.

The Prophet did not meet with the same hostility from the Christian community as from the Jewish. Indeed in a verse revealed in an early Medinese Sura he sets off the sympathetic attitude of the Christians against the unfriendliness of the Jews. 'You will find that the most implacable of men in their enmity to the faithful are the Jews and the pagans, and that the nearest in affection to them are those who say "We are Christians" ... When they listen to that which was revealed to the Prophet you will see their eyes fill with tears as they recognise its truth' (V.85,86). But he argued with them against the dogmas of Sonship and the Trinity, and disapproved of their inclination towards monasticism. Furthermore, the sympathetic feelings of the Christians fell short of the Prophet's expectation that they would accept him as the Paraclete (V.17, LXI.6). Finally, clashes with Christian Byzantium and its allies among the Arabs caused a change of attitude on the Prophet's part. He persevered in his confirmation of the Old and New Testaments, but essentially as containing an announcement of his own coming (VII.156). A Judaism or a Christianity not regarded as a harbinger of the coming of Muhammad was not an acceptable creed in spite of its monotheistic foundation. That fundamental belief could be found in another creed believed to be more autochthonous: that of Abrahamic Hanifism. 'They say "Accept the Jewish or the Christian faith, and you shall be rightly guided." Say "By no means! We believe in the faith of Abraham, the [Hanif] upright one." ' (II.129).

Notes to Chapter Six

1. Investigation as to what the word 'Hanif' means and how it connects with
    the faith of Abraham has resulted in various interpretations including the
    following: the word meant in Arabic (and also in Hebrew and Syriac)
    originally one who limps and, derivatively, one who abandons his faith.
    How this term of reproach came to mean one who worships the one true
    God, and in particular how it became associated with Abraham, is ex-
    plained by the following development which is described by the earliest
    biographers of the Prophet. Early in the 7th century, before the rise of
    Islam, a number of Arabs, particularly four distinguished Meccans
    (named Waraqa, 'Ubaidullah, 'Uthman and Zaid) became aware of the
    falsity of idol worship, met secretly and decided to go in search of a new
    religion which would recognise only one God. As it happened, an ancient
    tradition was current among the Arabs to the effect that Abraham, whom
    they considered as their ancestor, had rejected idol worship and believed
    in one God. The four reformers and a growing number of their sym-
    pathisers found in this Abrahamic tradition the mainstay that they were
    seeking for transferring their allegiance from idols to a unique God.
    Because of this apostasy they came to be called 'Hanif' (renegade) by the
    uncompromising pagans. The most devout of these reformers was Zaid
    son of 'Amr, who lived in forced retirement in a cave on Mount Hira
    where the Meccans used to spend one month in the year in the practice
    of penance and self-purification. According to tradition, Muhammad also
    paid a yearly visit to Mount Hira, and there he came into contact with
    Zaid, who prided himself on being the most devoted adherent to the
    Abrahamic cult. Muhammad felt a special reverence for him and shared
    his Abrahamic enthusiasm. Zaid died about 607. Some five or six years
    later Muhammad declared his mission and it is significant that in a Sura
    (XXX), revealed shortly afterwards, reference was made to the religion
    which he was preaching as the Hanif (which had now come to mean 'the
    true') faith, the natural and immutable religion of mankind, going back
    to Abraham. 'Stand firm in your devotion to the true [Hanif] faith, the
    upright nature with which Allah has endowed man; Allah's creation
    cannot be changed. This is surely the steadfast religion' (verses 20 and
    30). Thereafter the word Hanif was used in several verses as an antonym
    of 'polytheist' (XXII.32, X.105, XCVIII.4) and an epithet of the Abrahamic
    creed (XVI.121, VI.162, II.129, III.60 and 89).
2. John Penrice, *Dictionary and Glossary of the Koran*, Lahore, Law Publishing
    Company, 1873.
3. The punishment to be inflicted on the apostate in this life has not been
    specified in the Qur'an, but a succession of Moslem jurists, relying on the
    general condemnation laid down in the Qur'an, and on Tradition, have
    declared it to be death. Opinions differ as to whether the apostate should
    be executed immediately on conviction or should be allowed a respite (of
    three days according to Omar) to return to faith.
4. For a summarised description of these defections, based on Baidawi's
    commentary, see George Sale's translation of the Qur'an, *The Koran*,
    London, Frederick Warne, 1877 p. 107.
5. *Kashf al-asrar*, vol. 2, p. 77.
6. The unforgivability of idolaters is so emphatic that the Qur'an forbids the
    Prophet and believers from praying for their forgiveness. Even Abraham

renounces a promise which he had made to pray for his father's forgive-ness (IX.114–115 and XIX.49).

7. *Kash al-asrar*, vol. 5, p.386.

8. Flesh of swine is unlawful for Moslems according to verse V.4; it is also unlawful for Jews according to the rule in Leviticus XI.7 and 8. But the situation in Christianity is different. Indeed, according to the words of Christ in Matthew XV.11 no food is unlawful: 'What goes into a man's mouth does not make him unclean, but what comes out of his mouth, that is what makes him unclean.' And it is well known that Christians do not consider pork unlawful food. Should verse 7 of Sura V be construed therefore as relaxing in any sense the interdiction in verse 4?

9. Verse II.100 says: 'If We abrogate any verse or cause it to be forgotten We will replace it by a better one or one similar.'

10. The consequences of apostasy as laid down on the basis of traditions and jurisprudence are particularly dire: the apostate loses all civil rights, his marriage is annulled, he is put to death, his corpse may not be buried in the cemetery of Moslems, the reward of his good deeds is lost, and he is doomed to eternal hell-fire.

11. It is sometimes argued that the Qur'an commands Moslems to fight only those who make war on them and drive them from their homes (LX.9), but this is incorrect; for instance one verse (IX.29) requires Moslems to fight (among others) the People of the Book if they do not surrender to Islam, until they pay jizya. The duty to fight idolaters, unbelievers and infidels until they surrender to Islam is absolute and not conditional on any act of violence having been committed by the unbelievers.

CHAPTER SEVEN

THE OTHER WORLD

The Hereafter

A crucial distinction that the Qur'an establishes with special emphasis is that between this world and the Hereafter. It is crucial because without it the Qur'anic conception of the universe loses much of its significance. Even the Qur'anic rules of worldly conduct have their foundation in the Hereafter because their ultimate sanction consists of rewards and punishment in the world to come. Again and again the Qur'an affirms that compared to the life to come the present life is worthless. 'The life of this world is but play and amusement' (XLVII.38). 'Know that the life of this world is but a sport and a pastime ... What is the life of this world but goods and chattels of deception?' (LVII.19 and 20). 'What is the life of this world but play and amusement? Best is the Home in the Hereafter for those who are righteous' (VI.32). 'You look for the temporal goods of this world; but God looks to the Hereafter' (VIII.68). 'You prefer the life of this world, but the Hereafter is better and more lasting' (LXXXVII.17). 'What is the life of this world but amusement and play; it is the life to come that is the true life, if they but knew it' (XXIX.64). Belief in the Hereafter and in all the concepts that accompany it or underlie it is a *sine qua non* of faith; absence of this belief entails eternal damnation. 'Truly those who deny the life to come are doomed, for they have grossly erred' (XXXIV.8). Numerous other verses brand this life as unworthy and transitory and attribute worth and permanence only to the life to come. The Qur'an warns the believers against being seduced by the joys and pleasures of this world, and emphasises that life in this world, with all its attractions and ornaments is a passing mirage. An elaborate parable illustrates this theme. Verse 24 of Sura X characterises the divine work of construction and destruction in the following simile: God sends down rain which produces vegetation, providing food for men and animals, decking out the earth in a golden robe and causing men to imagine that they have powers of disposal over what the earth bears for them, but no sooner do the inhabitants of the earth prepare themselves for the rich harvest than God sends down His scourge upon the earth by night or by day, laying it waste as if it had not flourished only the day before. Whoever is deluded by the world and prefers it to the next incurs God's wrath and is doomed to eternal torment (XVI.109). The Qur'an cites examples of the deceptive sources of joy in this life: women, sons, treasures of gold and silver, horses, cattle and well-tilled land. The believer must resist the temptation of such possessions and must seek nearness to God, living in the hope of higher blessings prepared for the virtuous in the Hereafter; i.e. eternal life in Paradise under which flow rivers and in which pure companions wait for the believers (III.14 and 15). Verse 28 of Sura VIII says: 'Know that your children and your worldly goods are but a temptation and that Allah's rewards are great.' The same admonition is contained in verse 15 of Sura LXIV.

Resurrection

The Qur'an abounds in passages concerning Resurrection and the Last Judgement, emphasising again and again that that culminating event shall surely come to pass. No less than 67 Suras (56 Meccan and 11 Medinese) contain verses relating to this subject; a summary of the substance of these verses follows:

A point to be specially noted is that warnings to the effect that the Fateful Hour is near, and the description of Resurrection occur in particular in the Meccan Suras. A European writer expresses the opinion that if the Qur'an was not compiled during the life of the Prophet it was because the Qur'anic predictions had given rise to a general belief that the world would soon come to an end. The writer, P. Casanova, develops his view in this respect in a book entitled *Mohammad et la fin du monde.* Quoting verse 1 of Sura XXI which says: 'The day of reckoning is drawing near, yet the people persist in unbelief;' and other verses to the same effect, and also recalling the Prophet's saying that the distance between his appearance and that of Resurrection was equal to the distance between his middle and index fingers, he states that the expectation of this imminent event which would turn the world upside down had deeply affected the conscience of the early believers, and had made them regard the Qur'an more as an apocalyptic revelation than as a book of guidance for life on earth. The writer concludes that the early Moslems felt that it would serve no purpose to collect the revelations of the Qur'an in a world that was on the point of extinction.

Resurrection means the raising up of the dead when every soul shall

be tried and justice shall be rendered to all. The course of justice in
the Hereafter seems to correspond to the course of justice in the world
below, in the sense that it comprises the same procedural stages:
summons (raising up of the dead), trial (delivery of each man's
Record into his hand: LXIX.19 and 25), pronouncement of judgement
(justifying the virtuous and condemning the sinners) and enforcement
(admitting the former to Paradise and subjecting the latter to the
eternal torments of Hell). How this celestial design unfolds itself will
appear from what follows.

The Qur'an applies different names to Resurrection, each denoting
one of its characteristics: the Great Day, the Grand News, the Last Day,
the Appointed Time, the Sure Reality, the Inevitable Event, the Day
of Noise and Clamour, the Overwhelming Event, the Doom, the
Raising Up, the Reunion, the Gathering Together, the Resuscitation,
the Day of Meeting, the Day of Judgement, the Day of Reckoning, the
Day of Sorting Out (separation of the virtuous from the sinners), the
Day on which Men call out one to another, the Day of Mutual Loss
and Gain, the Inevitable Torment, the Very Great Calamity.

Resurrection is a future event the occurrence of which has been
clearly and emphatically foretold in numerous verses. No one must
doubt that it shall come to pass, but only God knows when it will occur.
The Hour is known to no one, not even to the Prophet. Addressing
the Prophet, God says: 'They question you about the hour of Doom.
"When will it come?" they ask. But how are you to know? Your Lord
alone knows when it will come. Your duty is but to warn those that
fear it' (LXXIX.42–44). The Prophet goes no further than saying that
the event is inevitable and the hour unexpected, but that it may be
near. Thus at the beginning of Sura LIV he says: 'The hour of Doom
is drawing near.' Elsewhere also, sounding a note of warning, he says
that the hour of torment is near.

A subject abundantly treated in the Traditions and various exegeti-
cal treatises is that of the signs which will appear at the end of time,
foreshadowing the advent of Resurrection and Last Judgement. Outstanding among these are: the sun rising in the west, the eclipse of
the moon, the coming of Antichrist, the eruption of Gog and Magog,
and the appearance of the Beast. This last sign is clearly mentioned
in the Qur'an. Verse XXVII.84 says: 'When the doom shall be ready
to fall upon them [the unjust] We will cause a Beast to come forth to
them out of the earth and speak to them saying "Verily men did not
firmly believe in Our signs." ' It has been suggested that the appearance of this Beast corresponds to St John's vision in Revelation (chapters XI to XIII) where, upon the sounding of the trumpet by the
seventh angel and the announcement that 'the time has come for
judging the dead' (XI.18), three signs appear consecutively: a dragon

(XII.3), a Beast coming out of the sea (XIII.1), and another Beast coming out of the earth (XIII.11). It is true that there are points of resemblance between the two Beasts: they both have an eschatological role; they both come out of the earth; they both speak; and just as the Revelation Beast imprints a mark on everyone's hand or forehead, so also the Beast mentioned in the Qur'an (according to tradition but not the Qur'anic text) stamps between everyone's eyes a mark to identify those who believe and those who do not. However, there is a fundamental difference between the two Beasts. The former appears in the role of a warner who, addressing mankind on the approach of the Day of Judgement, reproaches it for not having believed in the signs of God. The latter, the earth Beast described in Revelation XIII.11, is an alter ego of the devil, the serpent or Antichrist. Endowed with prodigious power transmitted to it from the dragon and the sea Beast, it revives the blasphemous cult of the latter (XIII.14–15), deceives the inhabitants of the earth, and helps bring about the anarchy which is to usher in the Resurrection. Finally with the advent of the Day of Judgement, the bowl containing the wrath of God is poured over the throne of the Beast, whose kingdom is thereby plunged into darkness (XVI.10).

The events described in the Qur'an as accompanying Resurrection conform to the spirit and also prominently to the letter of the predictions contained in the book of Revelation (VI.12–16 and elsewhere).

The cataclysm begins with the sounding of the Last Trump. That sudden, terrifying blast announces an upheaval which overwhelms the whole universe and all creatures, animate and inanimate. Everything including heaven and earth will change. The gates of the sky will swing open. The stars will fall, scatter and vanish. The sun will cease to shine. The moon will be cleft asunder and will be buried in darkness. The sun and the moon will be joined together. The heavens, rent asunder, will swim in the clouds. The sky will take on the colour of molten brass and will emit a smoke which will envelop all creatures. God will hold the entire world in His grasp and will fold up the heavens in His right hand. The mountains, uprooted, will fly hither and thither, becoming like tufts of carded wool, and will pass away just as the clouds pass away. The oceans will burst forth inflamed. The earth will be flattened out and, with a violent convulsion, will shake off its burdens. Hell will be made to burn fiercely. Both Paradise and Hell will be brought near.

At the sound of the Trumpet other phenomena occur: the earth will shine with the light of the Lord. The graves will be hurled about, vomiting forth the corpses that they contain. The first blast of the Trumpet will be followed by a second: all earthly affairs will then cease. Camels big with young will be left untended, nursing mothers will stop giving suck to their babes, pregnant women will lay down their burden, children's hair will grow white. The corpses thrown up from the tombs will come forth like locusts scattered about, and will rush in haste, as if racing each other in a contest, towards the arena of the Last Judgement. There God is seated on His Throne which is borne aloft by eight angels, other angels standing all around. All animals also, whether living on land, in water or in the air will be among those gathered together.

But what is the condition of those who have thus been called before the court of the Last Judgement? Those who in this life denied that the dead could be resurrected are specially stricken with remorse. The Qur'an contains many verses in which the unbelievers ask the Prophet how it is possible that a corpse which decays and rots in the earth should again become alive. The Prophet answers that He who created in the first place is able to create anew, and that He who revives the dried up soil by sending down rain can likewise bring the dead back to life. But the questioners remain unconvinced until the Day of Judgement when they are brought face to face with the truth. But then nothing will avail them: neither remorse nor repentance. In vain would they implore pardon or seek help from friend, parent or intercessor. The unbelievers and the unjust will recall their deeds and will bitterly reproach themselves for not having heeded the Prophet's warnings. Now, with downcast eyes, mournful faces and aching hearts they await their punishment while the believers look towards Paradise with radiant faces and eyes beaming in brightness.

The multitude as they arrive are brought into the presence of Allah. The register of the deeds of all creatures has been preserved. The records of the virtuous are kept in an exalted place, those of the wicked lie, as it were, in the depths of a gloomy dungeon.[1] All records are unfolded. Each person's fate is already determined by virtue of his record. Nothing is hidden from Allah. He gives to each person the record of his deeds, delivering it into his right hand if he is virtuous, and from behind his back if he is wicked. Since what is recorded is undeniable, and since every creature has received ample warning, there is no need for inquiry and debate, nor is anyone given a chance to put up a defence or to call witnesses. His very soul, his eyes, his ears and his skin, which are resuscitated for this purpose, give testimony against him.

Indeed, each sinner is already doomed on being raised up, for he comes out of the grave blind, deaf and dumb, and his punishment begins from that very moment. He is dragged face downwards, in chains, to the arena of the Last Judgement. The false gods are also raised up together with their worshippers, but they turn against their followers. In answer to God's question 'Why did you lead my servants astray?' they will say: 'We did not lead them astray; they were corrupted by the favours and bounties which Thou didst bestow upon them and their fathers.'

A characteristic name given to Resurrection is the Day of Sorting Out, meaning that on that day the virtuous are separated from the wicked, and the believers from the infidels. All souls are brought before Allah: Prophets, martyrs and true believers, as well as unbelievers, false gods and demons. The deeds of everyone are weighed in the balance. Those whose scale of good deeds proves heavy go to Paradise; those whose scale is light are consigned to Hell.[2] The multitudes are divided into three groups: the Foremost among the Blest, the Companions of the Right Hand and the Companions of the Left Hand. The first group is an exalted class consisting of those nearest to God. The second comprises the righteous people in general. A grandiose description is given of the state of bliss which awaits those blessed souls (verses 10–40 of Sura LVI). The third group consists of unbelievers and wrongdoers who are doomed to eternal misery. Their agony is described in gruesome terms to which reference is made in the section headed Hell and the Doomed below.

In several verses it is emphasised that the leading rebel against Allah is Iblis (Satan) who not only prides himself on disobeying the divine command, but affirms boldly his intention of leading all creatures astray. The Qur'an relates in detail how Iblis refuses God's command, and how he receives Allah's malediction. He is, however, granted a respite till the Day of Judgement during which time he is at liberty to put temptation in the path of God's creatures except true believers. God tells him that Hell will be filled with him and his followers, but in the description of the events of the Last Judgement no special mention is made of Satan and the punishment that he incurs for having led mankind astray during the entire period of creation to the day of the Last Judgement.

With the accomplishment of Resurrection, God's promises will have come true. All creatures are tried by the supreme and absolute Judge, and everyone reaps the harvest of his deeds. Time comes to an end, the universe disappears, and nothing shall remain thereafter except Allah, Paradise for the blest and Hell for the doomed.

Responsibility

In describing the conditions which determine man's state in the life to come, the Qur'an dwells on the concept of faith and its opposite, i.e. unbelief, and also on two other pairs of opposites (following the right path as against going astray, and gratefully acknowledging God's bounties as against obstinately denying them) which differentiate between the blessed and the doomed.

According to the principles of justice, punishment is of course awarded where a reprehensible act is committed wilfully; and rewards are given where meritorious deeds are performed freely. Man reaps the result of his deliberate actions. But does this criterion apply, in the Qur'anic perspective, to the determination of man's fate in the Hereafter? A number of verses would seem to imply that qualifying for heavenly rewards or incurring divine retribution is often a consequence of God's will rather than of man's action.

The position as described in the Qur'an is briefly as follows: God reveals His signs to mankind through His messengers. Man's reaction is either to recognise or to ignore these signs: recognition makes him a 'believer', rejection makes him an 'infidel'. God having shown the straight path to man, he who follows it is 'rightly guided', and he who does not 'goes astray'. Again, God points one by one to the wonders that He has performed in the act of creation, and in particular to the favours that He has bestowed on man. He who shows gratitude and praises God in all humility day and night is saved; he who desists from such response is doomed.

A serious problem arises when consideration is given to man's choice between faith and unbelief or between following the straight path and going astray. Here, according to numerous verses of the Qur'an, God's will or predestination largely replaces man's freedom of choice. Neither he who follows the straight path nor he who goes astray acts as a free agent; both are instruments of divine providence. The following passage is repeated in three verses (XIV.4, XXXV.9 and LXXIV.34): 'God leads astray whom He pleases and guides whom He pleases.' The same statement, expressed in different terms, appears in many other verses, in which it is emphasised that he whom God leads astray will have no one to help or guide him, and also that had God so willed, all peoples would have followed the straight path. Verse 16 of Sura XVIII says: 'He whom Allah guides is rightly guided; but he whom He leads astray shall find no friend to guide him.' Verses 33 and 34 of Sura XIII says: 'None can guide those whom Allah has led astray. They shall be punished in this life, but more painful is the punishment of the life to come.' An imposing number of other verses make it clear that man's going astray is the consequence of God's act in leading him astray, and that none can resist God's will. Verses 99 and 100 of Sura X say: 'Had your Lord pleased, all the people of the earth would have believed in Him. Would you then force faith upon men? None can have faith except by the will of Allah.' Verse 90 of Sura IV says: 'Would you guide those whom God has caused to err?

He whom Allah has led astray cannot be guided.' In verse 36 of Sura XI Noah addressed his people thus: 'Allah will visit His scourge upon you when He pleases, and you shall not escape it. Nor will my counsel profit you if Allah seeks to lead you astray, willing though I am to guide you.' Some verses state clearly that although it is by God's will that men go astray, yet God punishes those who do not follow the straight path, both in this life and the next. Verse 95 of Sura XVI says: 'Had Allah pleased He would have united you into one nation. But He leads astray whom He pleases and gives guidance to whom He pleases, and you shall surely be called to account for all your actions.' Verse 99 of Sura XVII says: 'Those whom Allah guides are rightly guided; but those whom He leads astray shall find no friends besides Him. We shall gather them all on the Day of Resurrection, prostrate upon their faces, deaf, dumb and blind. Hell shall be their home; whenever its flames die down We shall rekindle them into a greater fire.' Verse 120 of Sura XI says: 'Had your Lord pleased, He would have united all mankind . . . But the word of your Lord shall be fulfilled: I will fill the pit of Hell with Jinn and men all together.' Likewise verse 13 of Sura XXXII says: 'Had it been Our will We could have guided every soul. But My word shall be fulfilled: I will fill the pit of Hell with Jinns and men all together.' Verse 41 of Sura V says: 'Those whose hearts He does not please to purify shall be rewarded with disgrace in this world and a grievous punishment in the next.' Similarly verse 25 of Sura VI says: 'We have cast veils over their hearts and made them hard of hearing lest they understand your words. Referring to unbelievers, verse II.6 says: 'God has set a seal on their hearts and on their hearing, and on their eyes is a veil'; and verse VI.110 adds: 'We will turn away their hearts and eyes from the truth just as they refused to believe in it at first.' The same meaning is conveyed in at least 30 other verses, of which two may aptly be quoted to round off the argument of this paragraph: 'He whom Allah guides is on the right path, but he who is led astray by God shall surely perish. We have created for Hell many of the Jinn and many of men; they have hearts with which they do not understand, eyes with which they do not see, ears with which they do not hear. They are like cattle, indeed more misguided; such are the heedless' (VII.177–178).

This is not to say, however, that the Qur'anic outlook is throughout one of unmitigated determinism, for there are a number of verses which affirm that man 'earns' (the result of) his deeds, namely that he is free in his actions to choose between good and evil and is rewarded or punished accordingly. Attempts have been made by theologians to reconcile the two seemingly opposed doctrines, but the discussion of the arguments advanced is outside the scope of this study. All that can be attempted here is to explain in summary the actual contents of the Qur'an concerning the themes of Necessity and Free Will.

Necessity

Predestination (Qada' wa Qadar) appears in the Qur'an as the unalterable law of the universe as well as of human destiny, having been decreed by Allah from all eternity and recorded in His Glorious Book preserved in Heaven (VI.38 and 59, XXXIV.3, LXXXV.22). In it are also inscribed some attributes of Allah Himself: 'Your Lord has decreed mercy for Himself' (VI.12 and 54). Allah's Words are unchangeable (VI.34 and 115).

The Qur'anic concept of predestination is deduced from the use of the twin terms of Qada' and Qadar. The elaborate inquiries which have been made into the meanings of these terms have led to the following distinction: the two together signify Allah's eternal and unchangeable decree concerning all things; Qada' is the primordial act of foreordination; Qadar is its gradual realisation in the course of time.[3] By Qada' Allah decrees His Will (III.42, XIX.36, VI.2). By Qadar He 'measures it out' as befitting each occasion (XXXIV.17, LXXVI.16, LIV.12, XIII.26, XVII.32, XXIX.12, XXX.36). Because of Allah's undisputed Dominion, He cannot be questioned for His acts (XXI.23) nor can His decree be warded off (XIII.12).

Fatalism

The Qur'anic emphasis on predestination naturally leads to a fatalistic attitude towards life. The Qur'an counsels resigned acceptance of the inevitable, as everything is foreordained by Allah's decree. Man cannot will except by the will of Allah (LXXVI.30, LXXXI.29). 'Say "I have not the power to acquire benefits or to avert evil from myself except by leave of Allah"' (VII.188). 'No kind of calamity can occur except by the leave of Allah' (LXIV.11). 'Every misfortune that befalls the earth or your own persons is ordained before We bring it into being.' And the reason for this reminder is made clear: 'So that you may not grieve for the good things you miss or be overjoyed at what you gain' (LVII.22,23). The time and place of every man's death is preordained; the believer who is called upon to fight for the cause of Allah but who shuns the battlefield for fear of death does not escape his fate. To such lingerer the Prophet is commanded to say: 'Even if you had remained in your homes those for whom death was decreed would certainly have gone forth to the place of their death' (III.148). Man is not allowed to choose his death: 'None dies except as Allah permits; the term of every life is fixed as by writing' (III.139).

Human acts

Allah's supreme power extends to the determination of man's will, i.e. man cannot will except in the sense already willed by Allah. He who desires to take the straight path to his Lord is reminded twice: 'You shall not will except as God wills' (LXXVI.30 and LXXXI.29). There are those who desire to keep God's word in remembrance, but 'none will keep it in remembrance except as God wills' (LXXIV.55). In matters of faith and unbelief in particular there are numerous verses as already pointed out, which state that it is not man who decides, but Allah who guides him or leads him astray. To add one more instance to those already mentioned: verse XXXVI.7 says: 'We have bound their necks with chains of iron reaching to their chins so that they cannot bow their heads. We have put barriers before them and behind them and covered them over so that they cannot see.' In the face of the all-embracing will of Allah, there would seem to be no room for the exercise of independent will and power by man: if Allah is the agent of everything, man can hardly be the agent of his own acts. A question thus arises as to why, if man goes astray[4] because God so wills, should he suffer punishment in this world and the next? Reference may be made in passing to a comment on this subject which appears in a book entitled *God and Man in the Koran.*[5] It says '. . . man in this view is no longer considered free to choose . . . Everything would seem to be already fixed and decided from the very beginning. So man's going astray is nothing but the direct and necessary result of God's "leading astray". And this divine act of leading astray none can resist, and in such a case not even the Prophet himself can ever hope to lead anybody back to the right path, as the Koran itself repeatedly emphasises . . . The contrast . . . in the Koran could not but raise later among the Moslem thinkers grave problems regarding the concept of human freedom and moral responsibility. For once you adopt a strictly logical point of view you must recognise the existence of a logical contradiction between these two systems. Only the standpoint of the Koran is not that of pure logic; the Koranic thought unfolds itself on a plane which is essentially different from that of the logic of human reason.'

Referring to the repeated affirmation in the Qur'an that Allah is no oppressor of men, and that He is not unjust and will wrong no one (XLV.21, IV.52) one writer observes: 'But – the pious soul would ask . . . Can it be that God deprives men of all freedom and all autonomy in their acts, that He determines their conduct even in the minutest details, that He takes away from the sinner the possibility of doing good, putting a seal on his heart and covering his ears and his eyes with a thick veil (II.6) and yet punishes him for his disobedience and consigns him to eternal damnation?'[6] In answer to this question emphasis is naturally laid on those verses of the Qur'an which endow man with free will.

Free will

The Qur'an can be appealed to in support of the doctrines both of necessity and of free will. On this latter theme it refers, in a number of verses, to man's deeds as his 'acquisitions' and thus connects them logically with their consequences. 'Every soul will be given what it has earned, with no injustice' (III.24). 'Allah created the heavens and the earth to ... reward each soul according to its deeds' (XLV.21). Each soul is the hostage of its own deeds and shall be requited for whatever evil it has done (II.286). The same meaning is conveyed by verses LII.21, LXXIV.41, XIV.51, LIII.32, VI.164). He who seeks guidance will surely receive it; he who goes astray does so by his own choice and at his own peril (XVII.16). Allah does not in any way wrong mankind; men wrong themselves (X.44, XI.103). 'On their hearts is the stain of the ill which they do' (LXXXIII.14). He who fears Allah 'We will indeed make smooth for him the path to Bliss', and he who thinks himself self-sufficient 'We will indeed smooth for him the path to misery' (XCII.7–10). The same idea can be found in historical examples: for instance God guided the people of Thamud on the straight path, but they preferred to err and were therefore punished, except those who feared God and were saved (XLI.16). If there is a responsible agent outside of man himself it is not Allah but Satan (XXII.4, XXXV.5).

In the face of the two divergent doctrines outlined, each interested group has naturally chosen the one that suits it. Thus the rationalists (in particular the Mutazelites)[7] who maintained that man cannot in his moral and legal activity be the slave of predestination, dwelt on the free-will verses, while the holders of autocratic power (e.g. the Umayyad Caliphs)[8] placed emphasis on the other group of verses. Each party has claimed to be the holder of the ultimate truth, and as no decisive criterion is provided by the Qur'an the difference in question, the oldest dogmatic dissidence within Islam continues unresolved, though orthodoxy leans to the side of determinism.[9]

Hell and the Doomed

Infidels, those who commit sacrilege and blasphemy, hypocrites, polytheists, those who go astray, those who deny God's signs, those who doubt that they will ever meet their Lord, tyrants, transgressors, sinners, those who walk in arrogance, are all companions of Hell. When they enter the other world, the record of their deeds is placed in their left hand. Then, bound in chains and fetters, prostrate upon their faces, deaf, dumb and blind, they are dragged in a crowd to Hell. When they arrive, the gates of Hell are opened and its Keepers will say: enter your everlasting abode! Hell is guarded by 19 fierce and mighty angels. God has made this number a test and a subject of dispute among unbelievers. The true believers will have no doubt, but the infidels will question why Allah has chosen this number, and in this way God causes them to err (verse 30 of Sura LXXIV).

On the Day of Judgement Hell, an ever-blazing furnace fanned by scorching winds, and equipped with every conceivable means of torturing the damned, is brought near and placed in full view. Hell-fire, kindled by God, whose fuel consists of stones and men, roars and rages, its flames rising high in three columns, and throwing up sparks as large as towers. Hell is a bottomless pit, through which runs a stream of scalding water and over which hangs a pall of pitch-black smoke. God commands that the unbelievers, clothed in garments of liquid pitch, their necks bound with shackles and fetters, their faces blackened, their foreheads, sides and backs branded, shall be fastened together in great hordes and dragged through boiling water with a chain 70 cubits long. After being continuously lashed with a mace of iron, the unbelievers arrive at the place of doom. As each of them enters it a voice will cry: 'Seize him and drag him into the depths of Hell; then pour out boiling water over his head' (verses 43–50 of Sura XLIV).

Hell-fire spares nothing and no one. Skins are instantly consumed, but God says: 'No sooner will their skins be roasted through than We shall give them fresh skins so that they may truly taste Our scourge' (verse 56 of Sura IV).

At the bottom of Hell grows the cursed tree of Zaqqum, bearing a fruit like devils' heads. This fruit, bitter and pungent, is the food of the damned, together with thorns, festering blood, putrid and decaying filth. Then, when the doomed ask for a drink, they shall be given molten brass and boiling, stinking water. This food and drink will simmer and boil in their intestines. Groaning and wailing all the time, assaulted from above and from below, the tenants of Hell try to escape, but each time they are made to return and a voice cries: 'Taste the penalty of your misdeeds. Did We not send messengers to warn you and did you not reject them scornfully? Now is meted out to you the punishment which you refused to believe in.' The doomed bitterly lament their fate and say, 'Would that we had obeyed God and His Apostle; would that the record of our deeds had never been handed to us!' They beseech their keepers to intercede with God in their favour, but even the shortest respite is denied to them and they are told that their torment is eternal because it was they who in this world said: how can man be made to rise up again after death?

Whole multitudes of men and Jinns are doomed to hell-fire. In no less than four verses God declares that He intends to fill Hell to utmost capacity. In two verses it is said that had God so willed, He could have guided everyone and united mankind in one nation, but He resolved to fill Hell with Jinns and men (verse 120 of Sura XI and verse 13 of Sura XXXII). Finally, according to verse 29 of Sura L, God asks Hell: 'Are you full, and Hell answers: are there any more?'

Paradise and the Blest

The believers, the virtuous, the devout, the martyrs, the repentant souls, those who have suffered in the cause of God and have emigrated from their homes will go, as Allah has promised, to Paradise as a reward for their deeds in this life. Upon their arrival in the other world, the record of their deeds is delivered into their right hand and they are conducted to Paradise. The gates of Paradise swing open on their arrival. The guardians of Paradise greet them and invite them and their spouses to enter Paradise joyfully. Here is their everlasting home to which death has no access. Paradise consists of gardens in which fountains gush forth and rivers flow interminably. Verse 15 of Sura XLVII says: 'Here is a representation of the Paradise which the righteous have been promised: there shall flow in it rivers of incorruptible water, rivers of milk for ever fresh, rivers of delectable wine and rivers of clearest honey.' Clusters of fruits whose season is not limited, specially dates, grapes and pomegranates, as also all that the soul of man could desire or the eye could delight in are there in abundance and within easy reach. Among the numerous descriptions of Paradise which are given in the Qur'an perhaps the most picturesque is that contained in 30 verses of Sura LVI. In the 'gardens of delight' the blest shall recline on jewelled green couches raised high in the shade of thornless lote-trees, with gushing fountains all around. Waiting on them will be youths of perpetual freshness bearing goblets, beakers and cups of purest wine that cause neither after-ache nor intoxication. They will be served fruits of their choice and flesh of fowls. Theirs shall be dark-eyed maidens, undefiled by man or jinn, chaste as well-guarded pearls. They shall hear no idle talk, no sinful speech; 'Peace, Peace' is all they shall hear.

Other delectable features of Paradise as well as blessings with which the faithful shall be rewarded are described elsewhere in the Qur'an. 'Thus', says verse LXXVI.22, 'you shall be rewarded; your high endeavours are gratifying to Allah.' The blest shall feel neither the scorching heat of the sun nor the biting cold of the nether regions. They will be clothed in green garments of fine silk and brocade, and adorned with bracelets of silver. Round about them will pass youths of un-diminishing freshness like pearls, bringing them a pure beverage seasoned with camphor and ginger, served in silver vessels and crystal goblets. The pure wine of which the righteous will drink is described again and more vividly: 'They shall drink of a pure wine, securely sealed, whose very dregs are musk (for this let all men emulously strive); a wine tempered with the waters of Fount Tasnim, a spring at which those nearest to Allah will refresh themselves' (LXXXIII.25–28).[10]

Rejoicing in the countless blessings conferred on them, the companions of Paradise will turn to speak to one another. 'One will say: I had a friend who used to ask: Do you really believe in Resurrection? "When we are dead and turned to dust and bones shall we be brought to judgement?" And he will say to those around him: "Come, let us look down." He will look down and see his friend in the midst of the Fire. "By the Lord," he will say, "you almost brought me to perdition. But for the grace of Allah I should certainly have been driven into Hell." '

Such has been described the everlasting abode of the righteous in the Hereafter; a habitation of peace and bliss which they will have inherited by reason of their faith and their good deeds in this life.

Purgatory

According to the Qur'an there is in the other world, in addition to Paradise and Hell, another place, referred to as 'the Heights', which is intermediate between the two. This place has not been clearly described, but it may be identified with Purgatory. Sura VII is entitled 'The Heights', but out of its 206 verses only 5 refer to the Heights.

But how are the Heights pictured in the Qur'an? They figure as a wall or barrier separating the blessed from the doomed, and across which the two groups address each other. But the Heights have their own dwellers, who are only described as 'men who would know every one by his distinctive marks'. There are thus three groups, each of which has something to say to the other.

The blessed ask the doomed: have God's words come true in your case as they have in ours? 'They have', answer the doomed, and thereupon a crier proclaims: 'The curse of God is on the wrongdoers and those who would hinder from the path of God.'

The doomed address the blessed in these words: 'Pour down to us water or anything that God provides for your sustenance.' The blessed reply: 'Both these things God has forbidden to those who reject Him.'

The dwellers of the Heights[11] turn, on the one side, to the blessed and greet them, and on the other to the doomed and utter these words: 'Of what profit to you were your hoards and your arrogant ways? Behold! Are these not the men whom you swore that God would never bless with His Mercy? See now, how they are invited to enter Paradise without fear and without grief.' The dwellers of the Heights, witnessing the torments of the doomed, implore God not to condemn them to the same fate.

Thus the Heights are a Purgatory between Paradise and Hell, in which there exist neither the blessings of the one nor the torments of the other. Its dwellers are souls whose deeds on earth have been such that the good in them is equal to the evil. God has placed them in the intermediate station, holding them in suspense so that when He will have sent the believers to Paradise and consigned the unbelievers to Hell, He will decide their fate.

Notes to Chapter Seven

1. The Arabic word translated as gloomy dungeon i 'sijn' meaning prison; it is differently interpreted as the seventh and lowest storey of Hell, where the record of the black deeds of sinners is kept by demons, or where sinners are confined pending judgement, or as the name of the Register in which black deeds are recorded. Just as the record of sinners is kept in the lowest place, so the record of the virtuous is kept in the highest place, which in contrast to the sijn is called the Illiyin (exalted place), this word being the Hebrew Eliyon or supreme God. Illiyin is interpreted either as a place name or as the name of the record of the righteous.

2. The eschatological scenario is portrayed in different verses of the Qur'an. Several verses (e.g. XXIII.103–106) indicate that upon the sounding of the Last Trump all creatures are gathered together, their deeds are weighed in the Balance, and the righteous are sent to Paradise and the wicked consigned to Hell forthwith. But according to one description, which has given rise to many interpretations, all must go to Hell at first, the separation of the righteous from the sinners occurring subsequently. The Qur'an, after reprimanding man for having forgotten that he was created out of nothing, relates how the eschatological scenery will unfold in accordance with a divine decree which is absolute. After all men and demons are assembled, Allah sets them on their knees around Hell. Then He drags out of each group the most rebellious towards God, for He knows best who merits to roast in hell-fire. But every one must pass through Hell at first: 'There is not one of you who shall not pass through the confines of Hell.' After this first arrival in Hell, Allah delivers those who fear Him and leaves the wicked to endure the torments of Hell on their knees (verses XIX.69–73).

3. An anecdote serves to illustrate the difference between Qada' and Qadar. It is related that once, when 'Umar, accompanied by a friend, was travelling to Damascus, he was informed that plague had broken out in that city. On hearing this news, he turned back. His friend said: 'O 'Umar, you are fleeing from Qada.' 'Umar replied: 'No, I am only fleeing from the Almighty's Qada' to His Qadar.'

4. In one English translation of the Qur'an (by Yusuf Ali) the Arabic words (different derivations from the root 'dalla') meaning 'to lead astray' or 'to cause to err' have been rendered by the words 'leaves to stray'. This translation is inaccurate and has obviously been adopted with a view to placing the blame for going astray on the human being concerned.

5. T. Izutsu, *God and Man in the Koran: Semantics of the Koranic Weltanschauung*, Tokyo, Keio Institute of Philological Studies, 1964, p. 142.

6. I. Goldziher, *Le dogme et la loi de l'Islam*, Paris, Geuthner 1973, pp. 70–1.

7. They started from the principle that man possesses an unlimited free will in his acts and is himself the creator of his actions; otherwise God would be unjust in holding him responsible.

8. Thus the Umayyad caliph Abdul Malik, having lured one of his rivals into his palace and assassinated him, threw his head into the middle of the crowd of the victim's followers and caused a public crier to announce: 'The commander of the Faithful has slain your chief as it had been ordained by eternal predestination and by God's inescapable Decree.'

9. Shii tradition attributes a saying to Imam Rida, the eighth Imam, on this

subject, which has the appearance of a solution He is reported to have said: 'Neither Necessity nor Free Will, but a thesis between the two theses.'

10. The nectar or celestial drink of the blest is the Beatific Wine which neither intoxicates nor confuses, and which is perfumed with musk and mixed now with camphor now with ginger at the three heavenly fountains named Tasnim (exalted), Kafur (camphor) and Salsabil.

11. There are different opinions as to the nature of the 'dwellers on the Heights'. The prevailing opinion is that they are angels or spiritually exalted beings, such as apostles and saints who look on from the Heights and greet the blest on their arrival in Heaven. Their description as men who would know everyone by his marks lends support to this opinion.

CHAPTER EIGHT

COMMANDMENTS

Religious Commandments

From the point of view of the Qur'an religious commandments and moral precepts are closely associated and complementary to each other: piety demands high morals, and high morals include piety. But to be deemed 'religious' in the strict sense one must hold certain beliefs and perform specific acts. One must believe in God, in His Prophets, in angels, in the Last Judgement and in the Holy Book. One must condemn any creed which attributes an associate or partner to God, must not commit any kind of blasphemy, profanation or sacrilege; must avoid 'idle tales' derogatory to religion, must fear God, must be constantly thankful for God's favours and bounties, not relaxing in this attitude at times of adversity, must obey unquestioningly the commandments of Allah and the Prophet, must recite the Qur'an, observe prayer, the fast, perform the pilgrimage with its accompanying rites, such as that of sacrifice, and must pay the mandatory alms (zakat). One must perform the ritual ablutions, must be always mindful of what is permitted and what is forbidden by the religious law. Outstanding examples of prohibited things are: dead meat, blood, flesh of swine or of any animal slaughtered in the name of a divinity other than Allah, wine and gambling (in the form most familiar to the Arabs, i.e. casting lots by means of arrows). Other injunctions are to avoid all kinds of sin, whether apparent or hidden, to repent promptly in the event of committing a prohibited act, to wear the veil (in the case of women), to prevent polytheists from entering holy places. On the subject of permitted and forbidden food there appears to be an inconsistency to which reference has already been made in Note 6 to Chapter Six. Flesh of swine is forbidden in four verses (II.168, IV.4, VI.146, XVI.116), but can be held to be allowed by logical inference from verse V.7, namely as being allowed to Christians (included in the term 'People of the Book').

The text of verse VI.154 shows clearly that religious commandments and moral injunctions are closely associated: 'Come, I will tell you what your Lord has prohibited you from. You shall serve no other gods besides Him, you shall show kindness to your parents, you shall not kill your children on a plea of want, for We provide sustenance for you and for them: you shall not commit shameful deeds whether openly or in secret; you shall not kill – for this is forbidden by Allah – except for just cause ... Do not tamper with the property of orphans except to improve it until they reach maturity; give just weight and full measure. We never charge a soul with more than it can bear. Speak for justice even if it affects your kinsmen. Be true to the covenant of Allah.'

The all-important commandment of fighting the infidels (jihad) is dealt with in a separate section of this book.

Prayer, Fasting and Pilgrimage

Prayer

A commandment which is addressed to the believer again and again in the Qur'an is that of praying regularly. The classical text of the Moslem prayer is the seven verses of the Opening Sura, accompanied by the four verses of Sura CXII, but there are many other passages which the believer may recite in praying, such as verses XVII.82, XXIII.118, III.191,192. The gist of all these passages is glorifying Allah, emphasising His Oneness and imploring for guidance, for the forgiveness of sins and for God's mercy on the Day of the Last Judgement. The timing of prayers is established from the wording of different verses to be: early morning, afternoon, late afternoon, dusk and night. The afternoon prayer (Middle Prayer) is especially dwelt on in verse II.239. Clear directions are given concerning ablutions to be performed preparatory to praying, and reference is made to the praying postures of genuflection and prostration. The wording of one passage is difficult to reconcile with the prohibition concerning wine. In verse II.216 (the drinking of) wine is referred to as a sin. In verses V.92 and 93 wine is mentioned as one of the abominations by which Satan seeks to hinder believers from praying. Verse IV.46 says: 'Believers, do not approach your prayers *when you are drunk* but wait till you can grasp the meaning of your words.' Thus the wine-drinker is not debarred from the sacrament of prayer, but is not allowed to pray until he returns to a sober state.

Ablution or self-purification preparatory to praying is a strict commandment (IV.46 and V.9). It consists of bathing the whole body in the case of sex pollution, washing after coming from offices of nature, and washing parts of the body, i.e. face, hands, feet and head in all cases. Where water cannot be easily found (as when travelling in the desert) fine clean sand or earth may be used instead.

Another prohibition in the context of prayer is contained in the passage of verse IV.46 which says: 'Do not approach prayer ... in the state of sexual impurity *except when passing on the way.*' Here it is obvious that the place of prayer (i.e. the mosque) is meant, and the explanation of the phrase 'when passing on the way' is the following: some believers lived in houses whose doors opened into the mosque and they were obliged to pass through the mosque on their way out. This embarrassed them greatly because they considered it an irreverence to enter the mosque while impure (on the way to the bath). The passage quoted from verse IV.46 set their mind at ease.

Prescriptions reminiscent of the early days of Islam, when the Moslem community lived in constant fear of attack from enemies, appear in verses IV.102 and 103. The formal prayer could be shortened when the believer was on a journey and in danger of being pursued by an enemy. And in the case of congregational prayer it was laid down that the congregation should be divided into two parties: at first one party prayed while the other kept watch, with its weapons ready for use; then the order was reversed, those holding the rear came forward to pray, while those who prayed first fell back to the line of defence.

Fasting

Fasting is one of the basic religious duties of Moslems, but the Qur'an deems it necessary to state that it is not an Islamic innovation, having been prescribed also in previous religions. The rules concerning it are contained in a few verses. The period prescribed is the whole month of Ramadan, 'in which the Qur'an was sent down'. Fasting, whose rationale is expressed to be to cultivate self-restraint, means abstaining from food, drink, and sexual intercourse from daybreak till sunset. Those who are unable to fast (for example, for reasons of old age) may substitute for it a charitable act, i.e. the feeding of an indigent person. Those who are prevented from fasting because of sickness or being on a journey must make up for the lost days when the impediment ceases.

In some cases fasting is prescribed by way of expiation for certain faults, i.e. involuntary homicide, hunting when wearing the pilgrim garb and breaking a solemn oath.

Pilgrimage

Pilgrimage to the Ka'ba (the House of Allah) and its sacred precincts is an act which was performed by pagan Arabs, together with its attendant ritual, from centuries before the rise of Islam. It was taken over almost bodily, developed and perpetuated by the Prophet, but with a fundamental difference. While in paganism the act was performed in honour of idols, the Prophet sanctified it as the cornerstone of the new cult of the One and Only Allah. The Qur'an lays it down as a religious duty of the Moslem to make the pilgrimage in the Greater form (Hajj) or the lesser ('Umra), the difference between the two consisting in the greater amplitude of the ritual of Hajj, and in the fact that it must be performed, as in ancient times, only in the sacred months, specifically in that of Dhu'l-Hijja, while in pagan times it could be fulfilled in any of the four sacred months of Dhu'l-Qa'da, Dhu'l-Hijja, Muharram and Rajab. The rites to be observed during the pilgrimage are referred to in the Qur'an as 'Symbols of Allah', and Moslems are commanded to respect their sanctity. These rites are mentioned only in part of the Qur'an:[1] 'Ihram' or the act of sacralisation by putting on the pilgrim's garment; injunctions to be observed throughout the period of pilgrimage, i.e. not to shave the head, not to indulge in obscenities, in wicked acts or in quarrelling, not to hunt; prescription of ritual acts to be performed, i.e. circumambulating the Ka'ba, praying at the Station of Abraham, proceeding to the nearby hills of Safa and Marwa,[2] visiting the hill of Arafat some 12 miles east of Mecca, attending a great sermon which is traditionally delivered at a place called the Sacred Monument, and offering animal sacrifice on the last day. It is recommended that the pilgrim should stay on for two or three additional days in order to commemorate Allah, as the pagans used to commemorate their ancestors. Finally the pilgrim desacralises himself by shaving his head and putting off the pilgrim's garment.

Sacrifice

The subject of sacrifice appears in the Qur'an principally in connection with the ritual of pilgrimage to the Holy Sanctuary of Islam. This ritual is a glorification of the role attributed in the Qur'an to Abraham as the precursor of Islam and to Abraham and Ismael as the first builders of the Sanctuary (II.121). The prominent feature of the Abraham/Ismael episode being the attempted sacrifice of Ismael by Abraham in obedience to a divinely-inspired dream and the divine intervention by which an animal was sacrificed in place of Ismael, a mythical repetition of the act of animal sacrifice becomes the keystone of the ritual of pilgrimage. The commandments concerning sacrifice are contained in a number of verses of the Qur'an and have been greatly developed by interpretation.

Upon donning the pilgrim's garb, and until the moment of desacralisation, the pilgrim binds himself to the performance of acts of sacrifice, whether or not he reaches his destination. Sacrifice is a duty prescribed in its own right, but it may also be a substitute for another part of the ritual which the pilgrim may have failed to observe. In one instance it serves as a penalty: when the pilgrim contravenes the commandment not to kill game he must offer as sacrifice a domestic beast equivalent to the one he has killed (V.96). The animals which may be sacrificed are cattle and camels; they must be designated as offering and led to the scene of performance of the ritual. There, after the name of Allah has been pronounced over them, they must be slaughtered and their flesh eaten or distributed to the needy (XXII. 29 *et seq.*).

The philosophy of sacrifice is not specifically stated in the Qur'an, but sacrifice is referred to as a 'divine symbol' (XXII.33 and 37) and as a means of attracting divine favour by testifying to man's piety: 'Their flesh and blood does not reach Allah; it is your piety that reaches Him' (XXII.38).

Apart from its connection with the ritual of pilgrimage, sacrifice has been mentioned in the Qur'an as a reproduction, somewhat modified, of two biblical episodes: the sacrifice offered by Abel and Cain, and the sacrifice of a heifer by the Israelites by order of Jehova transmitted by Moses (II.63 *et seq.*). Reference is also made to a misconception of the Israelites in rejecting the Prophet's mission. They argued that one who claims to be a prophet must produce an offering which will be accepted by God as shown by the descent of a flame from heaven which devours the offering (III.179).

In one instance Allah commands a specific person to offer sacrifice; the person is the Prophet himself, who is ordered to perform the act of sacrifice after praying, as an expression of his gratitude for the favours bestowed on him by Allah (Sura CVIII).

Purity

Great stress is laid in the Qur'an on purity, and the words used in this connection have both a physical and a spiritual meaning. When the Qur'an enjoins on believers to make and keep themselves pure and to avoid impurity little reflection is needed to read into the commandment purity of heart and mind, that of body being an outward sign of an inward state. This does not mean, however, that physical purity as such is not among the commandments. It forms the subject of verses V.8,9 and IV.46 although in the context of ritual ablution preparatory to praying, and not as a counsel of common cleanness.

In a passage prohibiting the Prophet from praying in a mosque which had been built by 'hypocrites', the Qur'an says that God loves those who make themselves pure (IX.109). Only the pure can touch the Book of God (LVI.78). Those who purify their souls are blessed, and those who corrupt them are doomed (XCI.9 and 10). God sends prophets to purify mankind (II.123,146, III.158). He purifies whom He wills (IV.52). He announces to Mary that he has purified her (III.37) and to the pious that they shall be awarded pure wine (LXXVI.21) and pure mates in Paradise (II.23, IV.60). The injunction addressed to the Prophet to purify his garment (LXXIV.4) has obviously a metaphorical sense.

The quality of 'pureness' is attributed to objects which are considered to be sacred, i.e. the leaves of the Qur'an (LXXX.14, XCVIII.2) and the abode of the pious in Paradise, and also to things ritually or legally permitted, such as food that may be eaten, booty taken in war, women that the believer may marry, and release from an obligation assumed on oath (LXVI.2).

Furthermore, things that promote man's virtue, safety or welfare are often called pure, such as fair words (XIV.29), a favourable wind (X.22), fertile land (VII.56), lawfully acquired goods (II.269), property of the impious taken and purified by the Prophet (IX.104).

Impurity in the moral sense is strongly reproved in the Qur'an. The words used for impurity, where applied to persons, denote in every case an absence of virtue and piety (XXIV.26); and, where applied to things, denote existence of qualities which repel either physically or morally. The godless, the sinner, the wicked are impure. Whatever falls within any conception of evil is impure (V.100, III.173). God's plan is to separate the pure from the impure and to 'pile all the impure [persons or things] into a heap to be consigned to Hell' (VIII.38). Evil words, like evil trees, are impure (XIV.31). Two terms used in the general context of evil (rijz and rujz) and usually translated as 'abomination' imply impurity but have no specific definition (LXXIV.5, IX.126, V.93). Worthless things (IV.2), barren soil (VII.56), bad produce of land (II.269) are impure.

Two terms which are translated as unclean do not imply physical impurity but have a distinctly ritual significance. 'Najes', used only once in verse IX.28, means unfit to participate in an act of worship; 'haram' means taboo or prohibited by religion, principally applied to food. This term also describes a sanctified state, as that of a person performing the rite of pilgrimage, when he is considered to be outside the world of profane existence, until he returns to normal life by putting off the pilgrim's garb.

Physical uncleanness as such is mentioned twice: that of women during periods of menstruation, referred to as a 'pollution' which makes women unapproachable (II.222); and that of men who 'come from offices of nature or who have been in contact with women' (V.9 and IV.46). Those conditions entail disabilities which terminate upon purification as prescribed.

Prohibition of Wine

The verses of the Qur'an containing references to wine do not appear to be self-consistent. Traditions describe the circumstances in which each verse was revealed varying a previous text. In establishing a final rule the authorities have had recourse to such traditions and to the doctrine of abrogation.

The four principal verses concerned are quoted below, in the chronological order which is generally recognised.

XVI.67: 'And (We give you) the fruits of the palms and the vines from which you obtain an intoxicant as well as wholesome food; surely in this is a sign for people who understand.'

II.219: 'They question you concerning wine and games of chance. Say: "In both are great sin and some uses for men. But the sin in them is greater than their usefulness."'

IV.46: 'O believers, do not approach prayer when you are intoxicated until you know what you are saying.'

V.90–91: 'O believers, wine, games of chance, idols and divining-arrows are a clear abomination and some of Satan's work. So avoid it! Perhaps you will then prosper. Satan desires only to precipitate enmity and hatred among you, with wine and games of chance and to bar you from the remembrance of God and from prayer. Will you then not desist?'

Of the above five verses, the first (XVI.67) was revealed in Mecca and the other form in Medina. The Meccan verse, far from prohibiting wine, praises the fruit of the vine from which the intoxicant beverage is extracted. According to tradition, some of the Prophet's companions, especially 'Umar, reflecting on the harmful effect of wine on the mind, asked the Prophet to give an opinion concerning it; thereupon was revealed Medinese verse II.219 which declares wine to be principally evil but occasionally also useful to man. There being no prohibition, the drinking of wine continued even in public. One day a notable believer (Abdul-Rahman Owf) invited some friends to his house, and the guests drank heavily and were still intoxicated when the time of prayer came. Then the person who led the prayer proceeded to quote verses from the Qur'an, but when reciting the verse (from Sura CIX) in which Allah tells the Prophet to say to the infidels 'I worship not that which you worship', he omitted the negative. When this was reported to the Prophet, verse IV.46 was revealed which prohibits believers from praying when under the influence of wine. However, this was of course no prohibition of drinking wine, but was rather prohibition of men from praying when intoxicated. Shortly afterwards there was another incident: the Prophet's uncle Hamza, having drunk wine at the house of a friend, came out, and seeing two camels which were loaded with some goods belonging to Ali, struck them with his sword and killed them. Ali complained to the Prophet, and then came the final strict prohibition of wine in verses V.90–91. According to tradition these verses gave full satisfaction to 'Umar who had persistently urged the Prophet to make pronouncements in condemnation of wine. In response to the final sentence of the verse: 'Will you then not desist?' 'Umar is reported to have said emphatically: 'We will desist.'

The Qur'an mentions also a wine other than the earthly beverage. Wine, which on earth is despised and prohibited, flows in rivers in Paradise, and is served to the faithful, who drink it with joy (XLVII.17). The righteous, reclining on jewelled couches, shall be waited upon by immortal youths who bring them cups of a pure wine which will not pain their heads or affect their reason (LVI.18). 'Their thirst will be slaked with a pure wine which is sealed with musk. To this wine let those aspire who aspire to happiness' (LXXXIII.25–28).

Fighting

The great expansion of Islam in the short time after its inception was largely due to the militant spirit of the new faith. A great many verses of the Qur'an enjoin on Moslems to take up arms against polytheists, unbelievers and hypocrites. The words used in expressing this commandment are 'Qital' (slaying, warfare) and 'Jihad' (going forth to fight in the holy war). This latter word is more typical as its original meaning is striving with might and main; and, as will be seen, the dedication of maximum effort to the holy undertaking characterises the commandment. Although the wording of one verse (II.186) implies that fighting is justified when the enemy has attacked first, this is by no means the general rule. Nor is there any substance in the argument which is sometimes advanced to the effect that Jihad should be understood primarily in the sense of moral endeavour and self-discipline in the cause of service to Islam, and only secondarily in that of holy war. The verses quoted below will show that the emphasis is distinctly on warring against non-believers with the object of propagating Islam, this being, by the express injunction of the Qur'an, one of the primary duties of Moslems.

'O Prophet, make war on the unbelievers and hypocrites and deal rigorously with them; their home shall be Hell . . .' (IX.73). 'O believers, fight the infidels who dwell around you, and deal rigorously with them' (IX.124). 'Do not yield to unbelievers, but strive against them in a strenuous Jihad' (XXV.54). 'Fight for the cause of Allah with the devotion due to Him' (XXII.77). 'Fight valiantly for His cause so that you may triumph' (V.39). 'Whether unarmed or well-equipped, march on and fight for the cause of Allah with your wealth and your persons' (IX.41). 'Fight in God's cause; you are accountable for none but yourself. Rouse the faithful . . .' (IV.86). 'Fight against them (the idolaters) until idolatry is no more and Allah's religion reigns supreme' (II.189 and VIII.40). 'Fighting is obligatory for you, and you dislike it. But you may dislike a thing although it is good for you, and love a thing although it is bad for you' (II.212). 'Allah loves those who fight for His cause in ranks as firm as a mighty edifice' (LXI.4). 'The true believers are those . . . who fight for His cause with their wealth and their persons' (XLIX.15). 'O Apostle, rouse the believers to the fight. If there are twenty amongst you, patient and persevering, they will vanquish two hundred; if a hundred, they will vanquish a thousand of the unbelievers' (VIII.67). 'When you meet the unbelievers, smite at their necks; at length when you have thoroughly subdued them, bind a bond firmly (on them), thereafter is the time either for generosity or for ransom until the war lays down its burdens' (XLVII.4).

In a number of verses the command to fight is supported by promise of rewards. 'Who is he that will loan to God a beautiful loan which God will double to their credit and multiply many times?' (II.245–246). 'Allah has given those that fight with their goods and their persons a higher rank than those who stay at home. He has promised all a good reward, but far richer is the recompense of those who fight for Him: rank of His own bestowal, forgiveness and mercy' (IV.97). 'Those who believe, suffer exile and strive with might and main in God's cause with their goods and their persons have the highest rank in the sight of God' (IX.20). 'Those who . . . fought in the path of God have the hope of the mercy of God . . .' (II.215). Those who fall on the battlefield in the course of holy war become martyrs. 'Those that . . . fought and died for My cause shall be forgiven their sins and admitted to gardens watered by running streams . . .' (III.194). 'Think not of those who are slain in God's way as dead; they are alive and well provided for by their Lord' (III.163 and II.149). 'As for those who are slain in the cause of Allah, He will not allow their works to perish . . . He will admit them to the Paradise He has made known to them' (XLVII.5).

Other verses show God's displeasure with those who shirk their duty of fighting. 'And how should you not fight in the cause of Allah and for the helpless . . . ?' (IV.77). 'Those who were left behind [in the Tobouk expedition] rejoiced in their inaction behind the back of the Apostle of God; they hated to strive and fight with their goods and their persons in the cause of God. They said, "do not go forth in the heat;" say, "the fire of Hell is fiercer in heat" ' (IX.81).

The above quotations are by no means exhaustive. Clearly the Qur'an makes it the inescapable duty of every Moslem to take part in fighting for the cause of God; only the blind, the lame and the sick are exempt (XLVIII.17).[3] Whoever disobeys this commandment or tries to compromise with the enemy is a 'hypocrite' and must be treated as an infidel. On the other hand whoever takes part in the fighting is not only promised the rewards of the Hereafter, but in addition receives here below a share of the booty taken.

Except for a few verses which are revealed with reference to particular events such as the battles of Badr and Uhud, all the texts concerning Qital and Jihad have a general import. The obligation to engage in holy warfare is meant to persist, in the words of the Qur'an cited above, until God's religion reigns supreme. Therefore if by God's religion is meant Islam in the specific sense, and if it is maintained that the commandments of the Qur'an go beyond the special circumstances and needs of the time of revelation, then it follows that the prescriptions concerning holy war place the Islamic community in a situation of potential hostility towards the non-Moslem world.

According to an ancient (pre-Islamic) custom of the Arab tribes, fighting was forbidden during four months of the year: these (Dhu'l-Qaʻda, Dhu'l-Hijja, Muharram and Rajab) were called the 'sacred months'. The Prophet confirmed and perpetuated this custom. Verse 36 of Sura IX says that God prescribed from the first that the year should contain twelve months and that four out of these should be treated as sacred. Therefore their sanctity must be respected and they should neither be added to nor reduced. Verse 5 of the same Sura says to believers that, once the sacred months are past, they must kill the pagans wherever found. The rule therefore is that the period of fighting is limited to eight months in the year. But an exception to this rule is laid down in verse 190 of Sura II: the law of talion applies even in cases protected by sanctity. Thus, although fighting is prohibited in holy places, yet if the pagans start war in such a place, the believers should fight back in that place also. Likewise if the pagans break the rule of sanctity of the four months, the believers too should fight them in those months. It is to confirm this rule that the verse quoted above says: 'If anyone transgresses against you, transgress likewise against him.' Verse 214 of the same Sura, referring to fighting in the sacred months, says: 'Fighting therein is a grave offence, but a graver offence in the sight of God is to prevent access to the path of God, to deny Him and to prevent access to the Holy Mosque and drive out its members; tumult and oppression are worse than slaughter.'

Emigration

God's approbation, love and munificence are promised to those who go forth to fight in His cause, and generally to those who emigrate, forsaking house and home for the sake of serving the true faith. All must emigrate, men, women and children, except, in the case of Jihad, those explicitly excused, i.e. the blind, the lame and the sick (XLVIII.17) and, in the case of non-fighters, women, children and those who suffer from a serious impediment (IV.97). God promises goodly rewards to all believers, but He distinguishes those who go forth to fight by a rank above those who sit at home (even if excused). Verses IX.20–21 say: 'Those who have believed, fled their homes and striven in the path of God with their wealth and their persons have the highest rank in the sight of God, and these are they who shall achieve salvation. The Lord shall give them glad tidings of Mercy from Himself, of His good pleasure, and of gardens wherein are lasting delights and in which they will dwell forever.' In explanation of the term 'a higher rank' commentators distinguish four ranks one above the other in the sight of Allah: being a Moslem, emigrating, taking part in Jihad, and being slain in it.

Verse IV.101 says: 'He who emigrates from his homeland in the cause of God shall find in the earth many a place of refuge, wide and spacious, and should he die emigrant, his reward from God shall be assured.' Even the hypocrites can redeem themselves by emigrating. Referring to them God says to the believers: 'Do not take friends from among them until they emigrate in the cause of God, but if they turn renegades seize them and slay them wherever you find them' (IV.91).

Thus the paramount commandment was that the believers must migrate from places where Islam was persecuted and proceed to places where they could join and strengthen the Moslem community. Those who failed in this duty would have to answer to the angels of death for their neglect, and when they would plead that they were oppressed in their homeland, the angels would reject their excuse, saying, 'Was not God's earth wide enough for you to migrate in it?' Reduced to silence, they would be consigned to Hell for not having emigrated when they could have done so (IV.99).

Two emigrations, a lesser and a greater, occurred in the Prophet's time. In 615 a number of believers left Mecca and sought refuge in the court of the Negus of Ethiopia in order, at least partly, to flee from the injury and insult which they suffered at the hands of the enemies of their faith. But this was a temporary and unimportant flight as compared to the epoch-making emigration to Medina in 622. Reference is made in Sura LIX to the condition of the emigrants to Medina (Muhajirun) in the context of their need for help, having been driven away from their homes in Mecca. A special share is allotted to them in the distribution of the booty taken from the Jewish tribe of Banu-Nadhir in 625. At the same time the Medinese believers (Ansar or Helpers) are extolled for giving them shelter in their homes and for not grudging them the favoured treatment which they received in the distribution of the spoils (LIX.8–9). Verse VIII.73 says: 'Those who have believed and have fled their homes and fought for the cause of God with their wealth and their persons, as well as those who gave them asylum and aid, these are protectors one of another. As to those who have believed but have not fled their homes, you owe no duty of protection to them until they too leave their homes, but if they seek your aid in religion, it is your duty to help them except against a people with whom you have a treaty of mutual assistance.'

In a number of other verses the Qur'an assures the emigrants from Mecca on the one hand and their hosts and helpers in Medina on the other, of Allah's bounty and of the everlasting bliss which shall be theirs in Paradise (II.215, III.194, VIII.75–76, XVI.43–112).

Booty

After the establishment of the Moslem community in Mecca, the wars with the Meccans and the raids on Bedouin and Jewish tribes which ensued resulted in the capture of spoils which proved an important resource for the sustenance of the community.

The taking of booty was the primary objective in the case of raids on caravans and tribes, and it was the result in the case of Jihad or holy war. The importance of booty as a means of attracting people to the new faith or of maintaining their allegiance has been mentioned in historical accounts.

From the general tenor of the verses relating to the spoils of war it may be inferred that the motive of the Arab bedouin who took part in the wars and the raids was often the expectation of a share in the trophy (captives, land, buildings, goods). Verses 145 and 146 of Sura III contain an implicit reproach addressed to some of those who fought for the Prophet at Uhud, for having shown themselves over-hasty in capturing booty. That the Prophet was well aware of the special attraction that capture of booty had for some of his followers is clear from the fact that their zeal was strengthened by promises of abundant spoils. Verse XLVIII.19–20 says: 'Allah rewarded them with a speedy victory and with the many spoils which they have taken ... Allah has promised you rich booty and has given you this [the spoils taken at Khaibar] with all promptness.'

The phrase 'abundant spoils' occurs also in another verse in the sense of rewards that Allah will bestow in heaven on believers who refrain from taking improper spoils on earth. The Prophet, fearing that those who went forth to combat for his cause might be over-hasty in treating as unbelievers those who made friendly overtures to them, so as to have an excuse for dispossessing them of their belongings, says: 'With Allah there are abundant spoils.'

In one case clear reference is made to the fact that the prospect of taking booty could be the sole motive of men who took part in expeditions. As stated in the section headed Some Historical Events in Chapter 5, when in 628 the Prophet was preparing to go on pilgrimage to Mecca, some of his followers stayed behind because there was no prospect of plunder. Referring to these, the Qur'an says (XLVIII.15): 'Those who lagged behind will say, "When you are free to march and take booty, permit us to follow you ..." Say, 'You shall not follow us." '

The first occasion on which a Moslem army took booty was at the battle of Badr (AD 624). The spoils taken then are reported to have been very considerable, consisting of camels, horses, equipage, armour, vestments, carpets and articles of fine leather. A serious dispute arose in the camp concerning the distribution of the spoils since the men who had remained behind the front line to serve the Prophet and protect the camp maintained that they were entitled to an equal share with those who had been actually on the field of battle. The dispute was settled by a divine revelation. It decreed that the entire trophy belonged to God and the Prophet. Verse 1 of Sura VIII ('The Booty') says to the Prophet: 'They ask you about the spoils. Say, "The spoils belong to Allah and the apostle; therefore have fear of Allah and end your disputes." ' Later on in the Sura (verse 42) the manner of disposal of the spoils is prescribed as follows: one-fifth is assigned to Allah, the Prophet, the Prophet's kinsfolk, orphans, the needy and the wayfarers. It was understood that the remaining four-fifths would be for distribution among the forces according to the Prophet's discretion.

The Sura in question also contains a reference to the taking of captives in the wars. Verse 68 says: 'It is not fitting for a prophet to take captives until he has thoroughly subdued the land.' The following explanation has been suggested for this not very clear pronouncement: in the course of the battle of Badr the Moslems took a large number of captives, some of whom were set free against ransom without the Prophet's permission. The Prophet considered this a premature and unwarranted act but in the circumstances it was legitimised by a special revelation. Verses 69 and 70 say: 'Had there not been a previous sanction from Allah you would have been sternly punished for what you have taken . . . But now enjoy what you took in war, lawful and good.'

As already mentioned, the rules concerning the distribution of booty were laid down on the occasion of the battle of Badr. But the dissatisfaction which arose among the troops concerning the disposal of booty did not end there. It continued below the surface, showed itself fitfully from time to time and finally burst aflame on the occasion of the distribution of the spoils taken at Hunain (AD 630) when the objectors went so far as to slander the Prophet.[4] 'There are some among you', says verse IX.58 addressing the Prophet, 'who blame you concerning the distribution of alms. If a share is given to them they are contented, but if they receive nothing they are indignant.' On this occasion a fuller description was given of the use which should be made, at the Prophet's discretion, of the spoils and alms. The beneficiaries were stated to be the poor, the needy, the wayfarers, the collectors of the alms, and the new converts to Islam. Part of the funds was also to be spent for ransoming prisoners, assisting debtors and generally serving the cause of Allah.

Morality and Social Behaviour

The conception of Islamic morality as reflected in the Qur'an is very similar to the principles underlying the code of ethics of any well-organised community. The specific rules laid down fall within the universally respected headings of conscience, virtue, honour, loyalty, and the sense of duty and responsibility.

Moral injunctions, namely what a Moslem should or should not do, figure throughout the Qur'an in various contexts, sometimes incidentally but always with emphasis. Extracted from those contexts, the moral qualities which a Moslem is required to possess are the following:

Doing good, avoiding evil, enjoining what is right and forbidding what is wrong, truthfulness and condemnation of falsehood, moderation and avoidance of excess in all things, justice, gentleness in speech, avoidance of evil language and defamation, readiness to forgive, avoidance of haughtiness and self-conceit, patience, restraint and reserve, non-violence, readiness to act as mediator and peace-maker, faithfulness, loyalty, generosity, dutifulness towards parents, good neighbourliness and fellowship with all, chastity, fulfilment of vows, avoidance of perjury. The highest quality is that of virtue. Verse XLIX.13 says 'The most honoured of you in the sight of God is the most virtuous amongst you.'

The subject of taking oaths as a guarantee of statements and promises solemnly made is treated in several verses. Oaths deliberately taken must be fulfilled (V.91), but believers are commanded not to make them an excuse for failing to do good or to act rightly (II.224). They are specifically commanded not to disable themselves by oath from assisting their kinsmen and other needy persons (XXIV.22). A person who has bound himself by oath but subsequently changes his mind may release himself from it by an act of expiation which consists of feeding ten indigent persons or freeing a slave or, if he is unable to do either, by fasting for three days (V.91). The Prophet himself was reminded of the availability of the remedy of expiation (in respect of an oath which he had taken in his relations with his wives) in verse LXVI.2. The Qur'an abrogated the oath called Ila' by which an Arab husband could forbid himself indefinitely from approaching his wife, but without divorcing her, and ruled that if within four months the husband did not go back on his oath the woman would be regarded as divorced (II.226–227). Thoughtless, vain oaths, such as unintentional swearing in ordinary conversation, are pronounced ineffective, and God overlooks them, although it has been held that they should be expiated by an act of charity. To treat oaths lightly, i.e. to take God's name in vain, is a sin. Those who swear falsely are strongly condemned by the Qur'an, which includes in the category of virtual outcasts 'the wretch of many oaths' (LXVIII.10).

Superstitions and sorcery are severely reproved. A few verses refer to superstitious practices and witchcraft and strongly deprecate them. Thus in the context of superstitious beliefs certain forms of dedication of camels to heathen gods, and customs by which animals were treated as taboo and their use as carriers or food was prohibited, are mentioned only to be ridiculed and condemned (V.102, VI.139). One superstitious act is specially forbidden. Verse II.185 reproves the pagan habit of entering one's home from the back on returning from a pilgrimage, and enjoins that entry must be made through the proper doors.

In the context of superstitions reference should be made to one verse which is often invoked in support of the belief in the influence of the evil eye. It was commonly believed in the Prophet's time, as it is even today, that if one admires or wonders at the excellence of any object without remembering that God alone is its giver and sustainer, some harm will inevitably occur to that object. And accordingly it was and is considered necessary, in order to protect the object, that such thought or word should be accompanied by an incantation which could neutralise the effect of the spell cast on it. It is due to this primitive reasoning that commentators generally give as one (and usually as the more probable) interpretation of verse LXVIII.51 that it contains a remedy against the evil eye.[5] The verse, addressing the Prophet, says: 'The unbelievers would almost strike you down with their eyes on hearing the Message recited, and they say "Surely he is possessed." ' But this statement does not necessarily mean that there was a power of enchantment in the unbelievers' stare; taken figuratively it can be construed to mean that the bitterness in their hostile stare would have unsteadied a less stable man. However, it is also stated elsewhere that failure to remember God as the true donor of one's possessions causes God's scourge to fall upon them (XVIII.37 and 40).

Reprobation of sorcery follows from a reference to the Babylonians' harmful practice of the secret art presumed to have been taught by two fallen angels, (II.102) as also from the fact that the Prophet takes refuge with God against the mischief done by witches through the magical practice of blowing on knots (CXIII.4).

A number of rules of social behaviour appear in certain verses. A Moslem should not enter the house of another without leave. A Moslem must salute others and respond to their greeting with courtesy; rules of decorum must be observed in the company of others, such as making room in public gatherings for new arrivals, and departing when ordered by the host to depart. Whispering is improper; the rules prescribed as to when and how servants and children may enter the presence of their master or mistress must be respected. Special directions are given as to how the Prophet may be approached. When the Prophet summoned anyone to his presence for consultation on a matter of public interest, he had to appear and was not allowed to depart without the Prophet's leave. Allah authorised the Prophet to give such leave, but commanded him to implore for the forgiveness of the person who asked for leave, because to ask for leave implied some measure of defection in duty. Anyone who slipped away surreptitiously would meet with punishment in this life or in the next (XXIV.62–63). Finally, women were required to observe certain strict rules concerning clothes, ornaments and attitude towards men as described below.

Verse XXIV.31 commands believing women to lower their gaze, guard their chastity, cover their ornaments except such as are normally displayed, draw their veils over their bosoms and hide their finery from all except their husbands, their father, their husbands' fathers, their sons, their step-sons, their brothers, their brothers' sons, their sisters' sons, their women-servants, their slaves, their male attendants who are free from physical needs, and children who have no carnal knowledge of women. When walking they must not stamp their feet so as to draw attention to their hidden ornaments.

Verses 57 *et seq.* of Sura XXIV contain prescriptions which prohibit servants and children from entering, without leave, the presence of women (or men) when they are undressed, at given times (before morning prayer, at midday and after the evening prayer). But one kind of woman may be intruded upon without leave when she has taken off her outer garment, i.e. a woman who is past the prospect of marriage, provided that she does not make a wanton display of her ornaments, but in this case also it is better to observe modesty.

The wives and daughters of the Prophet, and in general all believing women are commanded to cast their outer garments over their persons in order that they may be recognised as such and not molested.

One late Medinese Sura (XLIX) consists throughout of social and moral exhortation. Believers must, on pain of forfeiting Allah's favours, refrain from behaving presumptuously in the Prophet's presence, raising their voices above his, or addressing him from outside his apartments. They must avoid listening to idle talk and rumour, mocking, defaming, nicknaming, backbiting, spying on or unduly suspecting one another. They must try to make peace between warring factions among the faithful, and must cultivate mutual acquaintance and understanding with their fellow beings. They must act on sincere faith and not merely offer lip service. It is interesting to note that none of the 18 verses of the Sura is the expression of an abstract principle; they are all related to concrete incidents and situations. These have been described in detail in the Commentaries. A few examples may be given. Firstly, the commandment that believers must lower their voices in the presence of the Prophet resulted from an incident in which Abu Bakr and 'Umar, disputing about the appointment of a governor in the Prophet's presence, became too vociferous. Secondly, the rule that believers must not mock one another was enunciated when Safiah, one of the Prophet's wives, complained that women addressed her as 'O you Jewess!' Thirdly, the disparagement of lip service had its origin in the professions of faith which were made by the Arab Bedouins, and which were not sincere, but were politically motivated, as was shown by the numerous apostasies which occurred after the Prophet's death. An instance can also be cited in connection with verse V.101 which contains the following injunction: 'Do not ask about anything which if made known to you would only pain you.' The occasion for this pronouncement is reported to have arisen when someone asked the Prophet, 'Where shall I be in the world to come,' and the Prophet answered, 'You will be in Hell.' Another explanation of this injunction appears in a tradition in which the Prophet advises the believers not to ask about anything which is not prohibited lest it might come to be prohibited because of the asking (*Kashf al-asrar*, vol. III, page 246).

In another Sura (XXV.64–74) a series of precepts, formulated in the abstract, appear consecutively, setting forth the qualities which will procure for those who possess them and patiently persevere in them the reward of being admitted to the highest place in heaven. These are: modesty and dignity of deportment, courtesy even towards opponents, unceasing adoration of Allah, beseeching Allah, by constant prayer, to save one from the torments of Hell, observance of the golden mean in spending, avoidance of idolatry, unlawful killing and fornication, truthfulness in bearing witness, veneration of Allah's revelations, and leading a life which may be a model for all those who fear God.

Evil talk of any kind is displeasing to Allah, and this is not confined to defamation, which is specifically condemned in Suras LXVIII and CIV. It also covers any mention in public of evil words spoken or evil acts committed by anyone, except where the victim of such speech or action speaks by way of complaint seeking redress, or even pronounces a curse against a wrongdoer. 'Allah does not love', says verse IV.147, 'that evil should be divulged in open speech except by one who has been wronged.' That recourse to abusive language is condemned by Qur'anic morality finds emphasis in the fact that verse VI.106 prohibits it even against idols.

With reference to misdeeds a special treatment is reserved for the three crimes of idolatry, homicide and fornication as specially detestable. On the one hand emphasis is laid on the punishment which the sinner will incur in this life and the double and everlasting penalty which will be inflicted on him on Judgement Day; and on the other there follows a saving clause by which the sinner, on repenting, will not only be forgiven, but will find his sins *converted into good deeds* (verse XXV.70). Thus is exalted the virtue of repentance, even at the risk of the possible cynical interpretation that the sinner, relying on the promised transformation, may be encouraged to increase the number of his sins in order proportionately to add to the number of his meritorious good deeds by virtue of his repentance.

In two important respects there is a contradiction which cannot be removed by recourse to interpretation. The attitude of Moslems towards the followers of other religions can be both tolerant and intolerant. This question has been discussed in the section on Attitude towards other Religions in Chapter 6. Secondly, the Moslem is told both to meet evil with evil and to return good for evil. Requiting evil with good is commended in verses XXVIII.54 and XXIII.98, but a contrary injunction is given three times. Verse X.27 says: 'Evil shall be rewarded with like evil.' 'Let evil be rewarded with evil,' says verse XLII.38. A similar rule is laid down in XVI.127. The law of talion, as explained in another Section, authorises the taking of vengeance or retaliation. In confirmation of this principle, verse XXII.59 says that he who repays an injury in kind is protected by Allah from being wronged by anyone for having caused injury to another. Verse II.190 says: 'If anyone attacks you, attack him as he attacked you.'

Usury

Verse 125 of Sura III forbids usury 'doubled and multiplied'. Verse 276 of Sura II says of usurers that they are confounded by Satan because they place usury on the same footing as trade, whereas God has permitted trade and forbidden usury. Whoever disobeys this commandment is doomed to hell-fire. God's blessing is denied to usury; therefore creditors must renounce part of their claim which consists of usury. If they do not they will be at war with Allah and His Apostle, but if they repent they may retain the capital sums they have laid out, suffering no loss and causing none. Furthermore, creditors must grant respites to debtors who are in difficulty, but it would be better for them to waive their claim altogether as an act of charity.

The word for the prohibited practice, translated as 'usury', is Riba (literally an increase or addition) which means both usury and interest, so that what is prohibited is not only lending at a usurious or excessive rate of interest, but lending on the understanding that the borrower will repay the loan plus something added thereto, however slight its value. It cannot, however, be inferred that the Qur'an condemns unconditionally the concept of giving in the expectation of receiving more than what is given. Indeed such transaction, strongly forbidden in the relations between man and man, is recommended, or even commanded, as between man and God. Verse LVII.11 says: 'Who will give a generous loan to Allah? He will repay him back twofold and he will receive (besides) a rich reward.' Verse LXIV.17 says: 'If you give a generous loan to Allah He will pay you back twofold and will grant you forgiveness.' The phrase 'multiplying many times' which occurs in the verse prohibiting usury, is also used in encouraging believers to lend to Allah. Verse II.246 says: 'Who will give Allah a generous loan? He will double it to his credit and multiply it many times.' The meaning of lending to Allah may be deduced from the wording of verse LXI.10 which says: 'O believers, shall I lead you to a bargain that will save you from a grievous penalty? . . . It is that you strive your utmost in the cause of God with your property and your person.'

Civil Law Matters

Part of the commandments of the Qur'an relate to matters of civil law, in regard to some of which rules are given at some length, while in regard to others only a few words have been said. In this book special sections are devoted to some of these subjects, i.e. marriage, divorce, succession and slavery. On other subjects of less extensive scope the Qur'an addresses to believers words of wisdom, admonition and guidance amounting generally to mandatory injunctions. A summary of these is given below.

Property

The right to acquire and own property is recognised equally for men and women, but the right to dispose of property is subject to strict conditions. Property must not be consumed in vanities; the owner must be neither extravagant nor niggardly in spending, but must observe a just balance between these extremes (XXV.67 and XVII.29); greed and avarice count as sins, and so do the inordinate pursuit of riches and the accumulation and hoarding of goods (LXX.18 and CIV.2); spending out of one's property on charity 'by night and by day, in secret and in public' is highly praised (II.274) but making a display thereof or humiliating the recipient in any way is condemned (II.266); dedication of wealth to the furtherance of God's cause is required of every Moslem as explained in the section on Fighting. These injunctions are not supported by any enforceable sanctions, but they follow from the supreme law that everything belongs to God, and that the owner's right is that of a trustee who can only dispose of his wealth in accordance with God's commandments and who must render an account of all his actions to God.

Commercial transactions

The use of property in enterprises of traffic and trade is particularly recommended on condition of reciprocity of benefit. When a contract is made for a transaction, big or small, involving future obligations, it must be put in writing and evidenced by two male witnesses.[6] If the party who is rendered liable is under any disability, he must be aided by a guardian. The scribe called upon to write down the deed must not refuse to do so, nor must the persons who have witnessed the deed refuse to give evidence when required. In the case of a bargain made 'on the spot', however, there is no need to observe the formalities described. Where a scribe cannot be found (as where the parties are on a journey) a pledge must be given.

The supreme transaction involving man's person and possessions is that which takes place between God and man, in which God purchases from him his person and his goods in exchange for eternal bliss. The Qur'an pledges its word as well as that of the Old and New Testaments to assure the believers that God will abide by His promises (IX.122). Verse XXXV.26 says that those who recite the Book of God, establish regular prayer and spend in charity secretly and openly engage in a trade that never fails. In the same vein verses LXI.10–11 show the believers the way to a bargain which will save them from perdition: 'You shall believe in God and His Apostle, and strive in the cause of God with your property and your persons.' Acts of charity and participation in Jihad are called loans that are given to Allah, which are liberally rewarded.

Honest dealing

The Qur'an lays emphasis on just dealing, by specifying the principle of giving full measure and weight. He who violates this rule incurs God's wrath. 'Woe to the unjust who when others measure for them exact in full, but when they measure or weigh for others defraud them' (LXXXIII.1). The commandment to give just measure and weight is also expressed, together with other religious and moral prescriptions, in verse VI.153. Fulfilment of vows and loyalty to pacts and promises are religious duties. Verses LXX.32, XXIII.8 and LXXVI.7 count among the blest all those who perform their vows and are faithful to their contracts and covenants. Verses XVI.92 *et seq.* liken those who break their vows to a woman who untwists the yarn which she has laboriously spun.

Testimony

Testimony is a subject which occurs frequently in the Qur'an, as much in relation to declaration of faith (I witness that Allah is one) as in connection with the giving of evidence in civil and criminal cases. The value of testimony as the surest means of distinguishing truth from falsehood or the most reliable guarantee of performance of obligations results from its sacred character. Even Allah himself appears in the Qur'an both as 'taker' and as 'giver' of testimony. He takes the testimony of the future generations of the human race binding themselves to eternal worship of Allah (VII.171). He bears witness to hypocrites being liars (LXIII.1). In verse VI.19 God commands the Prophet to say: 'God is witness between me and you.' Even the emanation of the Qur'an from Allah needs the probative support of testimony and such testimony is given by Allah Himself and by the angels (IV.164). Testimony plays an important role in the proceedings of the Last Judgement, when not only the register of the deeds of each person, but also his very skin and limbs bear witness against him, as do also the very false gods whom he worshipped on earth. As for the use of testimony in the transactions of the world, certain rules are prescribed in the Qur'an in respect of the accusation of adultery, as has been explained in another section. The need for testimony also arises in connection with wills, commercial transactions and divorce. The giving of true evidence is a religious duty, and 'to hide the evidence before God' is a sin (V.105).

Association

Association and partnership being tokens of good fellowship and understanding, as well as means of promoting business interests, are permitted and encouraged among believers, but a number of verses point to the view that this approval does not extend to relations between believers and non-believers. Indeed the formation of friend-ship between Moslems and unbelievers is expressly discouraged. Mar-riage is not permitted between a Moslem and a polytheist (II.220). Verse III.27 says that believers who make friends with infidels (except in self-defence or by way of precaution) have nothing to hope for from Allah. Verse IV.138 reproaches those who choose unbelievers rather than the faithful for friends. In verse 143 of the same Sura believers are warned against making friends with non-believers: 'Would you give Allah a clear proof against yourselves?' Verse IX.23 says: 'Believers, do not befriend your fathers or your brothers if they choose unbelief in preference to faith.' Consequently if friendly association with even one's father and brother (if not a believer) is forbidden, a fortiori any association with an unbeliever should be regarded as disallowed. Verse V.56 applies the prohibition even in the case of People of the Book if they exhibit an attitude of disrespect towards Islam.

Oaths and Imprecations

A considerable number of verses of the Qur'an are, or refer to, vows, oaths and imprecations. Oaths and imprecations uttered by Allah have already been described in a special section in which it has been pointed out that these words in their common acceptation are not properly applicable to Allah's utterances, for they both mean appeal to a supernatural being. When God swears or curses, He appeals to no power beyond Himself, but pronounces a self-sufficient fiat or doom. Such declarations abound in the Qur'an. Apart from oaths to the number of 81, Allah frequently utters curses, a few examples of which may be given: 'God has cursed the unbelievers and prepared for them a Blazing Fire' (XXXIII.64); 'God's curse is on them for their blasphemy' (II.82); 'We cursed the Sabbath-breakers' (IV.50); 'Those whom God has cursed, He has made them deaf and blinded their sight' (XLVII.25); 'The wrath of God is on them (the hypocrites), He has cursed them and got Hell ready for them' (XLVII.6); 'For them is the curse of God and an enduring torment' (IX.69); 'Those who incurred God's curse and wrath, He transformed some of them into apes and swine' (V.65).

Prescriptions are given in the Qur'an concerning vows, oaths and imprecations in the context of man's actions. The fundamental, unbreakable vow that man must take on pain of eternal doom is that of worshipping the one and only God. The taking of this vow, expressed in the phrase 'making one's faith pure for Him alone' is a commandment which figures throughout the Qur'an. Verse XXXIX.14 addresses the Prophet in these words: 'Say: I am commanded to serve Allah, making my faith pure for Him.' Among numerous verses enjoining such self-dedication are XL.14 and 67.

Vain and inconsiderate oaths are treated as void and of no effect, and God does not call to account the breaker of such oaths (V.91). But an oath deliberately and solemnly taken must be kept unless its effect is to prevent the doing of a good deed (II.224). An oath taken in support of a vow to abstain from one's wife (not by way of divorce) is binding, but may be dissolved by an act of expiation (such as freeing a slave), as happened in the case of the Prophet (LXVI.2). But such a vow if intended as pseudo-divorce (as in the pronouncement of Zihar and Ila', explained in the section on Divorce) shall be void although its infringement entails the necessity of expiation (LVIII.4–5).

The curse, i.e. the expression of a wish that harm should befall a certain person or thing, was considered by the Jahili Arabs as having a magical effect, but Islam changed it to a conception of prayer or entreaty addressed to God to inflict such harm. But a curse was not always a wish that harm should befall another; it also took the form of self-imprecation. A person who was accused of a guilty act and wished to prove his innocence could clear himself, in a judicial proceeding, by taking an oath of innocence, combined with a curse calling down the wrath of God upon himself if he should be lying.

This procedural device led to the practice of mutual imprecation between plaintiff and defendant. The practice by which each party asserted his innocence and uttered a curse against himself if he should be lying, found a specific application in the case of accusation of adultery by a husband against his wife, as explained in the paragraph on Adultery.

An instance of proposed mutual imprecation is mentioned in the Qur'an. In the year 632 a dispute arose between the Prophet and a Christian delegation from Najran (Yemen) concerning the true position of Jesus. The two parties agreed on the following means of settling the dispute, as quoted in verse III.54: 'Come, let us gather together, our sons and your sons, our women and your women, ourselves and yourselves; then let us earnestly pray and invoke the curse of God on those who lie.' However, tradition reports that the Christian delegation withdrew before the time fixed for the mutual imprecation.

Inheritance

The Qur'an contains rules concerning wills and the leaving of legacies to parents and relatives. When death approaches, those who have property to leave must make a bequest to parents and next of kin in accordance with reasonable usage. This general directive is given in Sura II (verses 176–178), but in a later Sura (Sura IV.7 *et seq.*) definite shares are laid down for the heirs, as described below.

A person making bequests must take two just witnesses from among his own people, or if he is on a journey, from among other people. If he doubts the word of the persons he chooses, he must make them take a solemn oath of fidelity. A person who after having heard a bequest changes it commits a crime, but if he discovers that the testator has in some way been unjust in ordering his bequests (such as by being unduly partial to one heir or by depriving a lawful creditor) he may intervene in order to bring about a satisfactory arrangement between the parties.

The Qur'anic provisions do not, by themselves, constitute a complete body of rules on testamentary disposition. They deal with the subject in broad outline, leaving gaps which have had to be filled by jurists on the basis of interpretation and analogy as well as the practice of the Prophet and his companions. The intention in this section is not to describe the whole system as thus developed, but only to quote the prescriptions contained in the Qur'an. However, one point which is essential to the understanding of the whole subject is that the jurists have held that the power of testamentary disposition is limited to one-third of the estate. The disposal of the rest is subject to mandatory rules.

The express rules laid down in the Qur'an regarding the division of the deceased's estate are the following, being the substance of verses IV.9,12–15,175.

Men as well as women are entitled to a share in what their parents and kinsmen leave.

If at the time of the division non-beneficiary relatives, or orphans or needy persons are present, they should be given a share of the estate, and should be treated with kindness.

The expenses of the maintenance of the widow together with residence for one year are a charge on the estate.

The male heir shall inherit twice as much as the female. If there are only daughters: if one daughter, her share is half the estate; if two or more, their share is two-thirds.

If the deceased leaves children, one-sixth of the estate goes to each of the parents. If he leaves no child and the parents are the only heirs, the mother's share in the estate is one-third. If the deceased has left brothers or sisters, the mother's share is one-sixth. In all cases distribution is made after payment of legacies and debts.

Where the deceased is a woman and she leaves no child, half the estate goes to the husband; if she leaves a child the husband takes one-fourth.

Where the husband dies leaving no child, the widow gets one-fourth of the estate; if he leaves a child she takes one-eighth.

Where the deceased, man or woman, has left neither children nor parents but has a brother or a sister, if there are two of them each takes one-sixth; if more than two they share one-third of the estate between them.

If the deceased is a man who has neither ascendants nor descendants but leaves a sister, the sister takes half the estate; if two sisters they share two-thirds of the estate between them.

If the deceased is a woman who leaves no parents or children, but has a brother he will be the sole inheritor. If there are two sisters, they shall have two-thirds of the estate, but if there are sisters and brothers they shall share the estate, the male taking twice the portion of the female.

An instance of abrogation occurs in the Qur'anic provisions concerning inheritance, related to the emigration from Mecca to Medina. Following that event the Qur'an penalised the Meccan believers who had not emigrated. Addressing the community of believers in Medina, it absolved them of any obligation resulting from kinship with the non-emigrants. 'As to those who believed but did not emigrate, they shall have no rights of kindred with you until they too emigrate'

(VIII.73). At the same time the same verse created a constructive bond of kinship between the Meccan emigrants and the Medinese helpers. Thus the Muhajirun and the Ansar became heirs to one another exclusive of the deceased's natural kindred (such relationship by fiction having existed in Arab society from ancient times). The obligation towards such contractual heirs was stipulated in verse IV.37: 'To those also to whom your right hand was pledged give them their due portion.' But these rules were abrogated subsequently when the community was solidly established in Medina and relations were resumed with the believers left behind in Mecca. 'Blood relations', says verse XXXIII.6, 'among each other have closer personal ties in the Decree of God than the brotherhood of ["Ansar"] believers and "Muhajirs" '.

Women Mentioned in the Qur'an

A few women, historical or legendary, have been mentioned in the Qur'an in different contexts. A lengthy account is given of the Queen of Sheba and of the woman enamoured of Joseph. Brief references are made to Abraham's wife, to the mother and sister of Moses, to Zachariah's wife and to Mary's mother. Some verses relate to certain of the Prophet's wives without mentioning them by name (e.g. Ayesha, Hafsa, Mary the Copt and Zainab). These allusions have all been described (some – as in the case of the Prophet's wives – in detail) elsewhere in this book. There remain a few instances which are explained in the following paragraphs.

The wives of Noah and Lot

These two women are mentioned in Sura LXVI as false wives of righteous husbands. They were doomed to hell-fire, and the fact that their husbands were among the elect of God did not stand in the way of their punishment. The nature of their misdeeds is not specified, but commentators suggest that Noah's wife endeavoured to persuade the people that her husband was distracted; and Lot's wife was in league with the corrupt men of Sodom, her husband's enemies. The mention of these women's fate, appearing in the Sura which relates the Prophet's grievance against two of his wives, was obviously intended to convey a lesson and a warning: those who swerve from the straight path should expect no mitigation of their punishment on account of their kinship with the Prophet or close relationship with believers.

The wife of Pharaoh

As an antithesis to the case of the two women just mentioned, the same Sura cites that of the virtuous wife of a miscreant, namely Pharaoh's wife who, averse to the impiety and worldly grandeur of her husband, prayed to God to save her from him and to 'build her a mansion in Paradise in nearness to Himself'. Coupled with the example of this virtuous woman is that of Mary, mother of Christ, the Sura thus contrasting the case of two pious women who were blest in the Hereafter with that of two impious women who were doomed to eternal damnation.

The wife of Abu Lahab

A bitter curse is pronounced in Sura CXI on the wife of the Prophet's uncle Abu Lahab, an enemy of the prophet and a relentless opponent of the new religion. The curse, uttered primarily against the husband, extends also to the wife, who 'carries a twisted cord of palm-leaf fibre round her neck'. Here again the wife's misdeed is not mentioned, but, according to commentators, she fomented the hatred which her husband bore to the Prophet, and used to carry twisted cords and strew them by night in the Prophet's path with the intention of injuring him.

The Condition of Women

The fact that Sura IV of the Qur'an is entitled 'Women' might lead the student to expect that a substantial part of the Sura would reflect the ideology, general conception and attitude of the Qur'an concerning womanhood. In fact, however, this is not the case. Out of the 176 verses of the Sura only 22 deal with a limited number of specific subjects concerning women: origin in creation, marriage, settlement of marital disputes, inheritance, punishment of immorality, dependent status of woman *vis-à-vis* her husband, contact with women necessitating recourse to purification. But Sura IV is by no means the only one which treats of the condition of women; prescriptions on this subject appear in several other Suras as well.

References to the special conditions applying to women in society are to be found in a large number of verses (more than 200) in a variety of contexts: rights and duties, civil and criminal prescriptions, social obligations, character and peculiarities of certain women as they figure in historical or legendary narratives. The student wishing to ascertain the overall outlook of the Qur'an in respect of womanhood must study all the specific instances in which women are mentioned or their status is provided for, and must arrive at his conclusions by carefully studying and coordinating these.

This section does not aim at proposing any such coordination or foreshadowing any general conclusion. Most instances of reference to women have already been described in the different sections of this book, as in the matter of marriage and divorce, succession, and punishment for immorality. Here we intend to mention instances which have not been dealt with elsewhere. The residual nature of the contents of this section explains the absence of any logical or other connection between the paragraphs that follow. However, in spite of any apparent incoherence in their presentation, it is believed that if they are read in conjunction with the relevant contents of other sections their value as a necessary component of the whole image will become evident.

Sura IV begins with the following verse: 'Men, have fear of your Lord who created you from a single person. *From that person he created his mate* and from the two he bestrewed the earth with countless men and women.' Obviously the 'person' is Adam and his mate is Eve. Accordingly the Qur'an confirms the Biblical account (chapter 2 of Genesis) which presents woman as a by-product so to speak, of man, but the Qur'an omits the allegory of Eve's creation from a rib of Adam. In both versions man precedes woman in the act of creation.

Some verses of the Qur'an contain a clear statement reflecting the superiority of men over women. An important text in this sense is contained in verse IV.34. It says: 'Men *have authority over women* because Allah has made the one superior to the other, and because they spend their wealth to maintain them. Good women are obedient. As for *those from whom you fear disobedience*, admonish them and send them to bed apart and *beat them.* Then if they obey you take no further action against them.'

In the context of the conditions relating to divorce where the Qur'an points to an equality of rights between husband and wife, there appears a phrase whose meaning is not clear, as it restricts the application of the first part of the sentence. Verse II.228 says: 'Women shall with justice have rights similar to those exercised against them, although men have a status above women.'

In two instances a woman counts clearly as half a man. Verse II.282 requires all transactions of contracting a debt to be put in writing. Such writing needs corroboration by two witnesses. The Qur'an rules that two male witnesses must be called in, but if two men cannot be found then there must be one man and two women. The obvious conclusion is (a) that women alone cannot be called as witnesses, and (b) that when one man is lacking only *two* women can replace him.

The other instance is of course the rule contained in verse IV.12 which fixes the share of a male inheritor as twice that of a female inheritor.

One verse defining the rights of man in respect of woman uses an expression which in the opinion of critics might be regarded as assigning to woman a distinctly subservient role in relation to man. Verse II.223 addressing men says, 'Women are your fields: go then into your fields as you please.'

Among the numerous verses of the Qur'an which denounce the pleasures of this life, one verse includes women in the enumeration of such pleasures. Verse III.12 mentions them, along with sons, gold and silver, horses and cattle, etc. as a source of temptation. 'These', says the verse, 'are the comforts of this life, but far better is the return to Allah.' It is in the same spirit that verse LXIV.14 warns believers that they have an enemy in their wives and children, of whom they should beware and whose offences they would do well to forgive.

In matters of faith or unbelief, virtue or sin, morality or immorality, and the enjoyment of worldly or other-worldly rewards or the application of punitive sanctions there is no difference between man and woman. Both are alike under the obligations imposed by religion and morality as laid down in the Qur'an. Verse XXXIII.35 enumerating the virtues which distinguish the pious and the godly places woman in an identical position with man. Each of the ten qualities mentioned there (Moslem, faithful, devout etc.) is expressed in both the masculine and feminine forms. Verse 36 makes men and women equally subject to the law of obedience to the commandments of Allah and the Prophet.

In the world to come, pure women have a specially exalted station. They form part of the symbols of felicity in the garden of Paradise. Verse II.23 announces to those who have faith and do good works that as their reward in the Hereafter they shall be wedded to chaste virgins.

In certain circumstances the Qur'an regards abstinence from sexual relations as a condition of piety. It appears that in the beginning such abstinence was an accompanying condition of keeping the fast. However, verse II.183 shows that this rule was later relaxed. The verse says: 'It is now lawful for you to lie with your wives on the night of the fast; they are a comfort to you as you are to them. Allah knows what you were doing secretly among yourselves, but He turned to you and pardoned you. Therefore you may now lie with them and seek what Allah has ordained for you.'

The Qur'an lays down rules regarding the women's period of menstruation. Verse II.222 says: 'They ask you about menstruation. Say: "It is an indisposition. Keep aloof from women during their menstrual periods. Do not touch them until they are clean again. Then have intercourse with them as Allah enjoined you." '

The equal right of a man or woman to enjoy the possession of what they acquire or earn is prescribed by verse IV.7 which says: 'To men is allotted what they earn and to women what they earn.'

Marriage

Verse XXIV.32 encourages men and women who are single, including male and female slaves, to marry. Fear of poverty, it says, 'must not deter a man and woman from contracting marriage, because Allah, in His munificence, will enrich them from His own plenty.' Nevertheless if considerations of poverty prevent a man from marrying he must remain chaste until God gives him means out of His grace. Verse V.7 says that a Moslem man may marry a woman from among either believers or People of the Book on condition of paying her dowry, and provided he is moved by a genuine desire for companionship and not prompted by motives of lust.

Virtue, faith and high morality are, in the perspective of the Qur'an, qualities which give to the union of man and woman the necessary sacred character. Pure women are destined only for pure men and vice versa. Lack of belief in Islam disqualifies a woman for union with a Moslem. An adulterer or adulteress, apparently even after having suffered the prescribed punishment, may not contract marriage except with persons guilty of the same crime.

Verse II.221 says: 'You shall not wed pagan women unless they embrace the faith. A believing slave-girl is better than an idolatress although she may please you. Nor shall you wed idolaters unless they embrace the faith. A believing slave is better than an idolater although he may please you.'

A full description of categories of women whom a believer is not permitted to marry is given in verse IV.26. The verse says: 'You are forbidden to take in marriage your mothers, your daughters, your sisters, your paternal and maternal aunts, the daughters of your brothers and sisters, the mothers of your wives, your step-daughters who are in your charge, born of the wives with whom you have lain (it is no offence for you to marry your step-daughters if you have not consummated your marriage with their mothers), and the wives of your own begotten sons. Henceforth you are also forbidden to take in marriage two sisters at one and the same time.'

As a rule it is forbidden to take in marriage married women except captives who are taken as slaves. But in one exceptional case which occurred during the life of the Prophet, as a result of the well-known pact of Hudaibiya marriage with a married woman was made lawful. As this matter has been mentioned in the Qur'an it needs to be explained. By virtue of the Hudaibiya Pact which was concluded in 628 between the Prophet and the representatives of the Quraish, it was mutually agreed that if a Meccan man or woman who was under the authority of a guardian emigrated to Medina without the permission of the guardian, the Moslem community would be under an obligation to return him or her to Mecca. Two years later the Moslems claimed that the Pact had lost its force because the Meccans had infringed it. It then became necessary to decide the fate of women who had emigrated from Mecca to Medina. The relevant rule was prescribed in Sura LX. Verses 10 *et seq.* of this Sura enjoined on the believers to test the Meccan émigrées to determine whether or not they were believers and their husbands non-believers, in which case it would not be proper to return them to Mecca. Such women were declared to be unlawful to their husbands and their husbands to them; consequently Moslems could take them in marriage on repaying to their husbands such sums as the latter had spent on them, and on paying them their dowries. Likewise believers were forbidden to keep non-Moslem women; they were required to return them to their kinsfolk, claiming from the latter the refund of sums expended on them, or allowing them to claim what they considered to be due to them to compensate for the retention of the women.

In cases where the wife of a believer left him to join a non-Moslem, compensation for the loss of his wife would be a charge on the community, which could eventually restore to him what he had spent on his wife, out of such booty as would be taken from the enemy tribe in the event of war.

At the end of the Sura LX God addresses the following command to the Prophet: 'If believing women come to you and pledge themselves to serve no other God besides Allah, to commit neither theft nor adultery, nor child murder, to utter no monstrous falsehood of their own invention and to disobey you in nothing just or reasonable, accept their allegiance and implore Allah to forgive them.'

According to an Arab custom of pre-Islamic times, when a man died, his widow became part of the deceased's estate and could be disposed of like other properties in accordance with the laws of succession. Verses V.23 and 26 repealed this custom and made it unlawful for believers to 'inherit' women against their will.

The approval of *polygamy* expressed in the Qur'an appears at the beginning of Sura IV. This approval is preceded by an injunction to the effect that believers must protect the rights of orphans. A connection is established between inability to act fairly towards *orphans* and permission to take up to four wives. In spite of several interpretations which have been suggested the juxtaposition of these two subjects remains obscure. The two verses concerned are worded thus: IV.2: 'Restore to orphans their property; do not give worthless things in exchange for good; do not devour their substance by mixing it up with yours, that would be a great sin.' IV.3: 'And if you fear that you shall not be able to deal justly with the orphans, then marry women of your choice, two or three of four . . .' Verse 2 orders a righteous conduct and warns against the commission of a sinful act; verse 3 prescribes, in the event of inability to act righteously as ordered in verse 2, the taking of up to four wives. The permission given to marry up to four wives is clear, but it does not appear how by benefiting from that permission a man is saved from being unfair to orphans.[7] Verse 3 goes on to say: 'If you fear that you cannot maintain equality among them [your wives] then marry only one or any slave-girls you may own.' As regards the rule of equality of treatment, it is interesting to note that elsewhere (verse IV.128) the Qur'an says that a man will never be able to maintain fairness as between women, however much he may desire to be fair and just.

A passage which occurs in verse IV.28 has been translated in two senses. As one of these has given rise to an important interpretation and practice within the Shii community, it is necessary to consider the implications of both translations.

The passage which causes the difficulty follows the description of the categories of women with whom a believer is not allowed to contract marriage. One translation of the passage reads as follows: 'Except for these, all others are lawful provided you seek them with gifts from your property, motivated by chastity and not lust; seeing that you derive benefit from them, give them their dowers as prescribed, but if after a dower is prescribed you agree mutually to vary it there is no blame on you.' In this translation the women referred to after the semi-colon are the same as those mentioned before, namely the women whom the believer weds in regular marriage. But according to the alternative translation a new type of union is introduced after the semi-colon. This translation reads as follows: 'And those among women *whom you have enjoyed* give them their lawful dowers.' This interpretation is taken to legalise 'temporary marriages', the term 'women whom you have enjoyed' being taken to mean precisely 'women (Mut'a) whom you have married for a limited period'. In this kind of marriage (literally a temporary marriage or marriage of enjoyment) on expiry of the period fixed, the validity of the union expires *ipso facto* without any separation formality.

The Sunnis generally adhere to the first interpretation, and those of them who recognise to some extent the validity of the second interpretation maintain that the permission givem therein to contract temporary marriages was withdrawn after a few years by the Prophet, or alternatively that the Caliph 'Umar vouched for its repeal after the Prophet's death. But the Shii sect adheres to the second interpretation, and regards temporary unions (with Sighehs or Mut'as) as legitimate.

Verse II.234 prescribes that if a man dies leaving a widow, she must wait, keeping herself apart from men, for four months and ten days after her husband's death. When she has reached the end of her waiting period she shall be free to contract another marriage.

Verse II.241 enjoins on believers to bequeath their widows a year's maintenance without causing them to leave their homes; but of course they may leave of their own accord.

Where it is feared that a breach may occur between a man and his wife, the Qur'an recommends that a reconciliation should be attempted by the intervention of arbiters to be chosen one from the family of the husband and one from that of the wife. Obviously if the attempt fails the husband will be free to exercise his right of divorce. In this situation if he refuses to divorce his wife while making peaceful life impossible for her, the Qur'an provides relief for the woman by allowing her to give the husband something for her freedom (verse II.229).

Furthermore, in the event that the wife fears ill-treatment or desertion on her husband's part, the two may come to an 'amicable arrangement' (i.e. an arrangement by which the wife gives some valuable consideration to her husband, e.g. forfeiting part of what she has received from him) in order to save the marriage tie from being broken. Verse IV.127 which lays down this rule indirectly recognises that such a situation may be brought about by the husband due to greed and avarice, but does not foresee the possibility that the husband, after having benefited from the 'valuable consideration' may revert to his cruel practices in the hope of receiving further consideration until the woman has exhausted all her resources.

It will be clear that these various prescriptions can in practice reduce the effect of the rule that a man divorcing his wife must not claim back from her any part of what he has given her in consideration of the marriage.

Finally it must be mentioned that, on the subject of matrimony, the Qur'an contains special stipulations which apply only to the Prophet. It must be remembered that there was no limitation to 'four wives' in the case of the Prophet. The categories of wives that God made lawful for him are described in verse XXXIII.50 and can be summarised as follows: the wives to whom he has paid their dowers, the women whom he has acquired as slaves or prisoners of war, his first cousins who had emigrated with him to Medina, and lastly any believing woman who offered herself to the Prophet. The exclusive application of this rule to the Prophet is emphasised as follows: 'This is only for you and not for the believers at large.'

Divorce

The Qur'anic law of divorce is contained partly in the first seven verses of Sura LXV (entitled 'Divorce') and partly in verses 228–232, 236–237 of Sura II.

An important instance of inequality between men and women in the prescriptions of the Qur'an arises out of the rules relating to divorce. A man may divorce his wife at will; a woman has no right to divorce her husband, although in certain circumstances she may 'purchase' a right of divorce by providing adequate consideration to her husband, as will be explained below.

A man who divorces his wife performs, strictly speaking, a *conditional* act. This means that divorce does not become absolute until after the lapse of three monthly courses (Idda), i.e. when it will have been established that the woman is not with child. A logical exception to this rule exists where the divorced woman is a virgin. During the waiting period of three monthly courses the husband may waive the divorce and take his wife back.

If a man wishes to divorce a woman in order to marry another he must not take away from her the dowry which he has given her. Such action would be grossly unjust. 'How can you', asks verse II.23, 'take it back when you have lain with each other and entered into a firm contract?' A man must not molest his wife so as to force her to give up a part of what he has given her, unless she be guilty of a proven crime.

A man who divorces his wife must upon expiry of the three monthly courses, either set her free on equitable terms or take her back but he must not take her back with the motive of injuring her or taking undue advantage of her.

A man may divorce his wife before the marriage is consummated or the dowry fixed. But the man must provide for her equitably, the rich man according to his means and the poor man according to his. If a man divorces his wife before consummation of the marriage but after the dowry has been fixed, he must pay her half the dowry unless she foregoes her half-share (receiving no dowry) or he foregoes his half-share (paying her the full dowry).

Where a man decides to divorce his wife before consummation of the marriage there will be no need to observe the waiting period of three monthly courses. The woman should be equitably provided for and released (XXXIII.48).

A man may divorce his wife twice. Each time he must either keep her honourably or put her away honourably. He shall not be entitled, on divorcing her, to claim back from her what he has given her.

A man who having divorced his wife twice takes her back, but then divorces her a third time will find himself in a peculiar situation. It will not be lawful for him to take her back again unless she first marries another man and is divorced by him. If then they feel that they can keep within the limits ordained by God, they may reunite (II.230). The second husband is called Mustahil in Arabic and Muhallel in Persian.[8]

In the midst of regulations on divorce, a rule is also laid down concerning the nursing of infants. Mothers are required to give suck to their children for two whole years. The duty of maintaining and suitably clothing the children falls on the father. Neither the father nor the mother should, however, be charged with more than he or she can bear. In the event of the father's death his responsibility devolves on his heir. Where the father and mother mutually agree to wean the child such arrangement shall be lawful. They may also naturally agree to engage a nurse for their child provided that she is paid a remuneration according to usage.

A woman whose husband dies cannot remarry until after a lapse of a special waiting period. The waiting period is longer (four months and ten days) in the case of widowhood than in the case of divorce (three monthly courses). The reason is the respect due to the deceased and the need for observing mourning ceremonies. In either case a new marriage cannot be contracted before the expiry of the prescribed waiting period.

During the waiting period it would be no offence for a man to make a proposal of marriage to the woman or to cherish such desire in his heart. However, he must not seek to meet her in secret and if he does meet her he must speak to her plainly and honourably.

In pre-Islamic times the Arabs had two customs which allowed a man to abandon his wife without properly divorcing her. These customs were most inhuman as they placed the woman in a state of suspense not being released or in any way provided for. One custom was called zihar: a man could, in a fit of anger, say solemnly to his wife: 'You are to me as the back of my mother.' This formula was taken to imply in effect a divorce but without any of the consequences of divorce in the matter of the husband's marital duties. Consequently the woman who was the victim of such a declaration was not able to claim from her husband even the expenses of her and her children's maintenance, nor, of course, was she able to contract a new marriage. Sura LVIII repealed the custom of zihar. A woman named Khaula went to the Prophet and complained that her husband had by the use of the formula of zihar, made her unlawful to himself, without in any way providing for her maintenance. The Sura emphasises that the term 'one's mother' can only correctly be applied to the woman who has given birth to one. It was prescribed that any man who had made a declaration of zihar could release himself from the oath by freeing one slave, or fasting for two consecutive months, or feeding sixty indigent persons. After the performance of one of these conditions the man would be able to resume relations with his wife. The condemnation of the custom of zihar is also expressed in verse XXXIII.4.

Another similar custom of the pagan Arabs enabled a man to sever all relations with his wife (without properly divorcing her) by uttering a formal oath called Ila'. This custom was also in effect repealed by Islam: verse II.226 laid down that a person who has taken an oath of abstention from his wife should wait four months, after which if he changes his mind he can resume relations with his wife; otherwise he must divorce her in the proper manner.

The Veil

Verse XXIV.31 says that believing women should restrain their eyes, preserve their chastity, cover their ornaments (except such as are normally displayed), draw their veils over their persons, and hide their finery except from their husbands, their fathers, their husbands' fathers, their sons, their step-sons, their brothers, their brothers' sons, their sisters' sons, their women servants, their slave girls, their male attendants who are free from physical needs, and children who have no carnal knowledge of women. When walking they should not stamp their feet so as to draw attention to their hidden ornaments.

The commandment to wear the veil is repeated with especial emphasis with reference to the Prophet's family. In verse XXXIII.59 Allah commands the Prophet to enjoin on his wives, his daughters and the wives of believers to draw their outer garments over their persons so that they may be recognised and not molested. The Arabic word translated as 'outer garment' is 'julbab', a long gown which covers the neck and bosom.

Verse XXIV.59 says that elderly women who are past the prospect of marriage may lay aside their outer garments when resting at home but likely to be visited unawares, provided that they do not make a wanton display of their ornaments.

The Prophet's Wives

The Qu'ran deals in part with the role of women in the life of the Prophet. The Prophet's wives are not mentioned by name in the Qur'an, but some of them are referred to without being named. The Prophet had nine wives at the time of his death. Matrimonial difficulties were often solved through Qur'anic verses which then assumed the form of a binding law. Therefore, in order to understand the rationale of such laws it is necessary to examine the events underlying them. Hence the following brief accounts of the relevant events. It will be noted that in ascertaining the circumstances relating to them it has been necessary to go beyond the text of the Qur'an and to make use of explanations provided in the official commentaries on the Qur'an.

The episode of Ayesha and Safwan ibn al-Muattal
In the fourth year of the Hijra (626) the Prophet left Medina with an army to attack the tribe of Banu Mustaliq who were settled in a place near the coast, a few stages from Medina. The attack was swift and successful; the Prophet then made haste to return. In this expedition Ayesha accompanied the caravan on a camel-litter. The night before the return the caravan stopped, one stage from Medina. There then occurred an incident which was fraught with important consequences. What follows is taken from a description given by Ayesha: 'I had to leave the resting place', she says, 'to attend to a call of nature. In the process a necklace that I was wearing slipped off and fell to the ground without my noticing it. When I returned to camp I became aware of the loss. I therefore hastened back to the place where I had lost it, felt for it in the dark and finally found it. I then made my way back to the camp, but in the meantime the caravan attendants had made ready to depart; the man assigned to me had taken up my litter, thinking that I was inside it, and had placed it on the camel's back, and the caravan had departed. The camp being entirely deserted, I decided to remain there expecting that the caravan would notice my absence and would send someone to find me. Towards morning a young man [the 25-year-old Safwan ibn-Muattal] who had remained behind to attend to some personal business, arrived, and was surprised to find that I had been left behind. He brought his camel close to me, and without looking at me placed me on the camel's back, took the reins in his hand and without himself mounting the camel, guided me back to Medina. In spite of our haste, we were not able to catch up with the caravan, which arrived in Medina some time before we did. Of course everyone noticed that we arrived separately from the caravan.'

This incident naturally gave rise to a great deal of backbiting. The accusation against Ayesha came to the Prophet's ear and saddened him. As for Ayesha, she either fell ill or feigned illness and went to her parents' house to be taken care of. In the meantime the rumours and the charges against Ayesha continued and even found receptive ears in the circle of those close to the Prophet, such as Ali and Hassan ibn Sabet, the poet. A few weeks passed and the Prophet resolved to make the matter public. He ascended the pulpit in the public square and severely condemned the slanderers, threatening them with punishment in this life and eternal damnation in the next. He then went to the house of Abu Bakr, called Ayesha and counselled her to repent if she had sinned, saying that God would forgive her, but she replied that she had committed no wrong and had nothing to repent of. A revelation substantiating Ayesha's innocence came to the Prophet, who, after a time, turned to Ayesha and announced that he had just received a revelation declaring her innocence. Soon afterwards the verses were recited in public as follows: 'Those who invented that slander were a number of your own people. Do not regard it as a misfortune, for it has proved an advantage. Each one of them shall be punished according to his crime. As for him who had the greater share in it, his punishment shall be terrible indeed. When you heard it, why did the faithful, men and women, not think well of their own people and say: "This is an evident falsehood?" Why did they not produce four witnesses? If they could not produce any witnesses, then they were surely lying in the sight of God . . . When you heard it, why did you not say: "It is not right for us to speak of this? Allah forbid! This is a monstrous slander!" Allah bids you never again to lend your ears to such scandals, if you are true believers . . . Those who delight in spreading slanders against the faithful shall be sternly punished in this life and in the next.'

Thus a divine utterance, contained in verses 11 to 19 of Sura XXIV, declares the innocence of Ayesha, and verse 23 adds that those who defame believing women shall be cursed in this world and in the next. But the importance of the episode lies in the fact that it is the source of the Islamic law concerning adultery. This law figures in the beginning of the Sura in these words: 'The adulterer and the adulteress shall each be given a hundred lashes. Let no pity for them cause you to disobey Allah . . . and let their punishment be witnessed by a number of believers . . . Those that defame honourable women and cannot produce four witnesses shall be given eighty lashes. No testimony of theirs shall be admissible.'

The episode of Zainab bint Jahsh
One incident involving a woman, to which the Qur'an makes reference,

concerns the celebrated case of Zainab bint Jahsh. In 626 a situation arose which led to the Prophet contracting a marriage which was incompatible with an established Arab custom; but the custom was abrogated by a divine revelation. Zainab was the wife of Zaid ibn Harith. Zaid belonged originally to a Christian family of southern Syria. Taken captive in a battle, he was sold and eventually became the property of Khadija, who gave him to the Prophet. The Prophet, feeling a special sympathy for the youth, took him to the Ka'ba and, in front of all, declared him to be his adopted son. According to a pre-Islamic traditional custom of the Arabs, an adopted son was regarded as a natural son, the act of adoption entailing application of all the normal laws and customs concerning the relations of parent and child. Thus it became the general rule to call the youth 'Zaid son of Muhammad'. Zaid proved himself a worthy servant to the Prophet and was one of the first to acknowledge Muhammad as a Prophet. Soon afterwards Zaid having become one of the closest and most trusted followers and attendants of the Prophet, the Prophet decided in favour of a marriage between his own cousin Zainab and Zaid. Since Zaid was a freed slave whilst Zainab belonged to a noble family, Zainab and her brother were reluctant for the match to take place. They consented at last in deference to the Prophet's wish. It seems that verse 36 of Sura XXXIII, with which the Qur'anic reference to this episode begins, is connected with this situation. 'It is not fitting for a believer, man or woman, when a matter has been decided by God and His apostle, to have any option about their decision.' The marriage took place in due course, but after a time Zaid became aware that Zainab's affections lay towards the Prophet. He therefore made known his feeling to the Prophet and requested leave to divorce Zainab and so leave her free to marry the Prophet, but the Prophet refused to give such permission and urged Zaid to keep his wife. This injunction, however, did not diminish Zaid's conviction that co-habitation with his wife was no longer possible, and he divorced her. There then arose the delicate problem of her marriage with the Prophet. The Prophet demurred for a time, but eventually he gave in and concluded a marriage which some historians have called the Prophet's only love-marriage. In so doing he overcame a very serious obstacle which only divine revelation could remove. A revelation soon came to the Prophet, prescribing that adopted sons should no longer be regarded as equal to natural sons. 'God has not made your adopted sons your own sons. These are mere words which you utter, but Allah declares the truth and guides to the right path. Name your adopted sons after their fathers. That is more just in the sight of Allah. If you do not know their fathers, regard them as your brothers in the faith and as your wards' (XXXIII.4 and 5). The Prophet is specifically vindicated:

'No blame shall be attached to the Prophet for doing what is sanctioned for him by Allah' (XXXIII.38). The story is related almost in detail in the Qur'an: 'You said to the man whom Allah and yourself have favoured: "Keep your wife and have fear of Allah." You sought to hide in your heart what Allah was to reveal' (i.e. his intention to marry Zainab). 'You were afraid of man, although it would have been right to fear Allah. And when Zaid ceased intercourse with his wife, We gave her to you in marriage, so that it should become legitimate for true believers to wed the wives of their adopted sons if they divorced them' (XXXIII.37). After this episode Zaid's presumed filial tie to the Prophet terminated; he was no longer called the son of Muhammad, but became known by his original name Zaid son of Haritha.

The episode of Mary the Copt

Although the name of Mary the Copt does not appear in the Qur'an, it is clear that her episode is the main subject of Sura LXVI titled 'The Prohibition'. In the sixth year of the Hijra (628) the Roman Governor of Egypt, answering a communication from the Prophet which invited the Governor to embrace Islam, sent presents to the Prophet so as to sweeten the effect of declining the invitation. One of these presents was a beautiful Coptic slave-girl Mary. The Prophet accepted the presents and showed special favour to Mary, but decided to lodge her, not in the apartment set apart for his wives, but in a garden outside the city where he visited her from time to time. Once, about a year later, when Hafsa the daughter of 'Umar and one of the Prophet's wives had gone to visit her parents, Mary went to Hafsa's apartment where the Prophet joined her. But Hafsa returned unawares and, finding the Prophet and Mary in her apartment, reacted violently, thereupon the Prophet took an oath by which he forbade himself all contact with Mary. He also received Hafsa's assurance that she would not divulge the incident.

Nevertheless, the Prophet continued to feel a great affection for Mary. At the same time he had noticed a change of attitude towards himself in Ayesha, which he attributed to a breach of confidence by Hafsa. Sura LXVI 'The Prohibition' provided the solution. In this Sura the first 6 of 12 verses describe the incident and its outcome without mentioning the names of the three women Mary, Hafsa and Ayesha. The text of the 6 verses is: 'Prophet, why do you prohibit that which Allah has made lawful to you, in seeking to please your wives? Allah is forgiving and merciful. Allah has given you absolution from such oaths. Allah is your master, He is the Wise One, the All-knowing. When the Prophet confided a secret to one of his wives, and when she disclosed it and Allah informed him of this he made known to her one part of it and said nothing about the other. And when he had acquainted her with it she said "Who told you this?" He replied: "The Wise One, the All-knowing told me." If you two turn to Allah in repentance (for your hearts have sinned) you shall be pardoned, but if you conspire against him, know that Allah is his protector, and so are Gabriel, and the righteous among the faithful. The angels too are his helpers. It may well be that, if he divorces you, his Lord will give him in your place better wives than yourselves, submissive to Allah and full of faith, devout, penitent, obedient and given to fasting; both widows and virgins.' In its last three verses the Sura says that Allah has set an example to unbelievers in the wife of Noah and the wife of Lot, who were subjected to hell-fire because of their disobedience, although their husbands were righteous servants of Allah; and has set an example to the faithful in the wife of Pharaoh who was admitted to the circle of the Blest because she prayed to God to deliver her from the wickedness of her husband.

A special class among the Prophet's wives
The Qur'an has laid down the conditions under which a man and a woman may lawfully marry. The conditions, explained elsewhere in this book, apply to all Moslems, but there is one instance which relates specifically and only to the person of the Prophet. This is the case where a woman gave herself (dedicated her soul) to the Prophet, and the Prophet was entitled to marry her regardless of the prescribed conditions. All historians agree that there were such women among the Prophet's wives, though they differ as to the number. The most celebrated case is that of Maimouna. When in the 7th year of the Hijra (629) the Prophet went on a pilgrimage to Mecca, this woman – then 26 years of age – whose husband had died and who was under the guardianship of Abbas, the Prophet's uncle, offered herself to the Prophet and was accepted without hesitation. Another in this category is said to be one Umm Sharik who, according to a tradition attributed to Ayesha, was at the root of the revelation in one of the verses of the Qur'an. The tradition says in effect that when Umm Sharik offered herself to the Prophet, Ayesha's jealousy prompted the remark that a woman who offers herself to a man is unworthy of esteem. The answer to this reproof came in the form of a verse declaring God's approval of such unions in the special case of the Prophet. The verse, listing the kinds of women that the Prophet could lawfully marry includes 'other believing women who give themselves to you and whom you wish to take in marriage; this privilege is yours alone, being granted to no other believer. We grant you this privilege so that none may blame you' (XXXIII.49).

Special rules concerning the Prophet's wives

Sura XXXIII contains many verses designed to encourage, warn, exhort and generally guide the Prophet's wives; to lay down rules on their treatment by others; and to prescribe the Prophet's rights and powers over them. The Prophet's wives are not like other women; they are mothers to all believers. They must remain at home; must not display ornaments of the kind that women wore in pre-Islamic times; must show discretion in what they say; must not be too complaisant in their speech lest they provoke men whose hearts are diseased; must draw their veils close round them (this commandment applies equally to the Prophet's daughters and to the wives of believers); must not be seen unveiled except by their husbands, fathers, sons, brothers, brothers' sons, sisters' sons, their women and their slaves; must attend to prayers, give alms to the poor and obey God and the Prophet and finally must commit to memory the revelations of God. They must be content with what the Prophet gives them. God commands the Prophet to say to his wives: 'If you seek this life and all its finery, come, I will make provision for you and release you honourably. But if you seek Allah and His Apostle and the Hereafter, know that Allah has prepared a rich reward for those of you who do good works' (XXXIII.28–29). He also commands the Prophet to say: 'Those of you who commit an evident sin shall be doubly punished; that is easy for God. But those of you who are devout in the service of God and His apostle and who do good works, shall be doubly rewarded. We have prepared for them a generous sustenance' (XXXIII.30–31). Men who have to ask the Prophet's wives for anything, must speak to them from behind a curtain. No man must wed the Prophet's widows after him. This would be a grievous offence in the sight of God (XXXIII.53). Verse 51 of the Sura tells the Prophet how to deal with his wives[9] when they trouble him: 'You may put off any of your wives you please and take to your bed any of them you please. Nor is it unlawful for you to receive any of those whom you have temporarily set aside. That is more proper so that they may be contented and not vexed, and may all be pleased with what you give them.'

Slavery

At the time of the appearance of Islam slavery was part of the social institutions of Arab tribes, and Islam did not forbid or reprove it. Indeed the Qur'an makes frequent reference to slavery and describes the nature of the rights possessed over slaves by their owners. The condition of slaves in relation to their master is significantly expressed in the phrase 'those whom his right hand possesses', which occurs frequently in the Qur'an. Thus the status of the slave as the 'property' of his or her master was recognised by the Qur'an as it was recognised in many parts of the world both at that time and for centuries afterwards.

Confirmation of the institution of slavery both in the economic and social contexts can be found in several parts of the Qur'an.[10] Verse XVI.73 says that those on whom God has bestowed His bounty do not give their slaves an equal share in their possessions; were they to do so, they would be denying Allah's goodness. Verse XXX.28 uses a parable to show to what extent God is exalted above His creatures. It says: 'Here is a comparison drawn from your own lives: do your slaves share in equal terms with you the riches that We have given you? Do you fear them as you fear one another?' Another example given in XVI.75 shows the contrast between the power of God and the helplessness of man. 'On the one hand there is a helpless slave, the property of his master. On the other a man on whom We have bestowed Our bounty so that he gives of it both in private and in public. Are the two alike? Allah forbid!' In yet another parable (verse 76 of the same Sura) it is asked: is there equality between on the one hand a dumb and helpless man, a burden on his master, and who returns from every errand with empty hands, and on the other hand one who enjoins justice and follows the right path? Fundamentally the Qur'an sees no injustice in that some should be servants to others; on the contrary it recognises that this is the very order established by Allah. Verse XLIII.31, referring to the manner in which God, in His wisdom, portions out the goods of this life to His creatures, says that He exalts some in rank over others, so that the one may take the other into his service.

Verse IV.29 recommends that he who cannot afford to marry a free woman should take a believing slave to wife, this being a less onerous charge. A slave girl, thus married, is less liable to rigorous punishment than a free woman if she commits adultery. The verse says: 'If any one of you cannot afford to marry a free believing woman, let him marry a slave-girl who is a believer ... Marry them with the permission of their masters and give them their dowry in all justice, provided they are honourable and chaste and have not entertained other men. If after marriage they commit adultery, they shall suffer half the penalty inflicted upon free adulteresses.'[11]

The Qur'an, in condemning extra-marital relations, makes an exception in the case of intercourse with slave girls. Verses XXIII.6 and LXX.30 say: 'Blessed are the believers ... who restrain their carnal desires (except with their wives and slave-girls, for these are lawful to them).' Verse XXXIII.52, pursuing the subject of the categories of women with whom the Prophet may cohabit, says that outside those categories no woman is lawful to the Prophet 'except his slaves'. Verse XXIV.31, which lays down the rule that women should conceal their persons and their finery from men (other than those specified within certain degrees of relationship) makes an exception in the case of slaves.

Provisions aimed at improving the condition of slaves and lessening their hardships are not lacking in the Qur'an. Thus verse XXIV.33 recommends to believers to help their slaves buy their liberty. This usually took place in the following manner: a slave who wished to purchase his liberty, would request his master to give him a deed promising manumission on condition of payment of the price of liberty. The verse quoted recommends that if the master knows the slave to be of good character he should not refuse such a deed, but should rather assist the slave to raise the amount required for buying himself out of slavery. The same verse affords an important protection to slave-girls against a particularly degrading form of abuse by the master, which was apparently common practice. The verse says: 'You shall not force your slave-girls into prostitution when they desire to preserve their chastity, in order to enrich yourselves thereby.' However, if they yield to force, God will be forgiving and merciful to them.

Finally, though a slave is under the full dominion of his or her master, the Qur'an recommends that he or she be treated humanely. Emancipation of a slave is prescribed on a number of occasions, either in the context of doing a good deed, or in that of expiating a fault or misdeed committed. As an illustration verse IV.94 may be quoted, which provides that the penalty in the case of a person who kills a believer by mistake is to set free a believing slave and to pay compensation to the family of the victim; but if the person killed belongs to a tribe at war with the Moslem community the penalty is only the emancipation of a believing slave.

Government

The state

'Government according to the Qur'an' may have one of two meanings. One meaning is that all aspects of life in society, i.e. religion, politics, law, morality and social relations must conform strictly and exclusively to the prescriptions of the Qur'an and the other recognised sources of the Islamic faith. The other meaning is that the ordering of society in its political and other aspects should take into account the general norms and principles of Islam. The first concept is that of an Islamic State, the second that of an Islamic Order. The difference between the two is the difference between a theocratic and a secular Moslem State. The defender of each theory can find support for his preference by drawing conclusions from the verses of the Qur'an. Accordingly the choice between these two conceptions of the State has for centuries been, and in particular at the present time is, a subject of debate in most Islamic countries. In the present study the intention is neither to evaluate and compare these concepts nor to examine the characteristics of an Islamic State in the strict and total sense. It is only intended to extract from the Qur'an such of its contents as relate to the various components of the State in the sense of an organised Islamic community. These components are: nation, sovereignty, obedience, law, politics and administration. The following paragraphs reproduce the contents of the Qur'an on these subjects, treating each theme separately. No attempt will be made to synthesise the different prescriptions into the concept of a model State, or to discuss their applicability to any given society.

The nation

To the question what is the Qur'anic conception of a 'nation' it is difficult to give a categorical answer. Indeed it has been contended in certain Islamic countries that the Qur'an does not recognise the concept of 'nation' as it is understood in our times. The Qur'an refers to groupings of men by a number of terms (differently translated as family, tribe, confederation, people, community, nation) each of which no doubt had a precise meaning in seventh-century Arabia, but none of which corresponds exactly to the modern concept of a 'nation' in the sense of a community established within fixed boundaries and united by ties of blood, a common language and culture, common traditions, habits and mentality. Among the terms used, the nearest to the concept of nation is that of 'umma', but this has a distinctly religious connotation, and does not include such characteristics of nationality as racial identity, geographical contiguity, or cultural affinity. The umma is the community of the faithful; these, whatever their origin or their country of residence form a single 'brotherhood' (verse LXIX.10). The superiority of such community to other communities is clearly expressed: 'You are the best nation [umma] that has ever been raised up for mankind. You enjoin what is right, forbid what is wrong and believe in Allah. Had the People of the Book believed (in Islam) it would surely have been better for them. Few of them have faith, and most of them are evil-doers' (III.106). Certain verses give an exclusive character to the community of the faithful and raise a question as to the nature of its relationship (whether friendly or hostile) to other communities. Furthermore, non-Moslems living in the same country with Moslems are not part of the nation in the Qur'anic sense, but form a minority for whom the state must devise a special status. The subject of relations between the Moslem umma and other peoples has been treated in the Section headed Attitude towards other Religions in Chapter 6, where it has been shown that the Qur'an contains both injunctions which give the Moslem umma an exclusive character as well as counsels which point to a spirit of fellowship with others. One verse which can be quoted in support of the latter view is: 'We have made you into nations and tribes so that you may know one another' (XLIX.13).

Sovereignty and obedience

In Islam sovereignty in the sense of unqualified and unreserved authority belongs to Allah. No part of sovereignty is invested in, or shared by, a human institution. 'Command', says a typical verse conveying this meaning, 'rests with none but Allah. He declares the truth and he is the best of judges' (VI.57). But Allah is not directly accessible to man; His will can only be known through the revelations which He makes to His messenger the Prophet. Just as authority belongs alone to Allah, so its corollary, obedience, is alone due to Him, but here also it is Allah's Messenger who exacts obedience in His name. This is why the injunction 'obey Allah' is always accompanied by the words 'and His Apostle'. This injunction is repeated 19 times in the Qur'an, followed by promises of salvation to those who obey and warnings of eternal torment to those that do not. Thus verse XXIV.63 in enjoining on believers not to address the Prophet in the same manner as they address one another, or (by an alternative translation) not to treat the Prophet's summons lightly as they would treat a summons made by one of them to another, says: 'Let those who withstand the Apostle's command take heed lest some calamity befall them (in this world) or a grievous punishment be inflicted on them (in the life to come).' Not only the making of laws but also the settlement of disputes is the exclusive province of Allah and His Messenger, and here again the judge who is directly accessible to man is the Messenger. 'If you differ in anything among yourselves refer it to Allah and His Apostle', says verse IV.62. A more precise ruling to this effect is given in verse XXXIII.36. 'It is not fitting for a believer, man or woman, when a matter has been decided by Allah and His Apostle to have any option about his decision; if anyone disobeys Allah and His Apostle he is indeed on a clearly wrong path.' Only twice is a third recipient of obedience mentioned in the Qur'an. Verse IV.62 begins by saying:

'Obey Allah and obey the Apostle and *those charged with authority* among you.' Verse 85 of the same Sura recommends that even the sifting of news affecting public or private safety should be referred to the Apostle and 'those charged with authority'. However, this latter phrase has not been defined in the Qur'an, and its interpretation in the ordering of Moslem States, as of course the question as to who exercises the divine powers of the Prophet after him, has always been a subject of dispute. In any event 'those charged with authority' have evidently no independent rules status, their claim to obedience being twice removed from the original divine source. Thus in the last analysis sovereignty belongs only to God and obedience is due only to God.

As if to give further emphasis to the affirmation that sovereignty belongs exclusively to God, the Qur'an reiterates in at least 20 verses that the heaven and earth and everything in between belong to God and are under His dominion. 'To God belong', says verse V.120, 'the dominion of the heavens and the earth, and all that is therein, and it is He who has power over all things.'

Law

From the premiss that God is the only Sovereign, it follows that He is the sole law-giver. He does not delegate law-making powers to anyone; the Prophet, in announcing the divine law, acts only as a messenger. Moslems maintain that the Qur'an constitutes a comprehensive code of laws and rules from which nothing whatever has been omitted. Indeed verse VI.59 says: 'There is not a grain in the depths of the earth, nor anything fresh or dry but is inscribed in the Clear Record.' An Iranian writer of a recent treatise advocating the constitution in Islamic countries of an all-Islamic State governed by the laws of the Qur'an says: 'That is a divine law which has brought within its purview in full detail all public and private matters affecting the life of man from birth to death, and legislating alike for the king's throne and the dead man's coffin. Here the legislator is the All-knowing God who is mindful of everything that relates to mankind.' Later on, taking up again the theme of the all-inclusiveness of divine laws, the writer says: 'All these general laws of Islam, on matters such as taxation, adminis-tration of justice, public order, marriage, divorce, punishment of crime by the law of talion and the infliction of bodily pain, interdiction of minstrelsy, amusements and sodomy, all varieties of ablution and self-purification, and the like are fixed and unalterable laws of God.' But this writer and others who discuss the corpus of Islamic law refer not only to the prescriptions contained in the Qur'an, but also to the voluminous body of rules which have been developed by jurists in the course of centuries by way of interpretation of those prescriptions. In this book, however, supplementary sources have not been taken into account, and what follows reflects only the actual contents of the Qur'an.

Constitution, politics and administration

The Fundamental Law of a Moslem State is necessarily the Qur'an. The organs of the state and its laws must conform to the prescriptions of the Holy Book, in the absence of which recourse must be had to the established traditions and the doctrines derived therefrom.[12]

The well-known Western theory of separation of powers summarises the essentials of state organisation. To the question as to how the Qur'an views and provides for the constituents of State organisation few specific answers can be found in the text of the Qur'an. A considerable body of principles and rules have been added to the relevant texts of the Qur'an by way of interpretation and deduction in order to formulate an all-inclusive conception of the state. But as this book does not take these latter sources into account, there will be gaps in the present study in treating the different subjects which are connected with the constitution of the State.

Regarding the structure of the state, i.e. whether it should be a kingship, a Republic or a religious autocracy no guidance can be found in the Qur'an. All three forms have been adopted at different times in Moslem States, claiming divine authority by inference from the terms such as 'caliph', 'imam', 'guardian' or 'holder of authority' used in the Qur'an. All that can be said is that absolutism and government by the will of one man are incompatible with the precepts of the Qur'an, for consultation is a fundamental restraint placed on the decision-making power of any ruler.

Recourse to consultation in the administration of affairs has been mentioned twice in the Qur'an. Verse III.153, praising the Prophet's demeanour in dealing gently with men, commands him to consult with them in the conduct of affairs. Verse XLII.36, mentioning the virtues that characterise believers (avoidance of sin, practice of forgiveness, observance of prayer, giving of alms, and general obedience to God) says that they resort to mutual consultation in the conduct of their affairs. These verses have been invoked by those Islamic countries which have adopted a parliamentary system.

It should be observed that in the Moslem State parliament is not, strictly speaking, a legislative body, because laws are not made by man, but have once and for all been laid down by God in the Qur'an. Divine or Qur'anic legislation is in theory absolutely exhaustive, leaving no matter, even of detail, for man to legislate on. Parliament can only be a planning body, in the sense that its function can only be that of formulating plans and programmes of actions, strictly within the framework of divine laws.

Although the modern concept of a political party as an organised group of persons acting together to promote a particular principle of government is of course absent from the Qur'an, nevertheless the idea of alliances in the form of factions or cliques formed principally, but not solely, for opposing a just cause, or of sects seceding from orthodoxy, is clearly reflected in the Qur'an. The word used for such combinations is hezb (party, faction, sect). This word appears on a number of occasions both in a good and a bad sense. The good party is of course the party of Allah (Hezbullah) which triumphs over its opponent, the party of Satan (Hezbushaitan). The former is promised admission to Paradise (V.61, LVIII.22); the latter is consigned to hell-fire (LVIII.20, XXXV.6,). Unfavourable references to hezbs outnumber the favourable ones. One Sura (XXXIII) is entitled ahzab (plural of hezb) as it deals in part with a confederacy of the Quraish, other tribes and the Jews against Islam. Even the community of the faithful has at times unwisely split into parties or sects, each wrongfully rejoicing in its separatist attitude (XXIII.55, XXX.31).

No directive is given in the Qur'an concerning the manner of disposition of the organs of the state, or the choice of rulers or 'those charged with authority', but it follows clearly from the precepts of the Qur'an that the affairs of the community must be in the hands of men well-versed in the laws of the Qur'an and who 'enjoin what is right and forbid what is wrong'.

In the matter of justice, if the divine law is silent on the organisation of the judicature, it is articulate and emphatic as far as the principle of just dealing is concerned. Justice is commended and injustice is reproved. God is strictly just with mankind and He enjoins on men to be just with one another (XVI.92 and LXXXIII.1–3). He commands His messengers to deal justly with men. David is made His vicegerent on earth to judge between men in truth and justice (XXXVIII.26). The same injunction is addressed to the Prophet (VII.28 and IV.106). All messengers have been sent to men in order that they shall deal justly with one another (LVII.25). Whoever is called upon to judge between man and man must apply justice, the law according to which judgment must be given being the divine law (V.51). One passage forbids pleading in defence of an act which may be regarded as treacherous: 'Do not plead on behalf of those who betray their souls' (IV.107). The occasion which gave rise to this commandment is reported to have been the following: One Ta'ma, a Moslem, stole a coat of mail and hid it in the house of a Jew whom he accused of theft. When the case came before the Prophet, members of Ta'ma's tribe pleaded in his defence, but the Prophet rejected their pleading and gave judgement for the Jew.

In so far as the conditions of administration of justice are concerned, the silence of the Qur'an has caused certain fundamentalist Moslems to advocate principles which are at variance with the juridical norms recognised by almost all countries. Thus it has been argued that in accordance with Islamic justice there is no need for appeals against, or revisions of, sentences, which must be executed immediately; there must be only one judge for each trial and he must be an Islamic judge; judge and investigator must be the same; the intervention of advocates and pleaders in the course of trials is unnecessary. In this connection it has also been argued that the defence of criminals is incompatible with the spirit of the Qur'an, in which Allah has forbidden the Prophet to plead for a traitor in a particular case (IV.106).

Concerning the economic regime that a Moslem State should adopt, only approximate and debatable conclusions can be drawn from the contents of the Qur'an. Here also absence of specific guidance makes it possible for contradictory opinions to be held in interpreting the spirit of the Qur'an. Thus the supporters of capitalism, communism and socialism have all been able to invoke the Qur'an in support of their theories. The political economist searching for criteria in the Qur'an on which to base an Islamic economic order has a wide range of possible conclusions to choose from, because the Qur'anic material which he can use lends itself to different interpretations.

The Qur'an recognises the right to possess property, to dispose of it subject to avoiding extravagance, and to utilise it in trade and traffic. 'Believers, do not consume your wealth among yourselves in vanity, but rather trade with it by mutual consent' (IV.33).

Inequality of men in wealth and fortune is expressly recognised as being God's decree. 'It is We who portion out between them their livelihood in the life of this world; and We raise some of them above others in ranks so that some may command work from others' (XLIII.31). Another verse says: 'God has bestowed His gifts of sustenance more freely on some of you than on others; those more favoured are not going to throw back their gifts to those whom their right hands possess (i.e. their slaves) so as to be equal in that respect. Will they then deny the favour of God?' (XVI.73). Two further allusions are made to the inequality of master and servant in verses XVI.77 and 78.

A pair of opposite terms used several times in the Qur'an, namely 'mustad'af' (meaning 'held to be weak, despised') and 'mustakber' (meaning 'arrogant, haughty') have been equated by certain modern political theorists with the polarised division of humanity into the exploiter and the exploited. The conclusion drawn from this interpretation is that the Qur'an enjoins on the Moslem State to make the liberation of the exploited masses its chief concern. But if we go back to the original meaning of the terms in question, we find that they were used, not in a politico-economic but in a religious sense. The mustad'af were believers in a religion who were persecuted by those in power, i.e. the mustakber, who treated them arrogantly out of opposition to God's messengers, and would not allow them to practise their faith or to depart (LXIII.5, XVI.22). The victims referred to in the Qur'an are the followers of Salih (VII.73), the Israelites in Egypt (XXVIII.4) and the early Moslem converts in Mecca (VIII.26). In the judgement of the Qur'an the mustad'af should have set out to fight in the cause of God or to emigrate. Indeed those who failed to do so are severely reprimanded (IV.77). When they plead before the angels who are about to take their soul and say that they were mustakd'af, the angels ask 'Was not God's earth wide enough for you to emigrate?' Unable to reply, they are consigned to hell-fire (IV.99) 'except those who did not have the means or the strength to emigrate.' It is thus evident that the Qur'anic 'mustad'af' and 'mustakber' are far removed from the present-day exploited and exploiter.[13]

On the subject of the financial administration of an Islamic State, the relevant principles can be determined by examining the meaning and application of a number of terms which have been used in the Qur'an. These are 'zakat'[14] or mandatory almsgiving; 'sadaqat' or voluntary charities; 'jizya' and 'kharaj' or tribute levied on the People of the Book and unbelievers. Each kind of revenue is supported by a philosophy. Zakat (purity) is the dedication of part of a man's wealth to the cause of God in order to 'purify' the rest. Sadaqat is the outward expression of an inner urge to benevolence. Kharaj and jizya (relating to the practice of early Moslem communities) were tributes collected from subdued tribes in return for protection, and from Jews and Christians living in a Moslem country for benefiting from its protection while enjoying exemption from military service. On the subject of jizya there is an express injunction in the Qur'an: 'Fight those who do not believe in God nor in the Last Day, who do not hold forbidden that which has been forbidden by Allah and His apostle, and do not acknowledge the true faith, even if they are the People of the Book, until they pay tribute with willing submission and are utterly subdued' (IX.29). Another source of revenue, which was of special importance during the early days of Islam, was 'anfal' or booty. It was regarded as a God-ordained imposition on the property of infidels whom the faithful were commanded to fight. Sura VIII bears the title of 'anfal' and contains rules concerning the distribution of the spoils of war. This subject has already been dealt with in a special section.

Criminal Law

Part of the prescriptions of the Qur'an concerns the punishment of acts that contravene religion, law or morality. The conception of punishment in the Qur'an is an inseparable part of its philosophy of the Hereafter. The greatest punishment of the wrongdoer is that which awaits him in the life to come, and this explains the outstanding place which the themes of Last Judgement, Paradise and Hell occupy in the Qur'an. Besides, as in the Qur'anic world-view religion, law and morality are all parts of a single reality, there is no need to make any distinction between sin, crime and immorality. All infringements of any nature are punished in this world and, inescapably, in the next. However, as man's loyalty is in the first place due to God, any breach of that loyalty constitutes an act of special gravity which in Islam, as in other religions, bears the condemning name of Sin.

Sin

Many verses of the Qur'an describe vividly the consequences of committing sin and blasphemy, and the terrible nature of those consequences will be apparent from the sections headed Resurrection and Hell and the Doomed in Chapter 7. The sinner has, however, the opportunity of escaping from his doom by repenting in time and not only at the point of death (IV.22). Verse XXXIX.54, addressing those who have sinned against their souls, says: 'Do not despair of Allah's mercy, for He forgives all sins. He is the Forgiving One, the Merciful. Turn in repentance to your Lord and surrender yourselves to Him before His scourge overtakes you, for then there will be none to help you.' But although Allah is 'ample in forgiveness' (LIII.33) His pardon does not extend to the sin of believing in more than one God.

According to the Qur'an there is a gradation of sins, some being greater than others. The verse just quoted refers to 'great sins' and sets them against 'small faults', but no criterion is given on the basis of which sins can be classified into 'great' and 'less great'. A number of words appear in the Qur'an which are more or less cognate with sin, but none of them has been defined. They have been translated as disobedience, shameful deed, act of transgression, iniquity, prohibited thing, profanity. No attempt can be made, within the limits of the relevant texts, to give a fixed meaning to any of these terms. All that can be said are that the greatest of them all is shirk (polytheism) and kufr (unbelief).

Crime

The Qur'an mentions certain ordinary crimes, and assigns punishments to them: wilful homicide, manslaughter, infliction of bodily injury, theft, adultery, false witness.

Homicide

The Qur'anic law of homicide is the law of retaliation (Qisas). Six verses deal specifically with the subject of taking life (II.173,174,175, IV.94,95, XVII.35), while three verses, *inter alia,* justify the principle of retribution and protect the taker of revenge from retaliatory aggression (II.190, XXII.59, XLII.38). In various respects, such as in its philosophy (private vengeance as against punishment at the hands of the community), the manner of its enforcement and its different stipulations depending on the nature of inter-tribal relations (obsolete since many centuries), the Qur'anic treatment of homicide is unique among systems of criminal law, and, particularly in so far as its vast jurisprudential development is concerned, difficult to understand.

The gist of the verses to which reference has been made is as follows: life must be respected since God has made it sacred (XVII.35); the preservation of life necessitates recourse to retribution (II.175); where wilful homicide occurs, for each person killed one person of similar sex and status should be slain by the victims' heir (II.173); such heir (referred to in the Qur'an as 'the brother of the slain', and in jurisprudence as 'the executor of the right of blood') is subject to one duty and is given one right, i.e. he must not exceed the permitted limits in slaying, and he may accept compensation in lieu of taking physical revenge (II.173,174, XVII.35); the 'brother' who elects not to accept compensation and kills the murderer is protected against any act of vengeance which others may commit on him, so that the cycle of vendettas is closed (XXII.59); the murderer of the believer incurs God's wrath and curse and is doomed to eternal hell-fire, but no mention is made of the murderer of an unbeliever (IV.94); where a person kills a believer by mistake (but again no mention is made of killing an unbeliever) he must pay compensation to the victim's heirs in addition to freeing one believing slave, or if he cannot do so, observance of two months' fast (IV.94). The latter prescription is the only sanction if the guilty party belongs to a tribe at war with the victim's tribe.

The principle of Qisas has been very considerably developed by jurisprudence. The explanation of such development does not fall within the scope of this work, but it may be useful to indicate some of its characteristic features. It is especially concerned with the concept of 'diyya' or blood-money. This term has been used in the Qur'an in the context of the obligation of a person who has killed by error (IV.94) to pay compensation to the heirs of the victim. The Qur'an contains no guidance as to the amount of compensation, but commentators report the following scale as having been fixed by the consensus of doctors: for a Moslem 100 camels, for a Jew or Christian one-third of the compensation due for a Moslem, for a Magian one-fifth of the compensation due for a Jew or Christian.[15] The blood-money for a woman is half of that for a man.

Jurisprudence seems to have given a curious extension to the concept of blood-money beyond the provisions of the Qur'an. Blood, whether *that of the killer* or the victim, has a price which must be paid. This stipulation appears in the Retaliation Bill promulgated by the Islamic Republic of Iran, which says in its Article 46: 'Where a man kills a woman, the executor of the right of blood may choose between (a) slaying the murderer *after paying him half a man's blood-money* and (b) settling for the receipt of the woman's blood-money from the murderer.' Articles 5 and 52 contain provisions to the same effect.

Bodily injury

The rule concerning the penalty for the infliction of bodily injury is contained in the statement of the law of talion which is very precise: '. . . an eye for an eye, a nose for a nose, an ear for an ear, a tooth for a tooth and a wound for a wound, but if a man charitably forbears from retaliation, his remission shall atone for him' (V.49). It follows that justice is done when the person who inflicts bodily injury on another has the same injury inflicted on him. 'If anyone attacks you attack him as he attacked you' (II.190). 'Let evil be rewarded with like evil' (XLII.38). 'If you punish, let the evil that you inflict be of the same kind as that which you have suffered' (XVI.127). It is unlawful to commit violence on a person for having taken vengeance. 'He that repays an injury in kind and then is wronged again shall be helped by Allah' (XXII.59).

Revenge

Revenge, which is the essence of the law of talion, is clearly permitted. 'We will surely take vengeance on the evil-doers' (XXXII.22 repeated in three other verses). 'Allah is the Lord of Vengeance' (III.3 repeated in three other verses). Likewise there are few Suras in which Allah does not recall how He took vengeance on peoples who refused to recognise His messengers.

It is true that pardon or leniency (by accepting monetary compensation) is recommended, but the difference between law and exhortation is obvious.

Theft

The punishment prescribed for theft is categorical: amputation of hands. 'As for the man or woman who is guilty of theft, cut off their hands to punish them for their crimes. That is the punishment enjoined by Allah' (V.38). Certain commentators have tried to mitigate the extreme harshness of this form of punishment by arguing that Allah forgives. Indeed the verse just quoted goes on to say, 'but whoever repents after his crime and mends his ways, Allah turns to him in forgiveness.' But the possibility of forgiveness does not reduce the severity of the punishment were it to be carried out.

Adultery

Here there is a striking contradiction between different verses of the Qur'an as well as between these and tradition. According to verse 19 of Sura IV a woman who commits fornication must be confined to her house till death overtakes her or till Allah ordains some other way for her. Here no reference is made to the *man* who fornicates. But verse XXIV.2 says: 'The adulterer and the adulteress shall each be given a hundred lashes; let no pity for them cause you to disobey Allah . . . and let their punishment be witnessed by a number of believers.' But these two prescriptions are in fact held to have been repealed by virtue of a tradition, and replaced by stoning. This punishment has been applied, even recently, in Islamic countries.

To prove adultery, four eyewitnesses must be produced. However, if a man accuses his wife and can produce no evidence other than his own, his solitary evidence can be received if he swears four times by Allah that he is solemnly telling the truth, and if he takes a fifth oath calling down the curse of Allah on himself if he should be telling a lie. Then if the wife denies the charge she can bear witness four times with an oath by Allah that her husband is telling a lie; she should then take a fifth oath calling down the curse of Allah on herself if her accuser should be telling the truth (Verses XXIV.2 *et seq.*).

In view of the severity of the punishment (stoning to death), it has been argued that the requirement of producing four eyewitnesses makes the application of the penalty practically impossible. However, this condition does not by any means eliminate occasions of recourse to stoning, because witnesses can be, and often have been produced, and besides, the accused person may confess. In fact it only weakens the seriousness and force of the Qur'anic injunctions to suggest that an order clearly and emphatically expressed was not meant to be carried out in practice and was only intended to deter.

Adultery, if committed by a slave-girl who has been legally taken to wife, is less severely punished. 'If after marriage they commit adultery, they shall suffer *half* the penalty inflicted upon free adulteresses' (IV.30). This means that as the woman cannot be *half* stoned, she must suffer the penalty of one hundred lashes. Consequently the married slave-girl has, thanks to her inferior status, an advantage over a free-born woman.

A person who accuses a woman of adultery and cannot produce four eyewitnesses shall receive eighty lashes and shall forever lose credibility as a witness.

Homosexuality

That homosexuality must be treated as a crime in a Moslem State is evident from the story of Lot and his people. Verse IV.20 says: 'If two men among you commit indecency punish them both; if they repent and mend their ways, let them be.' In this case no special penalty has been prescribed.

Fighting God and the Prophet and spreading corruption on earth

These two species of crime, which have been mentioned with special emphasis in many verses, have given rise to much debate from the point of view of compatibility with recognised principles of the philosophy of criminal law. According to these principles the legislator must clearly define all criminal acts, and in particular such acts as are punishable with death. Otherwise the judge would be free to bring within an ill-defined title any act of which, for personal reasons, he disapproves. Now, no definition has been given either for 'fighting God and His Prophet' or for 'corruption on earth'. The term 'fighting God and His Prophet' is so elastic that it even extends to the practice of usury (II.279). As for the term 'corruption' the Arabic word thus translated is so indeterminate that it has exercised the ingenuity of translators, producing such heterogeneous equivalents as 'mischief', 'scandal' and 'disorder'. This part of the Qur'anic criminal law is so important and can lead to such debatable consequences if literally carried out that it must be quoted in full. 'The punishment of those who wage war against Allah and His Apostle, and strive with might and main for mischief through the land is execution or crucifixion, or the cutting off of hands and feet from opposite sides, or exile from the land: that is their disgrace in this world, and a heavy punishment is theirs in the Hereafter' (V.37). The punishment of those guilty of these two crimes will be everlasting in the Hereafter (IX.64, LIX.4, LVIII.6 and 21).

One writer, commenting on the explanations which have been offered for the punishments prescribed in the Qur'an, comes to the following conclusion: 'None of these explanations are very convincing, and the reformist Moslem has yet to come to terms with the problem that although certain elements in Qur'anic legislation may have been suitable for seventh-century Arabia, and may even have represented advances on the customs of the time, they do not conform to the spirit of the times in the last quarter of the twentieth century.'[16]

Notes to Chapter Eight

1. The ceremonies not mentioned in the Qur'an are those of kissing the Black Stone embedded in the south-eastern corner of the Ka'ba, passing to and fro with hasty steps between Safa and Marwa, visiting the plain of Arafat, throwing seven pebbles at a pillar representing the Devil and staying the night at Mina.

2. The circumambulation of these two hills is prescribed in the Qur'an in the form of 'permission'. This is because Moslems were hesitant about the permissibility of this rite which the pre-Islamic Arabs had been in the habit of performing in honour of two idols placed on those hills.

3. The rule that all believers must participate in holy warfare does not override all other exigencies. On each occasion a contingent should stay behind to devote themselves to studies in religion and be ready to admonish the men when they return from the war (IX.123).

4. A vivid description is given of how on the occasion of the division of the Hunain spoils, the Prophet was mobbed and jostled by the people, who shouted 'divide the spoils', so that he had to take shelter under a tree. The people did not cease molesting him until he declared solemnly that the whole booty would be divided, and nothing would be held back (Muir, *The Life of Mohammed*, p. 407).

5. *Kashf al-asrar*, vol. 10, p. 199.

6. If two men cannot be found, one man and two women must be called, and instance in which a woman is considered half a man.

7. According to one interpretation the intention of this rule was to encourage men to marry the numerous orphaned girls or widows who were in a helpless condition, their bread-winners having perished in the course of the battle of Uhud, but in that case it is difficult to see the relevance of the mention of inability of acting fairly towards orphans. Another interpretation, obviously resulting from inability to connect convincingly the two terms of the proposition, suggests that an intermediate passage between verses IV.2 and 3 has been lost.

8. *Per contra*: the law of the Old Testament, according to Deuteronomy XXIV.4, if a man divorces a woman, and the woman marries another man and is divorced by him also, 'the first husband who divorced her is not allowed to marry her again after she has been defiled; that would be detestable in the eyes of the Lord'. The role of Muhallel (popularly referred to as 'the one-night husband') has been frequently treated by social critics as the subject of a scathing satire.

9. According to the commentaries, at the time of his death the Prophet had nine wives: Ayesha daughter of Abu Bakr, Hafsa daughter of 'Umar, Umm Habiba daughter of Abu Sufian, Umm Salma daughter of Abu Umayya, Sawda daughter of Zam'a, Zainab daughter of Jahsh, Maimuna daughter of Harith, Safiyya daughter of the chief of the Jewish community of Khaibar, Juwairiyya daughter of Harith (*Kashf al-asrar*, vol. 8, p. 41).

10. Certain Moslem reformers believe that the institution of slavery is essentially incompatible with Islam. Thus Amir Ali, author of *The Spirit of Islam*, writes: 'It is earnestly to be hoped that before long a general synod of Muslim doctors will authoritatively declare that polygamy, like slavery, is abhorrent to the laws of Islam' (quoted by G. H. Jansen in his *Militant Islam*, New York, Harper & Row, 1979, p. 202). Such reformers would no doubt face serious opposition from fundamentalists who are only too

ready to invoke the dogma of the unchangeability of the contents of the Qur'an, as stated in X.64, VI.115 and XVIII.26.

11. Thus a slave girl even when she becomes, through marriage, the equal of a free woman, does not achieve the same civil status, though in this particular case her inequality works in her favour. Incidentally this provision supports the view that the correct punishment for adultery is not stoning, but flogging, for the convicted woman cannot of course be half stoned

12. A typical statement of this fundamental principle is contained in the programme of one Islamic Brotherhood: 'Allah is our God, the Prophet is our Leader, the Qur'an is our Constitution, Jihad is our way.'

13. Attempts have been made in recent times to construe parts of the Qur'an in such manner as to find in them a prophecy or a justification of modern political, social or other conceptions. The proposed identification (mentioned in the text) of the Qur'anic antithesis mustakber–mustad'af with the present-day contrast of exploiter–exploited is an example of such interpretation, which an examination of the relevant verses of the Qur'an shows to be unfounded. In every one of 29 verses in which derivatives of the root 'istakbara' (of which 'mustakber' is the active participle) occur, the meaning is invariably arrogant denial of the signs of God and His message transmitted through Prophets. In five typical verses such arrogance is attributed to Satan who refused to obey Allah's command: 'Iblis swelled with rage (istakbara) and was one of those who reject faith' (II.32 *inter alia*). The phrase 'those who reject Our signs and show arrogance [yastakber]' occurs in several verses followed by threats of eternal damnation (e.g. IV.172, VII.34, XLV.5). A clear definition of 'mustakber' is given in XVI.23: 'Those who do not believe in the Hereafter and whose hearts are faithless.' The victim of the mustakber is the mustad'af. Here also in no less than 10 verses derivatives of the root 'istad'afa' (with mustad'af as the passive participle) occur with the clear meaning of being imposed upon to deny God. The contrast mustad'af–mustakber is well illustrated by the dialogue which according to verses XXXIV.30–32 is to take place between them in the Hereafter on Judgement Day. The first group blame the second: 'Had it not been for you, we would certainly have been believers.' The second group reply: 'Was it we who kept you back? . . . Not so, you yourselves were wrongdoers.' The first then retort: 'By no means; it was you who plotted day and night to make us deny God and attribute associates to Him.'

Another example of an unwarranted interpretation concerns verse XIII.12, which a late-19th-century pan-Islamist construed as giving permission to engage in political activism and insurrection. The verse says: 'God will not change the condition of a people until they change what is in their souls.' The meaning of the verse becomes clear from another verse (VIII.55) which shows, using practically the same words, that God destroyed Pharaoh and his people after they treated His signs as false. The verse says: 'God will not change the Grace which He has bestowed on a people until they change what is in their souls.' The *Kashf al-asrar* explains as follows the meaning of the two quoted verses: 'God does not take His favour away from a people unless they deprive themselves of it by sinning' (vol. 5, p. 172).

14. The concept of zakat, being the cornerstone of the financial edifice outlined in the Qur'an, calls for an explanation. It constitutes one of the

five fundamental religious duties of Moslems, but the Qur'an, which mentions it frequently, gives no guidance as to its definition or application. This is one of the instances in which tradition and jurisprudential reasoning have been resorted to for complementing the Qur'an. As a result of efforts of this kind made in the course of centuries, a number of rules have been evolved which give concrete form to the notion of zakat. A full explanation of this subject does not fall within the scope of this study, but we quote a few examples of these rules by way of illustration. The principal assets described as being liable to such pseudo-taxation are crops, gold coins and domestic animals. Crops (mainly wheat and barley) exceeding a tax-free allowance of about 850 kilos are liable to zakat at the rate of 10% if irrigation-fed, or 5% if rain-fed. Gold coins are, except for a free allowance of about 75 grammes, liable to an imposition of 2.5%. As to animals, the owner of 5 camels must give one sheep; a *pari passu* computation applies up to 25 camels; for 26 camels one camel must be given, and so on. The owner of 30 cows must give one calf. To pursue these bases of assessment would be most wearisome. Enough has been said to show the archaic and obsolete nature of the whole concept of zakat as a form of taxation.

15. *Kashf al-asrar*, vol. 2, p. 635.
16. G. H. Jansen, *Militant Islam*, p. 29.

BIBLIOGRAPHY

Translation of the Qur'an

English
Ali, A. Yusuf. *The Holy Qur'an*, Beirut, Dar al-Arabia, 1968
Dawood, N. J. *The Koran*, London, Penguin Books, 1956
Rodwell, J. M. *The Koran*, London, Everyman's Library, 1909 (reprinted in 1994)
Sale, George. *The Koran*, London, Frederick Warne, 1877

French
Blachère, Régis. *Le Coran*, Paris, G. P. Maisonneuve, 1947

General

Blachère, Régis. *Introduction au Coran*, Paris, Besson et Chantemerle, 1959
Gatje, Helmut. *The Qur'an and its Exegesis*, Routledge and Kegan Paul, 1971
Goldziher, I. *Le dogme et la loi de l'Islam*, Paris, Geuthner, 1973
Izutsu, Toshihiko. *Ethico-religious Concepts in the Qur'an*, Montreal, McGill University Press, 1966
— *God and Man in the Koran: Semantics of the Koranic Weltanschauung*, Tokyo, Keio Institute of Philological Studies, 1964
Jansen, G. H. *Militant Islam*, New York, Harper and Row, 1979
Kabir, Bongahe Amir. *Kashf al-asrar* (a commentary on the Qur'an in 10 volumes in Arabic and Persian), Teheran
Muir, Sir William. *The Life of Mohammed*, Edinburgh, J. Grant, 1912
Nöldeke, T. *Sketches from Eastern History*, Beirut, Khayats, 1963
Penrice, John. *Dictionary and Glossary of the Koran*, Lahore, Law Publishing Company, 1873
Rodinson, Maxime. *Mahomet*, Paris, Edition du Seuil, 1968
Sale, George. *The Preliminary Discourse to the Koran*, London, Frederick Warne, 1921

Tisdall, St Clair. *The Original Sources of the Qur'an*, London, Society for
    Promoting Christian Knowledge, 1911
Ward, Montgomery. *Mahomet*, Paris, Payot

INDEX TO VERSES

This index contains, in respect of each section of the book, a list of references to the verses relating to its subject. The references are given as Sura and verse numbers; Roman figures indicate the serial number of Suras and verses based, as stated in the text, on the Cairo (Arabic) edition of 1923.

221

The Qur'an

Adam

The Sons of Adam

Oaths Uttered by Allah

Noah

Qarun

XXVIII	76–82

Some Historical Events

II	136, 138–140, 250–252
III	11, 117–119, 140, 149, 150, 161, 162
VIII	50
IX	25, 111, 119
XVIII	8–25
XXX	1–5
XXXIII	13–20, 22–24, 26, 27
XLVIII	1, 18, 24–27
XLIX	2–6, 9–12
LX	1, 2
LXXXV	4–8
CV	1–5

The Destruction of Past Generations

II	210
III	9, 101
VI	6, 47, 141
VII	3, 4, 130, 132
X	13
XI	102–104, 118, 119
XIII	7, 31
XV	4, 5, 78, 79
XVI	28, 113
XVII	17, 18, 50, 70, 71
XIX	75, 98
XX	129, 134
XXI	6, 11, 95
XXII	44, 47
XXIV	39
XXV	39–42
XXVI	208, 212
XXVII	52–54, 58, 59, 71, 72
XXVIII	58, 59
XXX	8, 9, 41
XXXII	26
XXXIII	9

XXXVI	43
XXXVII	70, 71
XXXVIII	2
XL	5, 22, 23, 33, 82
XLIII	7
XLIV	36, 37
XLVI	26
XLVIII	14
L	35, 36
LXV	8–10
LXVII	17, 18
LXVIII	16–33
LXIX	11, 12
LXXI	26, 27
LXXVII	16–19

The Words Islam and Moslem

II	125, 127
III	17, 77, 79, 97
V	5
XXI	108
XXX	29
XXXIX	23, 55
XLIX	15

Faith (Belief)

II	4, 97, 99, 103, 105, 106, 115, 137, 197, 198, 202, 215, 257
III	6, 14–16, 27, 98, 99, 106, 133, 173, 190–193
IV	52, 58, 69, 70, 146, 151, 172–174
V	12, 13, 61, 104
VI	70, 122
VII	2, 38–40, 180, 200, 201, 204, 205
VIII	57, 58, 61
IX	23, 24, 51, 73, 100, 101, 110, 111, 126, 127
X	25, 35, 40, 62–65, 93–97, 104–109
XI	3, 4, 26, 111

INDEX: A GUIDE TO THE CONTENTS OF THE QUR'AN